The Complete Guide to ACT English

2nd Edition

Erica L. Meltzer

ISBN-13: 978-1530072804
ISBN-10: 1530072808

Table of Contents

Introduction   4

Cheat Sheet   5

Part I: Punctuation and Grammar

Parts of Speech   8

1. Apostrophes: Possessive vs. Plural   13

2. Sentences and Fragments   22

3. Joining and Separating Sentences: 37
   Periods, Semicolons & Comma + FANBOYS

4. Non-Essential and Essential Clauses   48

5. Additional Comma Uses and Misuses   65

6. Colons   75

7. Dashes   76

   Cumulative Review: Chapters 1-5   81

8. Verbs: Agreement and Tense   89

9. Pronouns: Agreement and Case   109

10. Adjectives and Adverbs   121

11. Word Pairs and Comparisons   128

12. Modification   135

13. Parallel Structure: Lists and Prepositions   142

14. Relative Pronouns: Who(se), Whom, Which, Where,   148
    and That

    Cumulative Review: Chapters 1-14   155

Part II: Rhetoric

15.   Shorter is Better: Redundancy and Wordiness   168

16.   Diction and Register   173

17.   Transitions   181

18.   Is it Relevant? Inserting, Deleting, and Replacing Information   201

19.   Sentence and Paragraph Order   213

20.   Suppose the Writer's Goal…   219

    Test 1   223

    Test 2   236

Answer Key   251

Score Conversion Chart   271

Appendix A: Questions by Category   272

Appendix B: Questions by Test   277

Appendix C: Who vs. Whom   281

Introduction

I first encountered the ACT® as a test-writer rather than a tutor. In 2009, I'd already written a number of practice SAT passages for WilsonPrep, a tutoring firm in Westchester County, New York, when the firm's owner, Laura Wilson, asked me whether I would be interesting in writing some ACT English passages. I'd never actually seen an ACT, but I figured that it probably didn't cover anything I hadn't encountered before. So I sat myself down with an official guide and began to learn the ins and outs of the test. Over the next couple of years, I wrote dozens of English passages; by the time I encountered my first ACT student, I knew the test pretty well. After I finished *The Ultimate Guide to SAT Grammar* in 2011, it seemed only natural to write an equivalent book for the ACT, and I immediately set to work as soon as I had published the former. About 20 pages in, however, I realized I had incorrectly explained a concept in my SAT book. What I thought would be a simple revision ended up taking three weeks – after which I decided I'd had enough of writing grammar books for the time being! Over the next few years, I returned to the book sporadically, but I always ended up shelving it in favor of other projects. In the meantime, though, I kept getting requests from tutors and students who had successfully used my SAT grammar book but needed a comparable guide for the ACT, and so I finally decided that it was time to sit down and finish.

This book is organized in two parts that correspond to the two types of questions on the English section of the ACT. The first half of the book deals with punctuation and grammar ("Usage and Mechanics"), while the second part deals with paragraph/passage content and organization ("Rhetoric"). Although I coordinated the contents of each chapter with the English questions in *The Real ACT Prep Guide*, 3rd Edition, I also drew on numerous additional recent exams while researching this book. Because the number of various types of questions can vary considerably from test to test, some concepts covered in detail here are not well-reflected in the breakdown of questions in the *Real Guide*. All the material in this book, however, is based on questions from administered tests. In addition, I have deliberately structured the chapters so that the most straightforward concepts are presented first, then returned to later and discussed in greater complexity. Since there is no way to cover the more sophisticated aspects without first explaining the basics, this organization seemed most logical to me. As a result, however, certain concepts that are commonly tested on the ACT are not covered until relatively late. For those who have limited time (or desire) to study, I have therefore included a "cheat sheet" on the following page; it provides a list of must-know concepts along with the chapters in which they are covered.

Finally, a note about the ACT as a test. While there is a kernel of truth to the idea that the ACT is a "curriculum-based test" that is largely immune to "tips and tricks," I find that that notion is largely a myth. Although ACT English questions are context-based and therefore less predictable than SAT grammar questions, they do nevertheless fall into a limited set of categories and often present the same concepts in virtually identical ways from test to test – a setup that can in fact make the ACT quite vulnerable to shortcuts (e.g. shorter is better, *being* = wrong). Whenever possible, I have tried to highlight these patterns. Furthermore, while ACT content may theoretically be intended to reflect a high school curriculum, the reality is that few schools provide comprehensive instruction in all of the grammar and rhetoric concepts tested on the exam. Few of my students have learned about dashes before the ACT, for example, and a surprising number have also lacked familiarity with common transition words such as *moreover* and *nevertheless*. My goal is thus not only to provide thorough and rigorous preparation that accurately reflects the content of the ACT but also to plug some of the gaps and misunderstandings that students may have inadvertently acquired along the way.

Erica Meltzer
February 2014

ACT English Cheat Sheet

Grammar

1. Period = Semicolon = Comma + and/but (ch. 2)

2. colon = dash; 2 commas = 2 dashes = non-essential clause, which can be crossed out (ch. 4, 6-7)

3. It's = It is; Its = Possessive form of *it* (ch. 1)

4. Colon = list or explanation. Need a complete sentence before but not necessarily after. (ch. 6)

5. *−ING* (gerunds), especially *Being* usually = WRONG (ch. 2)

6. Could/Would/Should/Might HAVE, not OF (ch. 16)   *could have, would have, should have*

7. No comma before or after a preposition, or the word *that* (ch. 5)   *prep· indicate place/time*   *about, above, across, after*

8. Comma before *it*, *he*, *she*, *they* usually = WRONG (ch. 3)

9. Singular **verbs** end in *−s*, plural **verbs** do not end in *−s* (e.g. *she reads*, *they read*) (ch. 8)

10. Keep pronouns consistent: one = one, you = you (ch. 9)

11. *Who* is for people, *which* is for things, *where* is for places (e.g. *the time/book where* = WRONG) (ch. 14)

12. Use *who* before a verb (*who went*, NOT *whom went*); use *whom* after a preposition (e.g. *by whom*, NOT *by who*) (ch. 14)

13. All items in a list must match (noun, noun, noun or verb, verb, verb)

14. Always underline NOT, LEAST, and EXCEPT

Rhetoric

1. Shorter is better (ch. 15)

2. Context is key: if you're not sure of the answer, read a sentence before and a sentence after. (ch. 17-19)

3. OMIT/DELETE: check that option first because it's usually right. (ch. 18)

4. Transitions within/between sentences: **physically cross out** the original transition and determine the relationship (e.g. continue, contradict, emphasize) between the two sentences or halves of a sentence BEFORE you look at the answer choices. (ch. 17)

5. Transitions between paragraphs: read at least a few sentences of the paragraph that the transition is intended to begin. The end of the previous paragraph might not be important. (ch. 17)

6. Insert/Delete: reread the paragraph and state the topic **in your own words** before checking the answers choices. If the sentence is directly relevant to that topic, it belongs. If not, it doesn't. (ch. 18)

7. Purpose of a passage: determine whether the topic is **specific** or **general**, then "yes" or "no." (ch. 20)

Part I:
Punctuation and Grammar

Parts of Speech

There are eight parts of speech in the English language, seven of which are tested on the ACT. If you are not comfortable identifying them, it is suggested that you begin by reviewing this section. Although portions of these definitions are repeated throughout the guide, familiarizing yourself with these terms before you begin will help you move through the explanations and exercises more easily.

The seven major parts of speech tested on the ACT are as follows:

1. Verb

Verbs indicate **actions** or **states of being**.

Examples: To be
To have
To seem
To go
To speak
To believe

The "to" form of a verb is known as the **infinitive**. All of the verbs listed above are infinitives. If you are uncertain whether a word can be used as a verb, try placing *to* in front of it to form an infinitive.

Verbs are not always used as infinitives, however. In order to indicate who is performing an action, we must **conjugate** the verb and provide its **subject**.

To be and *to have* are the most frequently tested verbs on the ACT. Because they are **irregular**, their conjugated forms are different from their infinitives; you must therefore make sure that you are comfortable distinguishing between their singular and plural forms.

Conjugation of the verb *to be:*

Singular	Plural
I am	We are
You are	You (pl.) are
He, She, It, One is	They are

Conjugation of the verb *to have:*

Singular	Plural
I have	We have
You have	You (pl.) have
He, She, It, One has	They have

The **number** of a verb tells us whether it is singular or plural.

   I, you, he, she, it, one speaks = Singular

   We, you, they speak = Plural

The **tense** of a verb tells us when an action occurred. *perfect- something occurred b4 another action in the past.*

   She speaks = Present   She would speak = Conditional *would= conditional*

   She has spoken = Present Perfect → *past* She would have spoken = Past Conditional

   She spoke = Simple Past   She will speak = Future

   She had spoken = Past Perfect   She will have spoken = Future Perfect

2. Noun

Nouns indicate people, places, objects, and ideas, and can always be preceded by *a(n)* or *the*. **Proper nouns** indicate specific people and places.

   Examples: house, bicycle, supervisor, idea, Julia Child, Chicago

   The **girl** rode her **bicycle** down the **street** to her **house**.

   In the **theater,** the **dancer** moved across the **stage** with her **arms** held above her **head**.

3. Pronoun

Pronouns replace nouns.

   Examples: she, you, one, we, him, it(s), their, this, that, which, both, some, few, many, (n)either

   Samantha loves basketball. **She** plays **it** every day after school.

   Marco walks to school with Sherri and Ann. **He** meets **them** at the corner.

Personal Pronouns are often referred to in the following manner:

   1st Person Singular = I   1st Person Plural = We
   2nd Person Singular = You   2nd Person Plural = You
   3rd Person Singular = He, She, It, One 3rd Person Plural = They

4. **Preposition**

Prepositions indicate where someone/something is, or when something happened.

> **Example:** The dog ran **under** the fence and jumped **into** the neighboring yard **in** only a matter **of** seconds.

Common prepositions include:

Of	To	Within/out	Over	Beside	Next to	Against
From	At	Between	Above	About	Toward(s)	Upon
In	For	Under	Along	Among	Before	Around
On	By	Beneath	Beyond	Near	After	Outside
Off	With	Below	Behind	Across	During	Through(out)

5. **Adjective**

Adjectives modify nouns and pronouns. (describes object)

> **Examples:** large, pretty, interesting, solid, wide, exceptional, smart, dull, caring, simple

> The class was so **boring** that I thought I would fall asleep.

> The **stunning** view left him at a loss for words.

6. **Adverb**

Adverbs modify verbs, adjectives, and other adverbs. They frequently end in –ly.

> **Examples:** rapidly, calmly, mildly, boldly, sharply, well, fast, very

> She smiled **brightly** at him when he entered the room.

> He received an **exceedingly** good grade on the test.

7. **Conjunction**

Conjunctions indicate relationships between words, phrases, and clauses.

> **Examples:** and, but, however, therefore, so, although, yet, when, because, since

> Alice went to the dentist, **but** first she went to the candy store.

> **Because** it rained yesterday, the ceremony was be held indoors.

10

Preliminary Exercise: Identifying Parts of Speech (answers p. 251)

Directions: identify and write the part of speech (e.g. noun, verb, adverb) for each underlined word.

Although igloos are usually associated with Alaskan Eskimos (Inuits), <u>they</u> have mostly been₁ constructed by people who lived in the central Arctic and Greenland's Thule region. Other Inuit peoples <u>tended</u> to use snow to insulate their₂ houses, which were constructed <u>from</u> whalebone₃ and hides.

Traditionally, three types of igloos <u>were</u>₄ constructed. Small igloos were constructed as temporary shelters <u>and</u> used only for one or two₅ nights. These were built and <u>used</u> during hunting₆ trips, often on open sea ice. Medium-sized igloos were <u>usually</u> single-room family dwellings that₇ housed one or two families. Often, several of these igloos were located in a small area, forming an <u>Inuit</u>₈ village. The largest igloos were normally built in pairs: one of the buildings was a <u>temporary</u>₉ structure for community feasts and dances, while the other was <u>intended</u> for living. These igloos₁₀ could be constructed from several smaller igloos attached <u>by</u> tunnels.₁₁

1. _pronoun_

2. _verb_

3. _prep._

4. _verb_

5. _conjunction_

6. _verb_

7. _adverb_

8. _Proper noun_
   adj. - village is noun. Inuit is describing village

9. _adj._

10. _verb_

11. _prep._

Today, igloos are used mostly for <u>brief</u> camping
                                      12
trips; however, the principles behind their

construction <u>remain</u> the same. The snow used to
                13
build an igloo must have enough strength to be cut

and stacked correctly. The best snow to use for this

<u>purpose</u> is snow blown by wind because <u>it</u>
     14   15
contains interlocking ice crystals, which increase

the amount <u>of</u> weight the ice can support.
            16
        Because of snow's excellent insulation

properties, inhabited igloos are <u>surprisingly</u>
                                      17
comfortable and warm inside. Sometimes, a short

tunnel is constructed at the entrance <u>to reduce</u>
                                         18
heat loss when the door <u>is</u> opened. Animal skins
                          19
can also be used as door flaps to keep warm air in.

        Architecturally, the igloo is unique <u>because</u> it
                                                20
is a dome that can be constructed without an

<u>additional</u> supporting structure. Independent
   21
blocks of ice lean on one another and are polished

to fit. <u>In</u> the traditional Inuit igloo, the <u>heat</u> from
        22   23
the *kudlik*, or stone lamp, causes the interior to

melt slightly, creating a layer of ice that

<u>contributes</u> to the igloo's strength. In fact, a
   24
correctly-built igloo will support the weight of a

person standing <u>on</u> the roof.
                 25

12. _adj_

13. _verb_

14. _noun_

15. _noun_ *pron*

16. _prep_

17. _adverb_

18. _verb_

19. _verb_

20. _conj_

21. _adverb_ *adj*

22. _prep_

23. _noun_

24. _verb_

25. _prep_

1. Apostrophes: Possessive vs. Plural

The possessive/plural distinction is one of the most frequently tested concepts on the ACT. You are more or less guaranteed to see at least two or three questions testing when – and when not – to use an apostrophe.

Nouns: Possessive and Plural

To form the **plural** of a noun, add –*s*. When a singular noun ends in –*s*, add –*es*. Do **not** add an apostrophe.

Correct: The **artists** are painting. = More than one artist is painting.

Correct: The **businesses** are open. = More than one business is open.

To form the **possessive of a singular noun**, add *apostrophe* + –*s*, even for nouns that end in –*s* in the singular.*

Correct: The **artist's** paintbrush = the paintbrush belonging to the artist

Correct: The **business's** policy = the policy of the business

To form the **possessive of a plural noun**, add –*s* + *apostrophe* (or –*es* + *apostrophe* if the singular ends in –*s*). Note that while the apostrophe comes **before** the –*s* when a noun is singular, it comes **after** the –*s* when a noun is plural.

Correct: The **artists'** <u>paintbrushes</u> = the paintbrushes belonging to the artists

Correct: The **businesses'** <u>policies</u> = the policies of the businesses

Contraction with Verb

The construction –*s* + *apostrophe* can also be used to form a **contraction** between a noun and the verb *is*.

Incorrect: The **artists** working in her studio.

Correct: The **artist's** working in her studio. = The **artist is** working in her studio.

The second sentence is correct because *apostrophe* + –*s* stands in for the verb *is*. The first sentence is incorrect because the lack of an apostrophe makes the word *artists* plural and eliminates the verb from the sentence.

Although this use is fair game for the ACT, it is not typically tested and should not be of primary concern.

---

*When well-known figures have names ending in –*s*, the possessive may be formed by adding only an apostrophe after the –*s* (e.g. Dickens' works = the works of Dickens). This use is **not**, however, tested on the ACT.

13

One of the ACT's favorite errors involves confusing the plural and possessive forms of nouns. While the distinction may seem straightforward, many test-takers do begin to second-guess themselves during the exam.

To minimize confusion, break these questions into two parts:

   1) Determine whether the noun is singular or plural. If singular, cross out plural answers and vice-versa.

   2) Determine whether the noun is possessive, and eliminate the remaining choice or choices that don't fit.

For two-noun questions, check each noun separately, starting with the one you're more certain about. In some cases, one noun will give you all the information you need to answer a question.

Let's look at an example. Break each question down, making sure to cross out incorrect answers as you go.

Since I was a child, my family has gathered

at my grandparent's home in Maine each
          1
summer. My grandmother and grandfather

bought it decades ago and still live

there from June to September. The houses'
                         2
rooms are bright and airy, and I love to
 2
sit on the deck and watch the waves roll in.

1. **A.** NO CHANGE
    B. grandparents'
    C. grandparents
    D. grandparent

2. **F.** NO CHANGE
    G. house's room's
    H. house's rooms
    J. houses rooms

Question 1: Singular or Plural? _____ P

                   Possessive? _____ Y

Question 2: Noun 1: Singular or Plural? _____ S   Noun 2: Singular or Plural? _____ P

                   Possessive? _____ Y   Possessive? _____ N

Solution:

1) Since the passage makes clear that the writer has both a grandmother and a grandfather, *grandparents* must be plural. That eliminates (A) and (D). Furthermore, the sentence indicates that the home belongs to the grandparents, so a possessive noun is required. (C) is plural but not possessive and can thus be eliminated. That leaves (B), which is correct because it is both plural and possessive.

2) Let's start with *houses*. The writer earlier refers to the grandparents' *home*, singular, so *house* must logically be singular as well. That eliminates (F) and (J), which are plural. Now, look at the second noun. There's nothing to indicate that anything belongs to the rooms, so that noun must be plural only. (G) incorrectly makes *room* possessive, so that answer can be eliminated as well. That leaves (H), which is correct.

Pronouns: Possessive, Plural, and Contraction with Verb

The ACT primarily focuses on the plural and possessive forms of just three pronouns: *it, they,* and *who.* Questions testing other pronouns such as *you* or *she* do appear from time to time, but they are quite rare.

The most important thing to understand is that apostrophes and *–s* **are used differently for pronouns than for nouns.** The addition of *–s* is **entirely unrelated** to whether a pronoun is **singular or plural**; it is **only related** to whether or not that pronoun is **possessive.**

- To form the **possessive** of a pronoun, add *–s.* **Do not add an apostrophe.** *its*

- To form a **contraction with a verb,** add *apostrophe + –s* or *–re.* (Contractions with other verbs are not generally tested on the ACT).

A. It's vs. Its

The *its vs. it's* distinction is one of the most frequently tested concepts on the ACT. You should therefore make sure that you are fully comfortable identifying which version is appropriate in any given situation.

It's = it is

Its = possessive of *it.* Used before a noun.

Its' = does not exist. The plural of *its* is *their.*

Its' can **always be eliminated immediately.** The easiest way to choose between the two remaining versions is simply to plug in *it is.* If it works, you need an apostrophe; if it doesn't work, the apostrophe is unnecessary.

Tip: because most of the confusion surrounding *its vs. it's* stems from the fact that people associate apostrophes with the possessive form, *it's* is most often used in place of *its.* As a result, *its* is usually the correct answer.

For example:

Since I was a child, my family has gathered

at my grandparents' home in Maine each

summer. My grandmother and grandfather

bought the house decades ago and still live

there from June to September. It's rooms are
                                  1

are bright and airy, and I love to sit on the deck

and watch the waves roll in.

1. **A.** NO CHANGE
   B. Its
   C. Its'
   D. There

Since you would not say "**it is** rooms are bright and airy," no apostrophe is necessary. In addition, the sentence refers to the rooms *of* the house, indicating that the possessive is required. (B) is therefore correct.

15

B. They're, Their, and There

They is the plural form of *it*, and *their* is the plural form of *its*. (Remember that *–s* has nothing to do with making pronouns plural!).

Although the same rules apply to *they're vs. their* as apply to other pronouns, an extra degree of confusion is often present because of a third identical-sounding pronoun: *there*.

They're = they are

Their = possessive of *they*. Used before a noun.

There = a place

In general, it's easiest to think of *there* as separate from *they're* and *their*, which are both forms of *they*. For *their vs. they're*, ask yourself whether you could plug in *they are*. If you can, you need the apostrophe; if not, you don't.

They're

Incorrect:	Although **their** usually powered by rowers, canoes may also contain sails or motors.
Incorrect:	Although **there** usually powered by rowers, canoes may also contain sails or motors.
Correct:	Although **they're** usually powered by rowers, canoes may also contain sails or motors.

Since you would say "Although **they are** usually powered by rowers," the apostrophe is required.

Their

Incorrect:	Deactivated viruses form the basis of many vaccines known for **they're** <u>effectiveness</u> in preventing disease.
Incorrect:	Deactivated viruses form the basis of many vaccines known for **there** <u>effectiveness</u> in preventing disease.
Correct:	Deactivated viruses form the basis of many vaccines known for **their** effectiveness in preventing disease.

Since you would not say "Deactivated viruses form the basis of many vaccines known for **they are** effectiveness," no apostrophe should be used. And since the sentence does not refer to a place, *there* cannot be correct either.

There

Incorrect:	Because the city of Munich is located close to the Alps, snow regularly falls **they're**.
Incorrect:	Because the city of Munich is located close to the Alps, snow regularly falls **their**.
Correct:	Because the city of Munich is located close to the Alps, snow regularly falls **there**.

Since the sentence is clearly talking about a place (the *city* of Munich), *there* is required.

C. Who's vs. Whose

The same rule regarding apostrophes applies to *who*.

Who's = who is

Whose = possessive form of *who*. Used before a noun. Unlike *who*, *whose* can be used to refer to both people and things.

To determine which version is correct, plug in *who is* and see whether it works.

> Incorrect: Jessye Norman is an American opera singer **whose** known for her moving performances.
>
> Correct: Jessye Norman is an American opera singer **who's** known for her moving performances.

Since you would say "Jessye Norman is an American opera singer **who is** known for her moving performances," the apostrophe is necessary.

On the other hand:

> Incorrect: Jessye Norman is an American opera singer **who's** performances many people find moving.
>
> Correct: Jessye Norman is an American opera singer **whose** performances many people find moving.

Since you would also not say "Jessye Norman is an American opera singer **who is** performances many people find moving," *whose* rather than *who's* must be used.

Very occasionally, questions testing possessive and plural will involve other pronouns (*you, that*). The same rule applies to those pronouns as applies to the ones discussed throughout this chapter:

- apostrophe + –*s* or –*re* = pronoun + *is* or *are*
- no apostrophe = possessive

	Pronoun + is/are	Possessive
You	You're	Your
That	That's	Thats = does not exist
She, He	She's, He's	Shes, hes = does not exist
Her, Him	Her's, hers' = does not exist His's, his' = does not exist	Hers His
Their	Their's = does not exist	Theirs

Drill 1: Apostrophes (answers p. 238)

1.   Despite <u>it's</u> brilliance and power, the sun grew out of tiny particles suspended in enormous clouds of dust and gas.

its

2.   The British scientist J.D. Bernal believed that human <u>beings'</u> would eventually be replaced by creatures <u>who's</u> bodies were half-human and half-machine.

→ beings / whose

3.   Instrument-makers have tried to reproduce a Stradivarius violin's precise sound for hundreds of years, but all of <u>they're attempts</u> have been unsuccessful.

their

4.   Bats can perceive and stalk <u>their</u> prey in complete darkness, using a system of ultrasonic sounds to produce <u>echo's that identify it's</u> location.

their / echoes / its

5.   A computer program devoted to facial recognition can determine people's emotions by following <u>there</u> faces' movements and linking <u>its</u> readings with a database of expressions.

their

its

6.   George Westinghouse was an electrical industry pioneer <u>who's</u> first major invention, the rotary steam engine, earned him many <u>scientists'</u> admiration when he was still a young man.

whose

scientists'

7.   Although Los Angeles has long been famous for <u>it's traffic jam's</u>, pedestrians are now able to walk in the <u>cities</u> center with much greater ease.

its / jams / city's

8. The peacock is a bird <u>who's</u> penchant for showing off <u>its</u> bright, multicolored plumage has made it a symbol of vanity and pride in many different cultures.

whose/its

9. The gray wolf, which once lived throughout much of North America, is now rarely spotted because <u>it's</u> habitat has been almost entirely destroyed.

its

_____

10. Every spring, New Orleans receives thousands of tourists for Mardi Gras, the <u>years</u> most important festival. Visitors arrive <u>their</u> from around the world.

years / there

Drill 2: Apostrophes (answers p. 251)

1. Thailand is full of bright colors. It's

    a country who's inhabitants spontaneously

    plant flowers, where the impressive and countless

    temples emit they're glory with an abundance of

    gold and red, and where the fruits at the market

    put every rainbow to shame.

1. A. NO CHANGE
   B. It's a country whose
   C. Its' a country who's
   D. Its a country whose

2. F. NO CHANGE
   G. there
   H. their
   J. it's

---

2. Although half of the Earths inhabitants now

    live within a hundred miles of an ocean, few people

    have a working knowledge of the sea. As a science,

    oceanography is still in its' infancy. Yet large

    numbers of people know the sea in other ways,

    through the arts and literature. Since the nineteenth

    century, fiction has described undersea world's

    that explorers were unable to reach.

1. A. NO CHANGE
   B. Earths's
   C. Earths'
   D. Earth's

2. F. NO CHANGE
   G. it's
   H. its
   J. their

3. A. NO CHANGE
   B. worlds that
   C. worlds and
   D. worlds' that

---

3. A few years ago, while writing an article about

    twentieth-century American literature, I consulted a

    literary encyclopedia to see how entries on authors

    were composed. Among the encyclopedia's articles

    was an entry about Amy Lowell, whose best known

    for her poem "Patterns." I didn't know much

    about Lowell, but as I read more about her, I

    found myself becoming intrigued.

1. A. NO CHANGE
   B. encyclopedia's articles'
   C. encyclopedias articles
   D. encyclopedias' articles

2. F. NO CHANGE
   G. Lowell, who's
   H. Lowell, she's
   J. Lowell and whose

20

4. One of the oldest pyramids in Egypt is the

Pyramid of Djoser, built around 2700 B.C. The

pyramid and <u>its'</u> surrounding complex, which were
      1

designed by the architect Imhotep, are generally

considered the <u>worlds'</u> oldest monuments built
                  2

with cut stone.

1. A. NO CHANGE
    B. it's
    C. its
    D. they're

2. F. NO CHANGE
    G. worlds
    H. world's
    J. it's

5. Caroline Maria Hewins, <u>who's best known for</u>
                              1

<u>helping to expand childrens</u> library services across
          1

the United States, also led the Harford Public

Library's transformation from a subscription library

to a free public library. In 1895, Hewins started her

own library branch in the North Street Social

Settlement House. She was extraordinarily

committed to <u>its success, moving in and eventually</u>
                              2

<u>residing there</u> for 12 years.
      2

1. A. NO CHANGE
    B. whose best known for helping to expand
       children's
    C. whose best known for helping to expand
       childrens
    D. who's best known for helping to expand
       children's

2. F. NO CHANGE
    G. it's success, moving in and eventually
       residing their
    H. its success, moving in and eventually
       residing they're
    J. its' success, moving in and eventually
       residing there

6. <u>Crocodile's</u> have many traits that make them
        1

successful predators. Their streamlined bodies

enable them to swim swiftly. They can also tuck

<u>their</u> feet to the side while swimming, allowing
  2

them to move faster by decreasing water resistance.

If a crocodile wants to make a sharp turn in the

water, <u>it's</u> webbed feet allow it to do so with ease.
        3

1. A. NO CHANGE
    B. Crocodiles
    C. Crocodiles'
    D. They

2. F. NO CHANGE
    G. there
    H. they're
    J. one's

3. A. NO CHANGE
    B. they're
    C. its
    D. their

21

2. Sentences and Fragments

Knowing how to distinguish between sentences and fragments is one of the most important skills necessary for success on the English portion of the ACT. The ability to correctly use most of the punctuation tested on the exam depends on your ability to consistently recognize what is and is not a sentence. Without that knowledge, you will find it extremely difficult to know when to use periods, commas, semicolons, and colons. At this point, you might be rolling your eyes and thinking, "Well *duh*, of course I know what a sentence is," but sometimes that isn't nearly as obvious as you might think.

Is it a Sentence?

We're going to try an exercise: For each statement below, circle "Sentence" if it can stand alone as an independent sentence and "Fragment" if it cannot. Once you've read the sentence carefully, spend no more than a few seconds deciding on your answer.

1. Louis Armstrong was one of the greatest jazz musicians of the twentieth century.

   (Sentence)   Fragment

2. He was one of the greatest jazz musicians of the twentieth century.

   (Sentence)   Fragment

3. Louis Armstrong, who was one of the greatest jazz musicians of the twentieth century.

   Sentence   (Fragment)

4. Who was one of the greatest jazz musicians of the twentieth century.

   Sentence   (Fragment)

5. Louis Armstrong, who was one of the greatest jazz musicians of the twentieth century, was a vocalist as well as a trumpet player.

   (Sentence)   Fragment

6. Today, he is considered one of the greatest jazz musicians of the twentieth century.

   (Sentence)   Fragment

22

7. He is, however, considered one of the greatest jazz musicians of the twentieth century.

   (Sentence)   Fragment

8. He is now considered one of the greatest jazz musicians of the twentieth century.

   (Sentence)   Fragment

9. Because of his virtuosic trumpet skills, Louis Armstrong is considered one of the greatest jazz musicians of the twentieth century.

   (Sentence)   Fragment

10. Although he was one of the most virtuosic trumpet players of his generation.

    Sentence   (Fragment)

11. Many people considering Louis Armstrong the greatest jazz musician of all time.

    Sentence   (Fragment)

12. Many of them consider him the greatest jazz musician of all time.

    (Sentence)   Fragment

13. Many consider him the greatest jazz musician of all time.

    (Sentence)   Fragment

14. Many of whom consider him the greatest jazz musician of all time.

    (Sentence)   Fragment

15. Having shown an unusual gift for music early in his childhood, Louis Armstrong, who was born in New Orleans on August 4, 1901.

    Sentence   (Fragment)

16. Having shown an unusual gift for music early in his childhood, Louis Armstrong, who was born in New Orleans on August 4, 1901, went on to become one of the greatest jazz musicians of the twentieth century.

    (Sentence)   Fragment

17. Moreover, Armstrong, who spent much of his early life in poverty, went on to become one of the greatest jazz musicians of the twentieth century.

    (Sentence)   Fragment

18. Nicknamed "Satchmo," Louis Armstrong, who was born in New Orleans on August 4, 1901, grew up to become one of the greatest jazz musicians of the twentieth century and, perhaps, one of the greatest musicians of all time.

    (Sentence)   Fragment

You might be wondering how much that exercise really has to do with the ACT – after all, ACT English questions are always presented in the context of a passage, and those are just random sentences. But if you can't consistently recognize when any given statement is and is not a sentence, you won't know what sort of punctuation to use when separating it from other sentences. In fact, dealing with sentences like the ones above in context can often make things *harder*, not easier, because you have all sorts of other information that can potentially distract you. And that means you're likely to get confused when you get to the ACT.

For example, let's say you weren't sure about #13 (*Many consider him the greatest jazz musician of all time*). If you saw the following question, you might get stuck.

In the decades since Armstrong retired from

performing, his fame has continued to grow. Jazz

fans and scholars now unanimously consider him

one of the greatest jazz musicians of the twentieth

century, many consider him to be among the
    1
greatest jazz musicians of all time.

1. **A.** NO CHANGE
   B. century, many would have considered
   C. century. Many consider
   D. century; many considering

Unfortunately, there's simply no way to answer this question for sure without knowing whether you're dealing with one sentence or two. You might recognize that (B) and (D) sound awkward and eliminate them on that basis. But with (A) and (C), you're stuck. If you think the second clause is a sentence, you'll want to put in a period and choose (C). But if it isn't a sentence, then the comma must be ok, and the answer must be (A).

You stare at the question for a while, thinking it over. *Many consider him to be among the greatest jazz musicians of all time...* That sounds kind of weird. Besides, what sort of sentence would just say *many*, without explaining many of *what?* You can say *many people*, that's fine, but not just *many*. It just sounds wrong. You don't even know who it's talking about. You can't start a sentence like that. Unless it's some kind of trick... But (C) is just too weird. No way can that be the answer.

So you pick (A).

But actually, the answer *is* (C).

You've just fallen into a classic trap – you thought that because *Many consider him to be among the greatest jazz musicians of all time* didn't make sense out of context, it couldn't be a sentence. But guess what: whether a statement is or is not a sentence has absolutely nothing to do with whether it makes sense out of context. Meaning is irrelevant; only grammar counts.

Starting on the next page, we're going to take a very simple sentence and look at the various elements that can get added onto it without changing the fact that it's a sentence. We're also going to look at some common types of fragments and how they get formed.

Building a Sentence

Every sentence, regardless of length, must contain two things:

1) A **subject**

2) A **conjugated verb** that corresponds to the subject.

A sentence can contain only one word (*Go!* is a sentence because the subject, *you*, is implied) or consist of many complex clauses, but provided it contains a subject and a verb, it can be considered grammatically complete – *regardless of whether it makes sense outside of any context.*

A. Simple Sentence

> Sentence: The tomato grows.

This is known as a simple sentence because it contains only a subject (*the tomato*) and a verb (*grows*), which tells us what the subject does. Because it can stand on its own as an independent sentence, it can also be called an **independent clause**.

B. Prepositional Phrase

If we want to make our sentence a little longer, we can add a **prepositional phrase**. A prepositional phrase is a phrase that begins with a preposition – a **time** or **location** word that comes **before a noun**. Common prepositions include *in*, *to*, *with*, *from*, *for*, *at*, *by*, and *on*. (For a complete list, see p. 10.)

> Sentence: The tomato grows **around the world.**

Sentences can contain many prepositional phrases, sometimes one after the other.

> Sentence: The tomato grows **in many shapes and varieties in greenhouses around the world**.

A prepositional phrase can also be placed between the subject and the verb. When that is the case, the prepositional phrase starts, as always, at the preposition and ends right before the verb.

> Sentence: The tomatoes **in the greenhouse** grow in many varieties and colors.

A prepositional phrase can also be placed at the **beginning** of a sentence:

> Sentence: **In the greenhouse,** the tomatoes grow in many varieties and colors.

A prepositional phrase **cannot**, however, stand alone as a complete sentence:

> Fragment: In the greenhouse

> Fragment: In many shapes and varieties in greenhouses around the world

C. Pronoun as a Subject

Nouns can also be replaced by **pronouns** – words such as *it*, *she*, and *they*. In the above sentence, we can replace the subject, the singular noun *tomato*, with the singular pronoun *it* and rewrite the sentence this way:

Sentence: It grows.

This is actually still a sentence because it has a subject (*it*) and a verb that corresponds to the subject (*grows*). The only difference between this version and the version with the noun is that here we do not know what the subject, *it*, refers to.

This is where a lot of people run into trouble. They assume that if a statement doesn't make sense out of context, then it can't be a sentence. But again, those two things are not necessarily related.

As is true for the original version, we can rewrite the longer versions of our sentence using pronouns:

Sentence: **It** grows around the world.

Sentence: **It** grows in many shapes and varieties in greenhouses around the world.

If we wanted to make the subject plural, we could replace it with the plural pronoun *they*.

Sentence: **Tomatoes** grow.

Sentence: **They** grow.

Sentence: **They** grow in many shapes and varieties in greenhouses around the world.

It and *they* are the most common **subject pronouns** (pronouns that can replace nouns as subjects), but there are a number of other pronouns that can be used as subjects as well. Some of them can refer only to people; some can refer only to things; and some can refer to both people and things.

People	Things	People or Things
I	It	None
You	Nothing	One
S/he	Anything	Each
We	Everything	Every
No one	Something	Any
Someone/somebody		Few
Anyone/anybody		Both
Everyone/everybody		Some
		Several
		Many
		More
		Most
		Other(s)
		All
		They

"Group" Pronouns

One very common point of confusion often involves **"group" pronouns** such as *some, several, few, many*, and *others*. These pronouns can be used to begin clauses in two different ways, one of which creates an independent clause and the other of which creates a dependent clause.

Let's start with these two sentences:

Sentence: Many tomatoes are grown in greenhouses around the world.

Sentence: Most people believe that the tomato is a vegetable.

People generally don't have too much trouble recognizing that these are sentences. They have pretty clear subjects (*many tomatoes, most people*) and verbs (*are, believe*), and they make sense by themselves. The problem arises when we take away the nouns, *tomatoes* and *people*, and start to deal with the pronouns on their own.

Pronoun (of them) = sentence

In this usage, the pronoun alone acts as a subject and is used to replace a noun. It is often followed by the phrase *of them*, but it can be used by itself as well.

Sentence: **Many (of them)** are grown in greenhouses around the world.

Sentence: **Most (of them)** believe that the tomato is a vegetable.

Taken out of any context, the above examples don't make much sense, nor do they provide any real information. Regardless of how odd you find these examples, however, **they are still sentences** because each one contains a subject (*many, most*) and a verb (*are, believe*) that corresponds to it.

Pronoun + "of which" or "of whom" = fragment

When an indefinite pronoun is followed by *of which* or *of whom*, it creates a **dependent clause** which, by definition, cannot stand alone as a full sentence.

Fragment: **Many of which** are grown in greenhouses around the world

Fragment: **Most of whom** believe that the tomato is a vegetable

Which means:

Incorrect: The tomato is used by cooks around the **world, most of them** believe that it is a vegetable rather than a fruit.

Correct: The tomato is used by cooks around the **world. Most of them** believe that it is a vegetable rather than a fruit.

Correct: The tomato is used by cooks around the **world, most of whom** believe that it is a vegetable rather than a fruit.

who vs whom – replace hi   ↑ not subject
        ↳ not subject

27

D. Adverbs

Adverbs **modify verbs** and **clauses**. Most adverbs are created by adding –*ly* onto adjectives. For example:

Slow	→	Slowly
Current	→	Currently
Important	→	Importantly

A second type of adverb, however, does not end in –*ly*. Some of these adverbs are **adverbs of time**, which tell you **when** or **how often** something occurs. Others are **transitions** that indicate relationships between ideas.

Again	Meanwhile	Next	Sometimes
Consequently	Moreover	Now	Then
Furthermore	Nevertheless	Often	Today

Important: Adverbs have <u>no grammatical effect whatsoever</u> on a sentence. A sentence to which an adverb is added will continue to be a sentence, regardless of where the adverb is placed.

Sentence: <u>**Now**</u>, the tomato grows in many shapes and varieties in greenhouses around the world.

Sentence: The tomato **<u>currently</u>** grows in many shapes and varieties in greenhouses around the world.

Sentence: The tomato grows in many shapes and varieties in greenhouses around the world **<u>today</u>**.

E. Non-Essential Clauses

Information can be inserted between the subject and the verb in the form of a **non-essential clause**:

Sentence: The tomato**<u>, which is one of the most popular salad ingredients,</u>** grows in many shapes and varieties in greenhouses around the world.

Non-essential clauses describe nouns (usually the subject of a sentence). They often begin with **"w-words"** such as *who(se)*, *which*, and *where*, and they are most often **followed by a verb**. They can consist of lengthy phrases, as in the example above, or of single words:

Sentence: The tomato**<u>, however,</u>** grows in many varieties in greenhouses around the world.

These clauses or words are called "non-essential" simply because they are not essential to the meaning of a sentence. When they are removed, the sentence still makes sense. For example:

Sentence: The tomato~~, which is one of the most popular salad ingredients,~~ grows in many shapes and varieties in greenhouses around the world.

Appositives

Although non-essential clauses frequently begin with "w-words" (also known as **relative pronouns**), they are not required to do so. You could also see a non-essential clause that looks like this:

> The tomato**, one of the most popular salad ingredients,** grows in many shapes and varieties in greenhouses around the world.

A non-essential clause that does not begin with a "w-word" is known as an **appositive**. Appositives can also appear as descriptions at the beginnings or ends of sentences, as in the examples below.

> Beginning: **One of the most popular salad ingredients,** the tomato grows in many shapes and varieties in greenhouses around the world.

> End: In greenhouses around the world grow many shapes and varieties of the tomato**, one of the most popular salad ingredients**.

A non-essential clause cannot stand alone as a complete sentence. As a **shortcut**, know that a statement beginning with a "w-word" like *which*, *who(se)*, or *where* will not be a complete sentence.

> Fragment: Which is one of the most popular salad ingredients

> Fragment: Who think that the tomato is a vegetable

> Sentence: One of the most popular salad ingredients, the tomato grows in many shapes and varieties in greenhouses around the world.

In addition, a sentence cannot **stop** right after a non-essential clause. If it does, it is no longer a complete sentence but rather a fragment, and it should not have a period or semicolon placed after it.

> Fragment: The tomato, which is one of the most popular salad ingredients

> Fragment: The tomato, one of the most popular salad ingredients

Although the first version contains the verb *is*, that verb does not correspond to the subject, *the tomato*. Instead, it corresponds to the pronoun *which* at the beginning of the new clause. In order to create a sentence, we must either remove *which* from the sentence, restoring the verb to the subject, *the tomato*:

> Sentence: The tomato **is** one of the most popular salad ingredients.

Or we must place a main verb after the non-essential clause and complete the sentence with more information:

> Sentence: The tomato, (which is) one of the most popular salad ingredients, **grows** in many shapes and varieties in greenhouses around the world.

F. Participles and Gerunds

Participles

Every verb has two **participles**:

1) Present participle

The present participle is formed by adding *–ing* to the verb

Talk	→	talking
Paint	→	painting
Throw	→	throwing

2) Past participle

The past participle is usually formed by adding *–ed* or *–n* to the verb

Talk	→	talked
Paint	→	painted
Throw	→	thrown

A **participial phrase begins with a participle** and can be formed in either the **present** or the **past**. While participial phrases on the ACT can involve past participles (*–ed* form), they are more likely to involve present participles (*–ing* form).

Let's get back to our sentence – now we're going to add a participial phrase at the beginning:

> **Originating in South America**, the tomato, one of the most popular salad ingredients, grows in many shapes and varieties in greenhouses around the world.

To form the past tense, we can use the present participle *having* + past participle of the main verb (*originated*):

> **Having originated in South America**, the tomato, one of the most popular salad ingredients, grows in many shapes and varieties in greenhouses around the world.

We can also use the past participle of the verb *grow*.

> **Grown originally in South America**, the tomato, one of the most popular salad ingredients, is now produced in many shapes and varieties in greenhouses around the world.

Participial phrases can appear in the beginning (as in the above examples), middle, or end of a sentence.

Middle: The tomato**, cultivated initially in South America during the first millennium B.C.,** is now grown in many shapes and varieties in greenhouses around the world.

End: The tomato is now grown in greenhouses around the world, **having first been cultivated in South America in the first millennium B.C.**

30

Participial phrases **cannot** stand alone as sentences, however:

Fragment: Originating in South America

Fragment: Having first been cultivated in South America in the first millennium B.C.

Fragment: Grown originally in South America

Fragment: Grown originally in South America, the tomato, one of the most popular salad ingredients

Gerunds

Gerunds are identical in appearance to present participles: they are created by adding –*ing* to the verb. (At this point, you do not need to worry about the grammatical distinction between gerunds and participles.)

Important: a word that ends in –*ing* cannot act as a main verb. A phrase that contains only an -*ing* word and no conjugated verb is a **fragment**.

Fragment: Tomatoes **growing** in many shapes and varieties in greenhouses around the world.

In order to turn the fragment into a sentence, we must eliminate the gerund by **conjugating** the verb.

Sentence: Tomatoes **grow** in many shapes and varieties in greenhouses around the world.

Important: Answer choices that contain –*ing* words, especially BEING, are usually wrong. *Being*, the gerund form of the verb *to be*, is the most commonly tested gerund on the ACT. It is also **irregular** – the conjugated forms look completely different from the gerund form. In order to easily correct errors with *being*, you should make sure to know all of that gerund's conjugated forms.

	Present	**Past**
Singular	Is	Was
Plural	Are	Were

Present

Fragment: Today, the tomato **being** grown in greenhouses around the world.
Sentence: Today, the tomato **is** grown in greenhouses around the world.

Past

Fragment: Originally, tomatoes **being** cultivated only in South America.
Sentence: Originally, tomatoes **were** cultivated only in South America.

31

G. Conjunctions

There are two main types of conjunctions:

1) **Coordinating conjunctions** join two independent clauses.

2) **Subordinating conjunctions** join an independent clause and a dependent clause.

Important: a single clause that begins with a conjunction cannot be independent, even though a sentence with more than one clause can sometimes begin with a conjunction.

Coordinating Conjunctions

There are seven coordinating conjunctions, collectively known by the acronym **FANBOYS**.

For, And, Nor, But, Or, Yet, So

The most commonly tested FANBOYS conjunctions are **AND & BUT**, so they should be your primary concern. We'll talk a lot more about FANBOYS in the next chapter, but for now, you need to know that a complete sentence **cannot** begin with a FANBOYS conjunction, regardless of how many clauses it contains. In real life, this rule is sometimes broken for stylistic reasons, but if the ACT asks you to choose between a version of a sentence that begins with a FANBOYS conjunction and one that does not, the latter will virtually always be correct.

Incorrect: **And today**, tomatoes are cultivated in greenhouses around the world.

Correct: **Today**, tomatoes are cultivated in greenhouses around the world.

Subordinating Conjunctions

Somewhere around third grade, you probably learned that you should never start a sentence with *because*. While this rule is taught with the best of intentions, it's unfortunately only half right. In reality, it's perfectly acceptable to begin a sentence with *because* – sometimes.

Here's the rule: *Because* is a type of conjunction known as a **subordinating conjunction**. A clause that begins with a subordinating conjunction cannot stand on its own as a sentence and is therefore **dependent**.

Sentence: Tomatoes are brightly colored and full of flavor.

Fragment: **Because** tomatoes are colorful and full of flavor.

If, however, we add that dependent clause to an independent clause (i.e. a complete sentence), it is perfectly acceptable to begin the whole sentence with the word *because*:

Sentence: **Because tomatoes are brightly colored and full of flavor,** they are one of the most popular salad ingredients.

Other common subordinating conjunctions include the following:

When	Although	Until	If
Whenever	Though	Whatever	Whether
Before	Despite	Because	Whereas
After	Unless	Since	While

Any of these words can be used to begin a sentence, as long as that sentence contains an independent clause in addition to the dependent clause.

Incorrect: **Although** tomatoes have been cultivated since the first millennium B.C.

Correct: **Although** tomatoes have been cultivated since the first millennium B.C., they did not become popular in the United States until the mid-nineteenth century.

Incorrect: **When** tomatoes were first brought to Europe from South America.

Correct: When tomatoes were first brought to Europe from South America, many people believed that they were poisonous.

Incorrect: **Despite** the fact that many people believe that the tomato is a vegetable.

Correct: **Despite** the fact that many people believe that the tomato is a vegetable, it is actually a fruit.

Drill: Punctuating Sentences and Fragments (answers p. 251)

1. Numismatics is the study or collection of

    currency. Including coins, tokens, paper money,
    _____
            1

    and related objects. Numismatists – more

    commonly known as coin collectors – also

    studying other types of payment used to resolve
    _____
       2

    debts and purchase goods, such as shells,

    precious metals, and gemstones.

1. A. NO CHANGE
    B. currency, including
    C. currency, this includes
    D. currency and including

2. F. NO CHANGE
    G. having studied
    H. would have studied
    J. study

2. Levittown is the name of four large suburban

    developments created in the United States by

    William Levitt and his company, Levitt & Sons.

    Built in the 1950s for World War II veterans and

    their families. These communities offered
         _____
                    1
    attractive alternatives to cramped city locations and

    apartments. Thousands of identical homes were

    produced, these came standard with a white picket
    _____
             2
    fence, green lawn, and kitchen with modern

    appliances. When sales began in March 1947, nearly

    1,500 homes being bought within the first three
              _____
                3
    hours.

1. A. NO CHANGE
    B. families, these communities offered
    C. families, and these communities offered
    D. families, these communities offering

2. F. NO CHANGE
    G. produced, they came
    H. produced and coming
    J. produced. They came

3. A. NO CHANGE
    B. having been
    C. has been
    D. were

34

3. The Globe Theatre was a theatre in London associated with William <u>Shakespeare, it was</u> built in 1599 by Shakespeare's playing company, the Lord Chamberlain's Men. Although the Globe's actual dimensions are <u>unknown. Evidence suggests that it was a three-story open-air amphitheater, which</u> could hold up to 3,000 spectators. For a long time, scholars thought that theater was <u>round. Now,</u> however, they believe that it was actually a 20-sided polygon.

1. **A.** NO CHANGE
    B. Shakespeare, this was
    C. Shakespeare. It was
    D. Shakespeare. And it was

2. **F.** NO CHANGE
    G. unknown, evidence suggests that it was a three-story, open-air amphitheater. Which
    H. unknown, evidence suggests that it was a three-story, open-air amphitheater that
    J. unknown; evidence suggests that it was a three-story, open-air amphitheater that

3. **A.** NO CHANGE
    B. round, now,
    C. round now,
    D. round, now

4. There are many ways to apply color to blown <u>glass, one of them involves</u> rolling molten glass in powdered color or larger pieces of colored glass called frit. Complex patterns with great detail can be created through the use of colored <u>rods, which</u> can be arranged in a pattern on a flat surface and then "picked up" by rolling a bubble of molten glass over them. One of the most exacting and complicated color techniques <u>being</u> "reticello," which involves creating two bubbles from cane, each twisted in a different direction.

1. **A.** NO CHANGE
    B. glass, one of which involves
    C. glass. One of which involves
    D. glass; one of them involving

2. Which of the following would be the LEAST acceptable alternative to the underlined portion?

    F. rods that
    G. rods. They
    H. rods, they
    J. rods. These rods

3. **A.** NO CHANGE
    B. having been
    C. will have been
    D. is

5. It might not be as famous as the Statue of Liberty, but the Verrazano–Narrows <u>Bridge, which is</u> also a New York City landmark. A double-decked suspension bridge that connects the boroughs of Staten Island and <u>Brooklyn, it is</u> named for both the Florentine explorer Giovanni da Verazzano, the first European to enter New York Harbor and the Hudson River, and for the body of water it spans: the Narrows. With a central length of nearly a mile, it was the longest suspension bridge in the world until <u>1981, when it was surpassed by the Humber Bridge in the United Kingdom, today</u> it is the tenth longest suspension bridge in the world. Every day, the Verazzano-Narrows bridge is crossed by thousands of <u>people. Many of whom</u> live in Staten Island and commute to work in Manhattan.

1. **A.** NO CHANGE
   B. Bridge is
   C. Bridge. It is
   D. Bridge, it is

2. **F.** NO CHANGE
   G. Brooklyn. It is
   H. Brooklyn, this is
   J. Brooklyn, the bridge is

3. **A.** NO CHANGE
   B. 1981. When it was surpassed by the Humber Bridge in the United Kingdom, today,
   C. 1981 when it was surpassed by the Humber Bridge in the United Kingdom today,
   D. 1981, when it was surpassed by the Humber Bridge in the United Kingdom. Today,

4. **F.** NO CHANGE
   G. people, many of whom
   H. people, many of them
   J. people. And many of them

36

3. Joining and Separating Sentences: Periods, Semicolons & Comma + FANBOYS

There are three ways to separate complete sentences (independent clauses) from one another:

1) Period

2) Semicolon

3) Comma + Coordinating (FANBOYS) Conjunction

A. Period = Semicolon

Periods and semicolons have the same function: to separate two complete sentences. Although the first letter after a period is capitalized while the first word after a semicolon is not, they are **grammatically identical**.

Correct: Tomatoes are used in many different types of **cooking. Farmers** around the world grow them in both fields and greenhouses.

Correct: Tomatoes are used in many different types of **cooking; farmers** around the world grow them in both fields and greenhouses.

"Strong" Transitions   ☆ has

Commonly tested "strong" transitions (formally known as conjunctive adverbs) include *however, therefore, consequently, moreover, nevertheless, meanwhile,* and *instead*. When these transitions begin a clause, the clause is **independent** – that is, the transition must come after either a period or a semicolon, **not** a comma.

When these transitions are tested on **grammar questions**, the correct answer can be given in the form of either "semicolon + transition" or "period + Transition."

When these transitions are tested on **rhetoric questions**, the answer will virtually always be given in the form of "period + Transition."

When they are used to begin a clause, these transitions should **never follow a comma**.

Incorrect: The tomato is one of the most popular salad **ingredients, however,** it is actually a fruit.

Correct: The tomato is one of the most popular salad **ingredients; however,** it is actually a fruit.

Correct: The tomato is one of the most popular salad **ingredients. However,** it is actually a fruit.

37

Very important: No matter where a sentence starts, make sure to read from the beginning all the way through to the period. Otherwise, you might not notice that there are two sentences rather than one. A phrase that makes sense at the end of one sentence might actually be the start of the following sentence.

Let's look at an example:

Since the early nineteenth century, doomsayers

have gloomily predicted that increasing populations

would exhaust their food <u>supplies in only a few</u>
1

<u>decades, they claimed</u> food shortages would result
1

in catastrophic famines. Yet the world currently

produces enough food to feed 10 billion people, and

there are only 7 billion of us.

1. **A.** NO CHANGE
    B. supplies. In only a few decades, they claimed,
    C. supplies, in only a few decades, they claimed
    D. supplies in only a few decades they claimed

Because the underlined phrase initially seems to make sense where it is, most test-takers will immediately pick NO CHANGE and move on to the next question without a second thought. (If you did that, don't worry – it just means you're normal.) What they will not do is read all the way to the period at the end of the paragraph. Take a moment now, and just read the entire sentence in isolation:

Since the early nineteenth century, doomsayers have gloomily predicted that increasing populations would exhaust their food <u>supplies in only a few decades,</u> they claimed food shortages would result in catastrophic famines.

Can you spot the problem now? If we leave the phrase *in only a few decades* without any punctuation, the sentence is way too long. In fact, there are two sentences, not one:

Sentence #1:   Since the early nineteenth century, doomsayers have gloomily predicted that increasing populations would exhaust their food supplies in only a few decades.

Sentence #2:   They claimed food shortages would result in catastrophic famines.

As discussed, two complete sentences must be divided by a period or a semicolon, not a comma. The only answer that divides the sentence into two is (B). When the underlined phrase is attached to the beginning of the second sentence rather than the end of the first, the sentences make perfect sense:

Sentence #1:   Since the early nineteenth century, doomsayers have gloomily predicted that increasing populations would exhaust their food supplies.

Sentence #2:   In only a few decades, they claimed, food shortages would result in catastrophic famines.

So (B) is correct.

Important: You can save time by checking answer choices that contain periods <u>first</u>. When you are given the option to use a period, that's often a hint that there are two sentences.

B. Comma + FANBOYS

As discussed in the previous chapter, complete sentences can also be joined by *comma + coordinating (FANBOYS) conjunction*: **F**or, **A**nd, **N**or, **B**ut, **O**r, **Y**et, **S**o.

To reiterate, the ACT tests primarily *and + but*. The conjunctions *so* and *yet* are tested very rarely, and *or* and *nor* are virtually never tested.

When a FANBOYS conjunction is used without a comma to join two sentences, the result is a **run-on sentence**. Note that a sentence does not have to be long to be a run-on.

> Run-on: Tomatoes are used in many different types of **cooking and they** are grown around the world in both fields and greenhouses.

> Correct: Tomatoes are used in many different types of **cooking, and they** are grown around the world in both fields and greenhouses.

Likewise, a FANBOYS conjunction should never be used after a period or a semicolon.* Any answer choice that contains one of those constructions can be automatically eliminated.

> Incorrect: Tomatoes are used in many different types of **cooking. And they** are grown around the world in both fields and greenhouses.

> Incorrect: Tomatoes are used in many different types of **cooking; and they are** grown around the world in both fields and greenhouses.

When the subject is the same in both clauses and is **not** repeated in the second clause, do **not** use a comma:

> Incorrect: Tomatoes are used in many different types of **cooking, and are** grown around the world in both fields and greenhouses.

> Correct: Tomatoes are used in many different types of **cooking and are** grown around the world in both fields and greenhouses.

You can also think of the above rule this way. Since *comma + and* = period, simply replace *comma + and* with a period and see if you have two complete sentences:

> Incorrect: Tomatoes are used in many different types of **cooking. Are** grown around the world in both fields and greenhouses.

Since the information after the period is not a sentence, no comma should be used before *and*.

*Occasionally, an ACT sentence will begin with a FANBOYS conjunction for stylistic effect. When this occurs, you will *not* be tested on the conjunction, although you may be tested on another aspect of the sentence. See *The Real Guide*, p. 292, fourth sentence (*So, when he has went…*) for an example.

Comma Splices

When a comma alone is used to separate independent clauses, the result is known as a **comma splice**. Comma splices are **always incorrect**.

Comma Splice:	Tomatoes are used in many different types of **cooking, farmers** around the world grow many varieties of them in both fields and greenhouses.

Remember from Chapter 2 that an independent clause can start with a pronoun (*it, they, she, many, some*) as well as a noun, and that it does not need to make sense out of context to be a grammatically complete sentence.

Sentence:	Tomatoes are used in many different types of cooking.
Sentence:	**They** are grown in both fields and greenhouses around the world.
Comma Splice:	Tomatoes are used in many different types of **cooking, they** are grown in both fields and greenhouses around the world.
Sentence:	Tomatoes come in a variety of colors.
Sentence:	**Some** (of them) are red, while others are green or yellow.
Comma Splice:	Tomatoes come in a variety of **colors, some** (of them) are red, while others are green or yellow.

Fixing Comma Splices

There are number of ways to fix comma splices, and the ACT does not favor any particular method over another. Some questions will require you to fix this error by using a period, while others will require you to fix them using a semicolon, *comma + FANBOYS conjunction*, or even another way entirely. As a result, you should be comfortable fixing comma splices a variety of ways.

The simplest way to correct a comma splice is to replace the comma with a period or semicolon:

Comma Splice:	Tomatoes were originally small and **multicolored, they** are mostly large and red today.
Correct:	Tomatoes were originally small and **multicolored. They** are mostly large and red today.
Correct:	Tomatoes were originally small and **multicolored; they** are mostly large and red today.

We can also leave the comma and add a FANBOYS conjunction, or add *semicolon + however*:

Correct:	Tomatoes were originally small and **multicolored, but** they are mostly large and red today.
Correct:	Tomatoes were originally small and **multicolored; however,** they are mostly large and red today.

Another option is to turn one of the independent clauses into a **dependent clause**. When a dependent clause is added to an independent clause to form a sentence, then a comma alone can be placed between the clauses.

Correct: **While tomatoes were originally small and multicolored,** they are mostly large and red today.

Correct: **Originally small and multicolored,** tomatoes are mostly large and red today.

Correct: Tomatoes are one of the most popular cooking ingredients, **used in soups, stews, and salads in many different cuisines**.

Correct: Tomatoes were originally small and multicolored, **<u>having</u> become large and red only during the nineteenth century.**

The last example above is notable because it involves an **exception to a common answer choice pattern,** namely that answers containing –*ing* are **usually wrong**.

When it comes to fixing comma splices, however, answers containing -*ing* are **often correct** because they create dependent clauses and thus prevent a comma from separating two independent clauses.

For example:

The large, lumpy tomato originated in

<u>Mesoamerica, it became</u> the direct ancestor of
            1
some modern cultivated tomatoes.

1. **A.** NO CHANGE
   B. Mesoamerica, becoming
   C. Mesoamerica; and it became
   D. Mesoamerica it became

Although (B) contains an –*ing* word, *becoming*, it corrects the comma splice in the original version of the sentence by making the second clause (*it became the direct ancestor of some modern cultivated tomatoes*) dependent.

(C) is incorrect because it places a semicolon rather than a comma before a FANBOYS conjunction, and (D) is incorrect because it places no punctuation whatsoever between the two independent clauses (fused sentence).

41

Very Important: Semicolon = Period = Comma + FANBOYS

Because a period, a semicolon, and "comma + FANBOYS" are grammatically identical, the ACT will never ask you to choose between them. **When more than one of these constructions appear as answer choices, you can eliminate all of them since no question can have more than one right answer.**

For example:

If you grow tomatoes to sell at a <u>market,</u>
$$1$$
<u>remember</u> that it will take about 70 to 80 days
$$1$$
from the time you set plants in the field until you

can pick ripe tomatoes from them.

1. **A.** NO CHANGE
   B. market, and remember
   C. market. Remember
   D. market; remember

Since (B), (C), and (D) are grammatically equivalent, all of them can be eliminated. When you encounter this pattern, you should of course double-check the remaining answer to make sure that it makes sense, but in general, you can assume that it will be right. In this case, (A) is correct because it places a comma between a dependent clause and an independent clause.

Very often, the semicolon = period = *comma + FANBOYS* rule will also be tested in "all of the following EXCEPT" questions.

For example:

There are many good varieties of tomatoes

available to <u>growers – each grower</u> should
$$1$$
try a few plants of several varieties to determine

which performs best.

1. All of the following would be acceptable alternatives to the underlined portion EXCEPT

   A. growers. Each grower
   B. growers, each grower
   C. growers; each grower
   D. growers, and each grower

Solution: Don't get too concerned about the dash; we'll talk about those later. If you know that the period in (A), the semicolon in (C), and the *comma + and* in (D) are the same, you can instantly eliminate all of them. Only (B) remains. Since it forms a comma splice, it is NOT an acceptable alternative to the underlined portion of the sentence.

While not every question will be nearly as straightforward as the examples above, many will contain this exact answer choice pattern, and most others will contain something close to it.

Drill: Periods, Semicolons, and Comma + FANBOYS (answers p. 251)

1. In 2006, the beverage marketing company

Power Brands was co-founded by Darin Ezra and

Martin <u>Molina. Both of whom</u> had prior experience
                    1
in the beverage industry. The company expanded

<u>rapidly. It currently employs</u> people in more than a
                    2
dozen countries on every continent except

Antarctica.

1. A. NO CHANGE
   B. Molina, both of them
   C. Molina; both of whom
   D. Molina, both of whom

2. Which of the following would NOT be an
   acceptable alternative to the underlined portion?

   F. rapidly; it currently employs
   G. rapidly and currently employs
   H. rapidly, currently employing
   J. rapidly, it currently employs

2. Since I learned to control a pencil at the

age of <u>four; writing</u> has been one of my favorite
       1
activities. As a child, I would sit for hours,

scribbling down stories about characters that I

had invented and insisting that my parents read

them aloud. Today, I keep a <u>journal. I set</u> aside
                             2
time to write in it every day.

1. A. NO CHANGE
   B. four, writing, which
   C. four. Writing
   D. four, writing

2. Which of the following would NOT be an
   acceptable alternative to the underlined portion?

   F. journal, I set
   G. journal, and I set
   H. journal; I set
   J. journal and set

3. For centuries, scientists believed in the existence

of planets beyond the solar <u>system, but</u> had no way
                            1
of knowing how common they were or how similar

they might be to better-known planets. Beginning

in the 1900s, many people insisted that they had

discovered <u>exoplanets; however, the first</u>
                    2
confirmed detection did not occur until 1992.

1. A. NO CHANGE
   B. system. But
   C. system but
   D. system but they

2. F. NO CHANGE
   G. exoplanets, however the first
   H. exoplanets, however, the first
   J. exoplanets; but the first

4. The kangaroo is an unofficial symbol of

Australia, as a result, there are numerous popular
         1
culture references to it. A kangaroo appears

as an emblem on the Australian coat of arms as

well as on some Australian currency, and is also
                                   2
used by some well known organizations, including

Qantas airline and the Royal Australian Air Force.

1. A.   NO CHANGE
    B.   Australia; as a result,
    C.   Australia as a result,
    D.   Australia as a result

2. F.   NO CHANGE
    G.   currency, it is
    H.   currency. It is
    J.   currency; it being

5. Sweet Honey in the Rock is an award-

winning a cappella troupe. Its members recount
                    1
African American history through song, dance, and

sign language. The group was originally a four-

person ensemble but has expanded to five-part
        2
harmonies, a sixth member acts as a sign-language
        2
interpreter. The members of the group
        2
have changed many times during the group's
                     3
30-year existence, more than 20 individuals have
        3
lent their voices to the group. Their music has

consistently combined contemporary rhythms and

narratives with a musical style rooted in traditional

African American spirituals.

1. Which of the following would NOT be an
    acceptable alternative to the underlined portion
    of the sentence?

    A.   troupe, its members
    B.   troupe whose members
    C.   troupe with members who
    D.   troupe; its members

2. F.   NO CHANGE
    G.   ensemble, but has expanded to five-part
         harmonies, a sixth member acts as a sign-
         language interpreter
    H.   ensemble, but has expanded to five-part
         harmonies; a sixth member acting as a
         sign-language interpreter
    J.   ensemble but has expanded to five-part
         harmonies. A sixth member acts as a sign-
         language interpreter

3. A.   NO CHANGE
    B.   times, during the group's 30-year existence
    C.   times. During the group's 30-year
         existence,
    D.   times, during the group's 30-year existence,

6. Historians of the crossword puzzle (yes, they do exist) generally date the brainteaser's first appearance to December 21, <u>1913. Shortly before</u> the end of World War I. That year, Arthur Wynne
₁
of the *New York World* published what he called a "word-cross" in his paper's Fun <u>section; however,</u> more than ten years would go by before the
₂
crossword, as it was known by that time, would become one of the biggest fads of the 1920s.

1. **A.** NO CHANGE
   B. 1913, shortly before
   C. 1913, this was shortly before
   D. 1913; shortly before

2. **F.** NO CHANGE
   G. section, however,
   H. section however,
   J. section; but

7. Seagrove, North Carolina has been a home to potters for hundreds of <u>years in the 1700s,</u> they
₁
were drawn to the town by two things all potters of that era needed: good clay and an abundant supply of trees for firewood to heat their kilns. These early potters primarily produced redware, an earthenware made of soft, porous red clay that turns red when <u>fired at the time, most</u> Seagrove area potters were
₂
farmers who earned a little extra income by producing wares that were sold regionally or traded. Most of their output was strictly functional and included pots, bowls, jugs, and even roof tiles. A few potters added simple decorations to their <u>pottery, but most</u> did not.
₃

1. **A.** NO CHANGE
   B. years, in the 1700s
   C. years. In the 1700s,
   D. years in the 1700s

2. **F.** NO CHANGE
   G. fired, at the time,
   H. fired at the time
   J. fired. At the time,

3. **A.** NO CHANGE
   B. pottery; but most
   C. pottery, most
   D. pottery, most of them

45

8. With its bright, round eyes, furry body, and vividly striped tail, the lemur is among the most fascinating and mysterious creatures in the animal kingdom. Because of its haunting stare and preference for nighttime <u>activity; the lemur</u> is
[1]
named after the Latin word for "ghost." Millions of years ago, this ancient primate is believed to have "sailed" on clumps of vegetation from the African mainland to the island of <u>Madagascar. Where</u> it has
[2]
lived largely in isolation ever since.

1. **A.** NO CHANGE
   B. activity the lemur
   C. activity, the lemur
   D. activity. The lemur

2. **F.** NO CHANGE
   G. Madagascar; where
   H. Madagascar, this is where
   J. Madagascar, where

9. Beautiful, glamorous and mysterious, Saturn's rings are among the most recognizable features in the solar system. While the solar systems' other three gas giants – Jupiter, Uranus and Neptune – have rings orbiting around <u>them, Saturn</u> is by far
[1]
the largest and most spectacular. The rings spread over hundreds of thousands of <u>miles, they consist</u>
[2]
consist of billions of individual particles that create waves, turbulence and other effects.

1. **A.** NO CHANGE
   B. them; Saturn
   C. them, but Saturn
   D. them. Saturn

2. **F.** NO CHANGE
   G. miles, and consist
   H. miles; and they consist
   J. miles, and they consist

10.   I've never been the world's most adventurous

eater. For most of my childhood, I ate plain

noodles with butter or grilled cheese while the rest

of my family dined on chicken cacciatore or grilled

<u>salmon occasionally</u>, my parents persuaded me to
    1
try a few bites of a new dish, but I could never

bring myself to finish an entire plate of asparagus

or steamed mussels.

    Last year, however, I was invited to spend a

month in Dijon, France, as an exchange student. I

would live with a local <u>family, and attend</u> classes at
                              2
a nearby high school. Although I'd studied French

for several <u>years; I had never</u> traveled to a French-
              3
speaking country. I was anxious meet my host

family and try out my language skills. The only

thing that worried me was the food.

1. **A.** NO CHANGE
   B. salmon. Occasionally,
   C. salmon, occasionally
   D. salmon, occasionally

2. **F.** NO CHANGE
   G. family and attend
   H. family and attending
   J. family, which I would attend

3. **A.** NO CHANGE
   B. years. I had never
   C. years, I had never
   D. years I had never

4. Non-Essential and Essential Clauses

As discussed in Chapter 2, non-essential words and phrases can be removed from a sentence without affecting its essential meaning. If these words or phrases are removed from a sentence, the sentence will still make grammatical sense. Consider the following sentence:

Correct: The Tower of London, **which was begun by William the Conqueror in 1078,** is one of the largest and most imposing fortifications in England.

The sentence contains a clause that is surrounded by commas and that begins with the word *which*. If we cross out that clause, we are left with this:

Correct: The Tower of London…is one of the largest and most imposing fortifications in England.

The sentence that remains makes complete sense on its own, indicating that the two commas were necessary.

Important: One of the ACT's absolute favorite ways to create errors is to give you a non-essential clause that is missing one or both of its commas. In such cases, you are responsible for recognizing where in the sentence the non-essential clause begins and ends – that is, where the missing comma or commas belong.

For example, it is very common to see sentences that look like these:

Incorrect: The Tower of London, **which was begun by William the Conqueror in 1078** is one of the largest and most imposing fortifications in England.

Incorrect: The Tower of London **which was begun by William the Conqueror in 1078,** is one of the largest and most imposing fortifications in England.

Incorrect: The Tower of London **which was begun by William the Conqueror in 1078** is one of the largest and most imposing fortifications in England.

In order to correct the sentence, you must recognize that it will still make sense if the clause *which was begun by William the Conqueror in 1078* is removed, and that commas must therefore be added around that clause.

Correct: The Tower of London, **which was begun by William the Conqueror in 1078,** is one of the largest and most imposing fortifications in England.

Sometimes non-essential clauses can be very long and confusing. In such cases, you must make sure to look all the way back to the beginning of the sentence and consider whether the sentence will still make sense if a particular section is removed. Keep in mind that you may have to cross out a lot of information to test out whether a non-essential clause is present.

Non-Essential Transition Words and Phrases

While non-essential clauses can be very long, they can also consist of single **transition** words and short phrases. Common examples include *however, in fact, moreover,* and *on the other hand.* Like longer non-essential clauses, these words and phrases must be surrounded by commas when they appear in the middle of a sentence:

Correct: The Tower of London was built during the Norman Conquest. It has**, in fact,** served as a treasury, an armory, and the home of the Royal Mint.

Correct: The Tower of London was built during the Norman Conquest. It still**, however,** remains standing nearly a thousand years later.

Although the placement of these words and phrases may seem odd to you, it is perfectly acceptable. Where commas are concerned, only grammar is important.

Important: Do not try to "cross out" information mentally. Take a pencil (not a pen!) and physically draw a line through the words on your test, as in the example below. You can always erase the line if necessary, but you're a lot more likely to miss something important if you don't actually cross out the words.

You should also make sure to look for key words such as *which, who(se),* and *where,* which often signal the start of a non-essential clause. In addition, you should think carefully about where in the sentence it is logical for the non-essential clause to end. This is particularly important when several lines of the passage are underlined, or when several questions asking about punctuation in a given section are presented consecutively.

For example:

Incorrect: London**, which was originally built by the Romans along the banks of the Thames more than two thousand years ago** contains some extremely modern neighborhoods.

Crossed Out: London**, ~~which was originally built by the Romans along the banks of the Thames more than two thousand years ago~~** contains some extremely modern neighborhoods.

The sentence that remains makes sense, so it is necessary to insert the second comma after *ago.*

Correct: London**, which was originally built by the Romans along the banks of the Thames more than two thousand years ago,** contains some extremely modern neighborhoods.

If you encounter a sentence such as this on the ACT and neglect to look back to the beginning, you may overlook the word *which,* which signals the start of a non-essential clause.

Important: two commas do not always equal a non-essential clause!

One common mistake is to assume that the presence of two commas in a sentence automatically indicates a non-essential clause. Compare the following two sentences:

Sentence #1:   London, which was one of the largest and most important cities in Europe during the Middle Ages, remains an important financial and cultural center today.

This sentence contains a non-essential clause that can be removed without altering its basic meaning:

London, ~~which was one of the largest and most important cities in Europe during the Middle Ages,~~ remains an important financial and cultural center today.

Now take a look at this sentence:

Sentence #2:   During the Middle Ages, London was one of the largest and most important cities in Europe, and today it remains an important financial and cultural center.

If we cross out the information between the commas, we get this:

During the Middle Ages, ~~London was one of the largest and most important cities in Europe,~~ and today it remains an important financial and cultural center.

The remaining sentence does not make sense, indicating that the information between the two commas is essential. The two commas are still necessary, however, just for different reasons.

In addition, some sentences containing commas that set off non-essential clauses may <u>also</u> contain commas that serve unrelated purposes. In such cases, it can be difficult to quickly tell where non-essential clauses are located.

Sumo wrestling, a full-contact sport in which competitors attempt to force one another out of a circular ring, originated in Japan, which remains the only country in the world where it is practiced.

The above sentence contains only one non-essential clause that can be removed without creating a problem:

Sumo wrestling, ~~a full-contact sport in which competitors attempt to force one another out of a circular ring,~~ originated in Japan, which remains the only country in the world where it is practiced.

If the information between a different set of commas is removed, however, we are left with nonsense:

Sumo wrestling, a full-contact sport in which competitors attempt to force one another out of a circular ring, ~~originated in Japan,~~ which remains the only country in the world where it is practiced.

If you cannot hear where the non-essential clause belongs, take your pencil, draw a line through the section you want to test out, and read the sentence without that section. If the remaining sentence does not make sense, erase the line, cross out a different section, and try again. It is very important that you go through this process because it is the only way you have of figuring out the answer logically.

Transitions: Two Commas vs. Semicolon or Period

Many of the transition words and phrases that are used non-essentially **within** clauses are also used to **begin** clauses. When this is the case, these words/phrases should not be surrounded by commas but rather should come after a semicolon or a period.

Compare the punctuation surrounding the word *however* when it is used non-essentially:

   Sentence #1:   London is a very old city. It does, **however,** contain some modern neighborhoods.

…and the punctuation surrounding the word *however* when it is used to begin a clause:

   Sentence #2:   London is a very old **city; however,** it does contain some modern neighborhoods.

Both of these constructions are perfectly acceptable; the punctuation simply changes because the grammatical role that the word *however* plays within the sentence changes.

In Sentence #1, the two commas around *however* tell us that if we cross the word out, the sentence will still make sense. And sure enough, if we cross out *however*, we are left with a grammatically acceptable sentence – even if that sentence does not make much sense outside of context:

   Correct: It does…contain some modern neighborhoods.

In Sentence #2, on the other hand, the semicolon indicates that *however* is being used to begin a clause. We cannot therefore do the following:

   Incorrect: London is a very old city, however, it does contain some modern neighborhoods.

In the above version of the sentence, the two commas imply that the word *however* can be removed without affecting the sentence's essential meaning. But if we remove those commas, we end up with a **fused sentence** – two independent clauses placed back-to-back without any punctuation between them. Fused sentences are always incorrect.

   Incorrect: London is a very old city it does contain some modern neighborhoods.

The need for two commas vs. a semicolon is determined solely by context. While there is no automatic "trick" for recognizing when one rather than the other is required, you should try crossing out the word or phrase in question and reading the sentence without it if you are uncertain which type of punctuation is required. If the sentence makes sense, the word or phrase is being used non-essentially, and two commas should be used; if the sentence does not make sense, you need a semicolon or a period.

Drill: Identifying Non-Essential Clauses (answers p. 252)

1. A tandem is a form of bicycle designed to be ridden by more than one <u>person, however,</u> the
    ₁
    term "tandem" refers to the seating arrangement (front to back), not the number of riders.

1. **A.** NO CHANGE
    B. person; however,
    C. person however,
    D. person, however

2. L. Frank Baum, who is best known for *The Wonderful Wizard of Oz* <u>actually wrote</u> thirteen
    ₁
    novels based on the land of Oz. When it was published in 1900, *The Wonderful Wizard of Oz* became an instant success, remaining the best-selling children's novel for two years. The other novels in the "Oz" <u>series, however,</u> did not
    ₂
    achieve the same degree of popularity.

X 1. **F.** NO CHANGE   *read closely*
       G. Oz actually, wrote
     ✓ **H.** Oz actually wrote
       J. Oz actually, wrote,

2. **A.** NO CHANGE
    B. series; however,
    C. series, however
    D. series however,

3. The red belt, ~~one of several colored belts used~~ <u>in some martial arts to indicate the practitioner's</u> <u>level,</u> is most commonly used in Judo, a martial art
    ₁
    that originated in Japan. Like the more commonly known black <u>belt, ~~which is used in Karate~~,</u> the red
    ₂
    belt can indicate Grandmaster status or other high <u>rank, in contrast,</u> other forms of martial arts use the
    ₃
    red belt to indicate pre-black belt rank or even to denote a beginner who holds no rank.

1. **A.** NO CHANGE
    B. level, is most commonly used in Judo a martial art
    C. level is most commonly used in Judo, a martial art
    D. level, is most commonly used in Judo. A martial art

2. **F.** NO CHANGE
    G. belt which is used in Karate
    H. belt. Which is used in Karate
    J. belt, which is used, in Karate,

3. **A.** NO CHANGE
    B. rank in contrast,
    C. rank, in contrast
    D. rank. In contrast,

52

4. George Barris, ~~who created the Batmobile for the Batman films~~ also built many other vehicles for movies and television programs. According to
1

Barris, some of his first film work consisted of
2
making soft aluminum fenders, for a Ford police
2
car that crashes into the rear of a Mercedes Benz convertible. The scene was a challenge for Barris who wanted to make the scene both comic and

thrilling, ~~nevertheless, he succeeded,~~ going on to
3
pursue a decades-long career in the big-screen automotive industry.

1. A. NO CHANGE
   B. films, also built
   C. films, he also built
   D. films; also built

2. F. NO CHANGE
   G. Barris, some of his first film work consisted of making soft aluminum fenders
   H. Barris; some of his first film work consisted of making soft aluminum fenders,
   J. Barris some of his first film work consisted of making soft aluminum fenders

3. A. NO CHANGE
   B. thrilling, nevertheless, he succeeded
   C. thrilling; nevertheless, he succeeded,
   D. thrilling nevertheless, he succeeded

5. Every year, nature-lovers flock to the Arnold Arboretum in Boston, Massachusetts. The arboretum founded in 1872, features
1
hundreds of tree, flower, and plant species;

however, ~~of all the plants in the arboretum's~~

collection, only one the lilac, is honored with an
2
entire day of celebration. That day, moreover, is the arboretum's biggest event of the year. Known as

Lilac Sunday, it is a day when the arboretum's
3
normally serene atmosphere gives way to fun and
3
festivities, in fact, it is the only day that visitors are
3
allowed to picnic on the arboretum's grounds.

1. A. NO CHANGE
   B. arboretum. Founded in 1872
   C. arboretum, founded in 1872,
   D. arboretum founded in 1872,

2. F. NO CHANGE
   G. collection, only one. The lilac is
   H. collection, only one the lilac is
   J. collection, only one, the lilac, is

3. A. NO CHANGE
   B. Sunday, it is a day when the arboretum's normally serene atmosphere gives way to fun and festivities. In fact,
   C. Sunday, it is a day when the arboretum's normally serene atmosphere gives way, to fun and festivities, in fact,
   D. Sunday. It is a day when the arboretum's normally serene atmosphere gives way to fun and festivities, in fact,

53

Essential Clauses With and Without "That"

Clauses beginning with *that* are always essential to the meaning of a sentence and should **never be set off by commas** (or any other form of punctuation, in most cases). The use of a comma before or after *that* is virtually always **incorrect**.

Incorrect: Parrots are one of the most difficult **pets, that** a person can have because they are intelligent, demanding, and live for up to 50 years.

Incorrect: Parrots are one of the most difficult **pets that,** a person can have because they are intelligent, demanding, and live for up to 50 years.

Correct: Parrots are one of the most difficult **pets that** a person can have because they are intelligent, demanding, and live for up to 50 years.

In the above sentence, the word *that* is optional. The sentence can be correctly written both with and without it.

Correct: Parrots are one of the most difficult **pets that** a person can have because they are intelligent, demanding, and live for up to 50 years.

Correct: Parrots are one of the most difficult **pets a** person can have because they are intelligent, demanding, and live for up to 50 years.

If the word *that* is deleted, however, no comma should be used in its place. When *that* is optional and is not used, it is always incorrect to insert a comma in its place.

Incorrect: Parrots are one of the most difficult **pets, a** person can have because they are intelligent, demanding, and live for up to 50 years.

This error usually appears at least once per test. It can also be difficult to catch, first because it often seems that a small pause is required at the comma, and second because most people would not naturally stop and consider whether the clause could also be written with *that*. Mastering this type of question is therefore largely a result of training yourself to spot clauses that can be written either way.

Otherwise, you can think of things this way: if you've mastered the key ways in which commas <u>should</u> be used (FANBOYS, non-essential clauses, lists) and encounter a comma used in a different way, you can be pretty sure that comma is wrong.

The Case of "Who:" Non-Essential vs. Essential Clauses

One potentially tricky concept that the ACT tests is the ability to distinguish between essential and non-essential information based on context. For example, it is possible to write the following sentence two different ways. **Both ways are grammatically correct**, but they have different emphases.

Correct: People**, who attend large open air events such as sporting matches and music festivals,** often turn to camping as a cheap form of accommodation.

The commas in the above sentence imply that the clause between them is not central to the meaning of the sentence. The emphasis is on the fact that people often turn to camping in order to save money. The fact that they attend large open air events such as sporting matches and music festivals is **less important**.

Correct: People **who attend large open air events such as sporting matches and music festivals** often turn to camping as a cheap form of accommodation.

The lack of commas in this version of the sentences indicates that it is not discussing people in general but rather **a specific group of people**: those who attend large open air events such as sporting matches and music festivals. While the first version of the sentence is grammatically correct, this version simply makes more sense.

Grammatically, these sentences can be written either way without a problem – the focus of the sentence merely shifts depending on whether the commas are used. When a sentence that can be written either with or without commas is considered in the context of a paragraph, however, things get a bit more complicated.

Consider the following:

The store where I work has a return policy I

have always found amusing. Normally, customers

have one year from the purchase date to return

unwanted or defective items; however, <u>customers,</u>
1

<u>who make purchases on February 29th</u>, have *four*
1

years to return their items. The store's owner

reasons that customers should have the right to

return an item until the next occurrence of the date

on which they bought it. Since February 29th occurs

only once every four years, customers should thus

be allowed nearly 1,500 days to decide whether

they truly want a toaster or a pair of shoes.

1. **A.** NO CHANGE
   B. customers, who make purchases on February 29th
   C. customers who make purchases on February 29th,
   D. customers who make purchases on February 29th

Solution: The phrase *who make purchases on February 29th* cannot be crossed out of the sentence because it specifies which customers are being discussed. The remainder of the paragraph talks *only* about those particular customers, not about customers in general. Furthermore, without the phrase, the passage would contradict itself because the previous sentence states that customers normally only have one year to return unwanted items. The underlined portion shifts toward an exception to that rule. No commas are thus necessary, and (A) is incorrect.

(B) is incorrect because the clause in question must either have two commas, indicating that it is non-essential, or no commas, indicating that it is essential. Only one comma is never an option.

(C) is incorrect for the same reason as (B), except that in this case the single comma is placed at the end of the clause rather than at the beginning. This answer is a little trickier, however: the **complete subject**, *customers who make purchases on February 29th*, is quite long. As a result, it might seem that a pause is needed before the verb, *have*. Even when a subject is very long, however, no comma should be placed between it and the verb.

(D) is correct because the lack of commas indicates that the underlined information is essential to the meaning of the sentence, and the subject is not separated from the verb.

Let's look at another example:

The hexacopter, a lump of steel propellers and

lenses, is both camera and flying machine. This

contraption is revolutionizing the way news is

reported. In the past, journalists, ~~who wanted to~~
                                    1
~~obtain aerial shots of events to accompany their~~
                         1
stories, were forced to rely on conventional
      1

helicopters, which often flew too high to capture

detailed images. The hexacopter, however, can

catapult itself into the air and hover right above the

scene the photographer wishes to record.

1. **A.** NO CHANGE
    B. journalists who wanted to obtain aerial shots to accompany their stories,
    C. journalists, who wanted to obtain aerial shots to accompany their stories
    D. journalists who wanted to obtain aerial shots to accompany their stories

Solution: (B) and C) can be eliminated pretty quickly because our options are two commas or no commas. If we were to cross out the information between the commas, the sentence would still make perfect grammatical sense (*In the past, journalists...were forced to rely on conventional helicopters*).

The problem is that by definition, the commas imply that the information between them is not essential – and in this case, the information is important. Based on the context, it is clear that the sentence is not talking about journalists in general, as the commas would imply, but rather about **specific** journalists: those who wanted to obtain aerial shots to accompany their stories. Because that information is necessary to define the type of journalists being discussed, no commas should be used. (D) is therefore correct.

It is also possible that you will encounter other types of clauses that can be either essential or non-essential. Such questions appear rarely, but you should be prepared for the possibility of encountering them.

For example, consider the following:

In 2004, while rummaging in a Seattle basement, historian and journalist J. Pennelope Goforth came across a silver shopping bag with **an envelope** inside. <u>The envelope marked "Alaska Commercial Company"</u> immediately caught her attention. For years, Goforth had researched the company, which had controlled Alaska's waters in the late nineteenth century.

1. **A.** NO CHANGE
    B. The envelope marked "Alaska Commercial Company,"
    C. The envelope, marked "Alaska Commercial Company,"
    D. The envelope, marked "Alaska Commercial Company"

Solution: The real question here is whether the clause *marked "Alaska Commercial Company"* is essential (no commas) or essential (two commas). If the sentence is crossed out, we're left with *The envelope…immediately caught her attention.* Since the envelope has already been mentioned in the previous sentence, the sentence still makes sense in context. Two commas should therefore be used, making (C) correct.

On the other hand, consider this version of the passage:

In 2004, while rummaging in a Seattle basement, historian and journalist J. Pennelope Goforth came across a silver shopping bag filled with **envelopes**. <u>The envelope marked "Alaska Commercial Company"</u> immediately caught her
1
attention. For years, Goforth had researched the company, which had controlled Alaska's waters in the late nineteenth century.

1. **A.** NO CHANGE
    B. The envelope marked "Alaska Commercial Company,"
    C. The envelope, marked "Alaska Commercial Company,"
    D. The envelope, marked "Alaska Commercial Company"

Solution: Crossing out the phrase *marked "Alaska Commercial Company"* again leaves us with *The envelope immediately caught her attention.* This time, however, the sentence no longer makes sense in context because the previous sentence only refers to "envelopes." As a result, we don't know which envelope caught Goforth's attention. The clause is therefore necessary, so no commas should be used. (A) is thus correct.

Commas with Names and Titles

Names and titles can be either essential or non-essential. While you may have learned in school that a comma should always be placed before a name or title, that is not the whole story. Commas should *sometimes* be placed before – and after – names and titles. Other times no commas at all should be used. It depends on the context.

Important: when a name or title appears in the middle of a sentence (that is, not as the first or last words), there are generally only two correct options.

    1) Two commas, one before and one after the name/title

    2) No commas at all

In rare instances, a single comma may be required after the name or title for other reasons, as discussed later in the chapter.

The simplest way to determine whether commas are necessary is to treat the name or title like any other non-essential word or clause. Take your pencil, cross the name/title out, and see whether the rest of the sentence makes sense **in context** without it. If it makes sense, the commas are necessary; if it does not make sense, the commas are not necessary.

Let's look at how this rule would play out in some test-style questions:

Ada Lovelace and her <u>acquaintance, Charles</u>
                         1

<u>Babbage,</u> were two of the most influential figures in
1
the history of computer science. After Babbage

sketched out his ideas for an "analytical engine,"

Lovelace demonstrated that the machine might be

able to carry out a variety of complex tasks.

1. **A.** NO CHANGE
   B. acquaintance Charles Babbage
   C. acquaintance Charles Babbage,
   D. acquaintances, Charles Babbage

Solution: Because the name *Charles Babbage* appears in the middle of a sentence, our options are two commas or no commas, eliminating (C) and (D). To decide between (A) and (B), we're going to cross out the name:

> **Ada Lovelace and her acquaintance were two of the most influential figures in the history of computer science.**

At this point, we need to be careful and consider the context. The sentence is still grammatically acceptable, but a crucial piece of information is lost: we do not know who Lovelace's acquaintance was. As a result, the reference to Babbage in the following sentence does not make sense. So the name is essential, and no commas are required. The answer is therefore (B).

Another way to think of this rule is as follows:

- Commas around a name or title imply that it is the **only** person or thing.

- No commas around a name or title imply that it is **one of many** people or things.

While approaching questions this way can be confusing, it does offer another way of thinking them through.

In the case of the question on the previous page, placing commas around *Charles Babbage* would imply that Babbage was Ada Lovelace's **only** acquaintance. Is that possible? Yes, theoretically. But it's probably not what the writer intended to say. Without the commas, the sentence implies that Ada Lovelace had multiple acquaintances, one of whom was Charles Babbage. That version simply makes more sense.

In some cases, knowing this rule may allow you determine the answer more quickly. Consider the following two sentences. Although both versions are grammatically acceptable, only the second one creates a logical meaning.

Incorrect: The controversy over baseball player Satchel Paige's true date of birth was stoked by Paige's **mother Lula**.

Correct: The controversy over baseball player Satchel Paige's true date of birth was stoked by Paige's **mother, Lula**.

In the first version, the missing comma before *Lula* implies that she was one of many mothers. Logically, though, Paige only had one mother! Although the sentence is acceptable, its meaning is nonsensical.

In contrast, the comma before *Lula* in the second version of the sentence implies that Paige only had one mother, and that her name was Lula – a far more reasonable implication.

Let's look at another example:

Caribbean-American <u>author, Jamaica Kincaid</u>
                                        1
is also known for being an enthusiastic essayist and

gardener. She was born Elaine Potter Richardson in

St. John's, Antigua but came to the United States at

the age of 17 to work as an au pair in Westchester

County, New York. She eventually won a scholarship

to Franconia College in New Hampshire but returned

to New York City to write. In 1985, she published the

novel, *Annie John*, a semiautobiographical story of a

young girl growing up in Antigua.

1. **A.** NO CHANGE
    B. author Jamaica Kincaid
    C. author, Jamaica Kincaid
    D. author Jamaica Kincaid

Solution: Once again, we're going to start by crossing the name out of the sentence.

Caribbean-American author...is also known for being an enthusiastic essayist and gardener.

No, that makes no sense. The name is clearly essential, so no commas are necessary. The answer is thus (B).

Now, however, consider this version of the passage:

I've always been interested in gardening, but until recently, I didn't have room for flowers or plants. When I moved into a new house last summer, however, I was thrilled to discover that there was enough space in the yard for a garden. There was just one problem – I'd never actually planted one. So I called a friend who had a lot more gardening experience than I did. Luckily, that <u>friend, Jane,</u> agreed to come over the next day.

1. **A.** NO CHANGE
   B. friend, Jane
   C. friend Jane,
   D. friend Jane

Solution: Again, our options are two commas or no commas. When we cross out *Jane*, the resulting sentence makes sense (*Luckily, that friend agreed to come over the next day*). The commas are necessary, making (A) correct.

Now let's look at an example of a title question. We're going to revisit this passage from a different angle:

Jamaica Kincaid (born May 25, 1949) is a novelist, essayist, and gardener. She was born Elaine Potter Richardson in St. John's, Antigua but came to the United States at the age of 17 to work as an au pair in Westchester County, New York. She eventually won a scholarship to Franconia College in New Hampshire but returned to New York City to write. In 1985, she published <u>the novel, *Annie John,*</u> a semiautobiographical story of a young girl growing up in Antigua.

1. **A.** NO CHANGE
   B. the novel *Annie John,*
   C. the novel, *Annie John*
   D. the novel *Annie John*

Solution: As always, we're going to start by crossing the title out of the sentence and reading the sentence without it.

> **In 1985, she published the novel...a semiautobiographical story of a young girl growing up in Antigua.**

No, this does not make sense in context because we do not know which novel the sentence is referring to. The information is therefore essential, meaning that commas should not be placed around the title.

But wait, there's a twist! This is the rare **exception** to the "two commas or no commas" rule. A comma is required to separate the independent first clause from the dependent second clause (*In 1985, she published the novel Annie John, a semiautobiographical story of a young girl growing up in Antigua*). Without the comma, we just get a big jumble. So the answer is (B).

If a name or title appears at the end of the sentence, the rule is similar: a comma indicates that the name or title can be crossed out, while no comma indicates that the name or title cannot be crossed out.

> Incorrect: Glass is the building material most often associated with **celebrated architect, I.M. Pei.**

The comma before I.M. Pei implies that the name can be crossed out of the sentence. If you cross it out, however, you get the following:

> Incorrect: Glass is the building material most often associated with celebrated architect.

Clearly, this version does not make any sense. The comma should therefore not be used.

> Correct: Glass is the building material most often associated with **celebrated architect I.M. Pei**.

You can also think of the sentence this way: even though the word *architect* is typically used as a noun, here it's actually acting as an adjective that **describes** I.M. Pei.

Since adjectives should never be separated from the nouns they describe by commas, no comma should be placed between *architect* and *I.M. Pei*.

Drill: Commas with Essential and Non-Essential Clauses (answers p. 252)

1. Lisa See, author of the <u>best-selling novel, *Snow*</u>
<u>*Flower and the Secret Fan,*</u> has always been intrigued
₁

by stories that have been lost, forgotten, or

deliberately covered up. To research the book, See

traveled to a remote area of China <u>that, ~~she was~~</u>
₂
~~told~~ only one foreigner before her had ever visited.
₂

While there, See was able to investigate a secret

type of writing that women had kept hidden for

over a thousand years.

1. **A.** NO CHANGE
   B. best-selling novel *Snow Flower and the Secret Fan*
   C. best-selling novel, *Snow Flower and the Secret Fan*
   D. best-selling novel *Snow Flower and the Secret Fan,*

2. **F.** NO CHANGE
   G. that she was told,
   H. that; she was told
   J. that, she was told,

2. Grant Wood's best known <u>painting, *American*</u>
₁
<u>*Gothic,*</u> is one of the few images to reach the status
₁
of universally recognized cultural icon. The work

depicts a severe-looking farmer and his daughter,

and it was first exhibited in 1930 at the Art

Institute of Chicago, where it is still located today.

Photographs of the painting, ~~which was awarded a~~

~~$300 prize~~ appeared in newspapers country-wide
₂
and brought Wood immediate recognition. Since

then, it has been borrowed and satirized endlessly

for advertisements and cartoons.

1. **A.** NO CHANGE
   B. painting *American Gothic*
   C. painting *American Gothic,*
   D. painting, and *American Gothic*

2. **F.** NO CHANGE
   G. prize, and appeared
   H. prize, appeared
   J. prize, appearing

3. Alfred Mosher Butts, the American architect, who created Scrabble™, intended it to be a variation on an existing word game Lexiko. The two games had the same set of letter tiles and point values, which Butts had worked out by analyzing the frequency with which letters appeared in newspapers and magazines. He decided, the new game should be called "Criss-Crosswords" and added the 15 x 15 game board. Butts created a few sets himself, but the first manufacturers, who inspected them, did not think that the game was likely to become very popular.

1. A. NO CHANGE
   B. architect, he created Scrabble™,
   C. architect who created Scrabble™,
   D. architect and who created Scrabble™

2. F. NO CHANGE
   G. values that, he had worked out
   H. values. He had worked out
   J. values, he had worked out,

3. A. NO CHANGE
   B. He decided the new game,
   C. He decided, the new game,
   D. He decided the new game

4. F. NO CHANGE
   G. himself; but the first manufacturers who inspected them,
   H. himself, but the first manufacturers. Who inspected them
   J. himself, but the first manufacturers who inspected them

4. In November 1895, German physicist, Wilhelm Roentgen accidentally discovered an image created by rays emanating from a vacuum tube. Further investigation showed, the rays penetrated many kinds of matter. A week after his discovery, Roentgen photographed the hand of his wife, Anna, clearly revealing her wedding ring and bones. The image electrified the general public and aroused great scientific interest in the new form of radiation, which Roentgen named the X-ray.

1. A. NO CHANGE
   B. physicist Wilhelm Roentgen,
   C. physicist Wilhelm Roentgen
   D. physicist, Wilhelm Roentgen,

2. F. NO CHANGE
   G. showed, that the rays
   H. showed; the rays
   J. showed that the rays

3. A. NO CHANGE
   B. wife Anna, clearly revealed
   C. wife Anna; clearly revealing
   D. wife Anna, it clearly revealed

5. First recorded in 1835, the <u>disease, polio,</u>
                                    1
baffled researchers for decades. According to

<u>historian William O'Neill,</u> "polio was, if not
       2
the most serious, easily the most frightening

public health problem of the 1940s and '50s."

As result, scientists found themselves in a frantic

race to find a cure. During the 1940s, <u>President</u>
                                         3
<u>Franklin D. Roosevelt,</u> was the world's most
           3
recognized polio victim. In 1938, he had

founded the <u>organization, the March of Dimes</u>
                    4
to fund the development of a cure. Before a

vaccine was finally discovered by the American

<u>scientist Jonas Salk</u> in 1955, more than 80 percent
        5
of polio patients were helped by the foundation.

1. A. NO CHANGE
   B. disease polio
   C. disease, polio
   D. disease: polio

2. F. NO CHANGE
   G. historian, William O'Neill,
   H. historian William O'Neill
   J. historian, William O'Neill

3. A. NO CHANGE
   B. President, Franklin D. Roosevelt
   C. President, Franklin D. Roosevelt,
   D. President Franklin D. Roosevelt

4. F. NO CHANGE
   G. organization the March of Dimes
   H. organization the March of Dimes,
   J. organization. The March of Dimes

5. A. NO CHANGE
   B. scientist Jonas Salk,
   C. scientist, Jonas Salk,
   D. scientist, Jonas Salk

6. Along with her <u>husband, Martin Luther King,</u>
                         1
Coretta Scott King played an important role in the

Civil Rights Movement. She was most active in the

years after 1968, when she took on the leadership

of the struggle for racial equality herself and

became a leading figure in the women's movement.

Although Mrs. King would object to the <u>term,</u>
                                          2
<u>"pacifism,"</u> she was a longtime activist for world
    2
peace.

1. A. NO CHANGE
   B. husband Martin Luther King
   C. husband Martin Luther King,
   D. husband, Martin Luther King

2. F. NO CHANGE
   G. term pacifism,
   H. term, pacifism
   J. term pacifism

64

5. Additional Comma Uses and Misuses

Commas <u>should</u> be used:

A. To Separate Items in a List

In any list of three or more items, each item must be followed by a comma. The comma before *and* is optional. The ACT will never ask you to choose between a version with the comma and a version without the comma.

Correct: The museum's new open-storage display brings some 900 vintage World's Fair souvenirs out of attics, desk drawers, **shoeboxes, and museum** archives for visitors to view.

Correct: The museum's new open-storage display brings some 900 vintage World's Fair souvenirs out of attics, desk drawers, **shoeboxes and museum** archives for visitors to view.

No comma should ever be used **after** the word *and*.

Incorrect: The museum's open-storage display brings over 900 vintage World's Fair souvenirs out of attics, desk drawers, **shoeboxes, and, museum** archives for visitors to view.

Incorrect: The museum's open-storage display brings over 900 vintage World's Fair souvenirs out of attics, desk drawers, **shoeboxes and, museum** archives for visitors to view.

B. To Separate Adjectives Whose Order Could be Reversed

When the order of the adjectives does not matter, then a comma should be used. You can also try placing the word *and* between the adjectives; if they can be separated that way, then the comma is correct.

Correct: One of the Queens Museum's recent exhibits featured works by contemporary artists from Japan, Taiwan, and Ireland, offering patrons the chance to see a kind of **innovative, passionate** art that larger museums often ignore.

Correct: One of the Queens Museum's recent exhibits featured works by contemporary artists from Japan, Taiwan, and Ireland, offering patrons the chance to see a kind of **passionate, innovative** art that larger museums often ignore.

Correct: One of the Queens Museum's recent exhibits featured works by contemporary artists from Japan, Taiwan, and Ireland, offering patrons the chance to see a kind of **innovative and passionate** art that larger museums often ignore.

If the order of the adjectives cannot be reversed, the word *and* cannot be placed between them, or one adjective is used to modify the other, no comma should be used:

Incorrect: Columbian artist Maria Fernanda Cardoso often makes use of **colorful, plastic objects** in her paintings and sculptures.

Incorrect: Columbian artist Maria Fernanda Cardoso often makes use of **colorful and plastic objects** in her paintings and sculptures.

Correct: Columbian artist Maria Fernanda Cardoso often makes use of **colorful plastic objects** in her paintings and sculptures.

In the above sentence, the adjective *colorful* describes *plastic objects*, so a comma should not be used between the two adjectives.

C. After a Close-Parenthesis Where a Comma Would Normally be Necessary

Sentences that test both commas and parentheses simultaneously are rare, but they do appear from time to time. In general, the best way to approach such sentences is to simply pretend the parentheses do not exist.

Correct: The Tower of London was constructed as a prison in the eleventh century (1078 to be exact), but over the centuries it has been used as everything from an armory to a treasury.

If we eliminate the parentheses, we are left with two independent clauses joined by a FANBOYS conjunction:

Correct: The Tower of London was constructed as a prison in the eleventh **century, but** over the centuries it has been used as everything from an armory to a treasury.

No comma should be used before an open-parenthesis, however:

Incorrect: The Tower of London was constructed as a prison in the eleventh **century, (1078 to be exact),** but over the centuries it has been used as everything from an armory to a treasury.

The reason is that the two commas indicate the presence of non-essential information, but the parentheses *already* serve that function. If we eliminate only the parentheses and leave the rest of the sentence exactly the same, the result is as follows:

Incorrect: The Tower of London was constructed as a prison in the eleventh **century,, but** over the centuries it has been used as everything from an armory to a treasury.

Removing the parentheses leaves us with two commas next to one another, a construction that cannot ever be correct.

66

D. After Introductory Words and Phrases

Introductory words and phrases (e.g. *in fact, essentially, moreover, as a result*) should be set off by commas.

For example:

Correct: **At first,** it looked as if the storm was going to miss us by a few hundred miles.

Correct: **Nevertheless,** Armstrong persisted and became one of the greatest jazz musicians of all time.

Note, however, that (subordinating conjunctions) *dependent* such as *although* and *because* <u>cannot</u> be used as introductory words. Only conjunctive adverbs (e.g. *however, therefore, moreover, furthermore, nevertheless, consequently, meanwhile*) can be used this way.

Incorrect: Desserts were traditionally characterized by their sweetness. **Although,** bakers are now creating ones that feature intriguing blends of sweet and savory.

Correct: Desserts were traditionally characterized by their sweetness. **However,** bakers are now creating ones that feature intriguing blends of sweet and savory.

Important: The use of commas after introductory words and phrases is not normally tested on the ACT. Whenever you are given a set of answer choices consisting of introductory words or phrases, all will typically include commas. In these cases, the focus will not be on the grammar but rather on finding the option whose meaning is most appropriate in context of the sentence/passage.

Commas should NOT be used:

A. Between Compound Subjects and Compound Objects

A **compound subject** consists of two or more nouns joined by the word *and*. A comma should never be placed between the items in a compound subject.

Incorrect: **Ada Lovelace, and Charles Babbage** were two of the most influential figures in the history of computer science and mathematics.

Correct: **Ada Lovelace and Charles Babbage** were two of the most influential figures in the history of computer science and mathematics.

This sentence also contains a compound object, *computer science and mathematics*. A sentence should also never contain a comma between the items in a compound object.

Incorrect: Ada Lovelace, and Charles Babbage were two of the most influential figures in the history of **computer science, and mathematics**.

Correct: Ada Lovelace and Charles Babbage were two of the most influential figures in the history of **computer science and mathematics**.

You can also think of it this way: because *comma* + *and* = period, you can plug in a period in place of *comma* + *and*, then check whether there are two sentences. Since *Ada Lovelace* in the first sentence and *mathematics* in the second are not complete sentences, no comma should be used.

B. Between Subjects and Verbs

Unless a subject and verb are separated by a non-essential clause, no comma should be placed between them.

Incorrect: Ada Lovelace and Charles Babbage, **were** two of the most influential figures in the history of computer science, and mathematics.

Correct: Ada Lovelace and Charles Babbage **were** two of the most influential figures in the history of computer science and mathematics.

This rule holds true even when subjects are extremely long and complex.

Incorrect: What is particularly remarkable about Ada Lovelace's work on Babbage's "analytical "engine," **is** that she foresaw many of the ways in which computers are used today.

Correct: What is particularly remarkable about Ada Lovelace's work on Babbage's "analytical "engine" **is** that she foresaw many of the ways in which computers are used today.

Even though you may feel that a pause is necessary before the verb (and even though it is acceptable to use one informally in order to break up long sentences), in strict grammatical terms, no comma should be used.

C. Before or After Prepositions

Prepositions are **location** and **time** words such as *of, for, from, to, in, with, by, before,* and *after*.

For the ACT, the most important thing to know about prepositions is that commas should not be used **before or after** them. Usually, the ACT will incorrectly place the comma before the preposition, but occasionally it will place the comma after the preposition. Although this error may not always appear in the passage itself, it will typically appear in incorrect answer choices multiple times on each test.

Incorrect: Ada Lovelace and Charles Babbage were two of the most influential **figures, in** the history of computer science and mathematics.

Incorrect: Ada Lovelace and Charles Babbage were two of the most influential **figures in,** the history of computer science and mathematics.

Correct: Ada Lovelace and Charles Babbage were two of the most influential **figures in** the history of computer science and mathematics.

The only **exception** to this rule occurs when a preposition is used to begin a non-essential clause. **This construction is tested rarely**, but questions including it have been included on past exams.

Correct: Although Ada Lovelace lived nearly a century before the first computer was built, she, **in a way that was unique among nineteenth century mathematicians,** predicted many of the modern computer's capabilities.

D. Between Adjectives and Nouns

Incorrect: Headquartered in New York, the National Academy of Television Arts and Sciences (NATAS) is a **national, organization** that has local chapters around the country.

Correct: Headquartered in New York, the National Academy of Television Arts and Sciences (NATAS) is a **national organization** that has local chapters around the country.

E. Between Two Adjectives Separated by "But" or "Yet"

Incorrect: Many modern architects choose to design buildings made of glass because it is a **strong, yet elegant** material.

Incorrect: Many modern architects choose to design buildings made of glass because it is a **strong, yet elegant,** material.

Correct: Many modern architects choose to design buildings made of glass because it is a **strong yet elegant** material.

In real life, this rule has a bit more flexibility – people often do use commas around *but/yet + adjective* – but the ACT applies it strictly. No comma should be used.

F. Before or Around an Emphatic Pronoun

Emphatic pronouns are used to **emphasize** that a particular person or people is being referred to. Each object pronoun has an emphatic counterpart.

Me	→	Myself
You	→	Yourself
It	→	Itself
One	→	Oneself
Her/Him	→	Her/himself
Us	→	Ourselves
Them	→	Themselves

Although constructions containing these words may sound strange to you, there is nothing inherently wrong with them. In fact, the only thing you need to know is that it is **incorrect** to place commas before them, or before and after them.

Incorrect: Although the Panama Canal opened nearly a hundred years ago, the idea of a waterway connecting the Atlantic and Pacific Oceans is significantly older than the **canal, itself**.

Correct: Although the Panama Canal opened nearly a hundred years ago, the idea of a waterway connecting the Atlantic and Pacific Oceans is significantly older than the **canal itself**.

Incorrect: The tower of London, which lies within the Borough of Tower Hamlets, is separated from the city, **itself,** by a stretch of open space.

Correct: The tower of London, which lies within the Borough of Tower Hamlets, is separated from the city **itself** by a stretch of open space.

In most cases, it is also incorrect to place a comma after an emphatic pronoun. For example:

Incorrect: The tower of London, which lies within the Borough of Tower Hamlets, is separated from the city **itself,** by a stretch of open space.

However, when a comma would normally be necessary (e.g. before a FANBOYS conjunction or to set off a non-essential clause), it is acceptable to place one after an emphatic pronoun. For example:

Correct: The tower of London is separated from the city **itself, but** it is nevertheless one of London's most popular tourist attractions.

Correct: The tower of London, which is separated from the city **itself,** is nevertheless one of London's most popular tourist attractions.

In the first example, *comma* + *but* is used to separated two independent clauses. The first independent clause just happens to ends with the word *itself*.

Likewise, in the second example, the comma after *itself* is used to mark the end of the non-essential clause.

Combined Drill: All Period, Semicolon, and Comma Rules (answers p. 252)

1. Throughout high school, one of my favorite activities was participating in my school's sailing team. It wasn't particularly glamorous, though, my teammates and I sometimes rose as early as five o'clock in the morning to practice. Furthermore, the water was choppy, and the wind was cold. Being out on the water was, however, exhilarating. Feeling the wind whip through my hair made me feel energized, and excited. By the time practice ended, I didn't want to leave.

Today, I still love sailing, (although the boats I sail in are only slightly larger than a bathtub) and I have even participated in competitions. So when I was invited to report, on a sailing race in California last year, I immediately said yes.

2. Ellen Clark Sargent, who became an early major link between suffragists in California and those in Washington was aided by her husband, Senator Aaron A. Sargent. Senator Sargent was the first member of Congress to utter the word "suffrage," and he even wrote a Constitutional amendment giving women the right to vote. The Sargents also

---

1. **A.** NO CHANGE
   B. glamorous though, my
   C. glamorous, though. My
   D. glamorous though

2. **F.** NO CHANGE
   G. was; however,
   H. was however,
   J. was, however

3. **A.** NO CHANGE
   B. energized; and excited
   C. energized and, excited
   D. energized and excited

4. **F.** NO CHANGE
   G. sailing (although the boats I sail in are only slightly larger than a bathtub)
   H. sailing, (although the boats I sail in are only slightly larger than a bathtub)
   J. sailing (although the boats I sail in are only slightly larger than a bathtub),

5. **A.** NO CHANGE
   B. report on
   C. report. On
   D. report on,

1. **A.** NO CHANGE
   B. Washington, was
   C. Washington; was
   D. Washington. She was

2. Which of the following would NOT be an acceptable alternative to the underlined portion?

   F. "suffrage;" he even wrote
   G. "suffrage" and even wrote
   H. "suffrage," he even wrote
   J. "suffrage." He even wrote

71

established a relationship with the famous

suffragist Susan B. Anthony, who was jailed for
<u>3</u>

registering to vote. When Ellen Sargent became

secretary of the National Suffrage Association in

1872. Her husband defended Anthony in court.
<u>4</u>

Eventually, Senator Sargent went to President

Grant, to intercede on Anthony's behalf and
<u>5</u>

"sprang" the great lady from jail.

(handwritten: 2 commas surrounding name or none at all)

3. A. NO CHANGE
  B. suffragist, ~~Susan B. Anthony,~~ who
  C. suffragist, Susan B. Anthony who
  D. suffragist Susan B. Anthony. Who

4. F. NO CHANGE
  G. 1872, her husband
  H. 1872; her husband
  J. 1872, and her husband

5. A. NO CHANGE
  B. Grant; to intercede
  C. Grant to intercede
  D. Grant to intercede,

---

3. Artist and sculptor Maria Fernanda Cardoso,

whose work makes use of many types of ready-

made material grew up in Colombia, studied in the
  <u>1</u>

United States, and now lives in Australia. Her

works, which have been exhibited around the

world, often contain unusual materials such as

trash, and Styrofoam. Her most famous installation
<u>2</u>

is the Cardoso Flea Circus. It featured live cat fleas
            <u>3</u>

as "performers" and "stunt fleas." They included

an escape artist, Harry Fleadini, and two tightrope

walkers. Because the fleas were so small, Cardoso

collaborated with media artist, Ross Harley, to
            <u>4</u>

add audio and video for a larger projection. The

circus was first displayed publicly in

October 1996 in San Francisco, later, it was
            <u>5</u>

acquired by the Tate Modern Gallery in London.

1. A. NO CHANGE
  B. material; grew
  C. material, grew
  D. material. Grew

2. F. NO CHANGE
  G. trash; and Styrofoam
  H. trash and, Styrofoam
  J. trash and Styrofoam

3. Which of the following would be the LEAST
    acceptable alternative to the underlined portion?

  A. Circus, which featured
  B. Circus, featuring
  C. Circus and featured
  D. Circus; it featured

4. F. NO CHANGE
  G. media artist Ross Harley
  H. media artist, Ross Harley
  J. media artist Ross Harley,

5. A. NO CHANGE
  B. San Francisco; and later, it was
  C. San Francisco later, it was
  D. San Francisco. Later, it was

4. Louisa May Alcott was an American author
best known as the author of the novel, *Little*
                                        1
Women. Raised in Concord, Massachusetts, she
   1
grew up among many of the well-known

writers of the day, including Ralph Waldo
                          2
Emerson; Henry David Thoreau, and Nathaniel
                 2
Hawthorne. Because her family suffered severe
   2
financial difficulties; Alcott worked to help
              3
support her parents and siblings from a young age.
               4

Early in her career, Alcott sometimes used the

pen name A. M. Barnard, but as she began to
                       5
receive critical success for her writing. She
                      5
increasingly chose to write under her own name.

The turning point in her career came in 1868,
                                          6
when she published *Little Women*. The novel,
  6
which is set in Orchard House, the Alcott family

home, is loosely based on Alcott's childhood

experiences with her three sisters. The novel was

very well received, it is still a popular children's
                 7
book today.

1. **A.** NO CHANGE
    B. novel *Little Women*. Raised
    C. novel; *Little Women* raised
    D. novel, *Little Women*, raised

2. **F.** NO CHANGE
    G. including, Ralph Waldo Emerson, Henry
            David Thoreau, and, Nathaniel Hawthorne
    H. including Ralph Waldo Emerson, Henry
            David Thoreau, and Nathaniel Hawthorne
    J. including Ralph Waldo Emerson, Henry
            David Thoreau; and Nathaniel Hawthorne

3. **A.** NO CHANGE
    B. difficulties. Alcott
    C. difficulties Alcott
    D. difficulties, Alcott

4. **F.** NO CHANGE
    G. parents, and siblings
    H. parents and siblings,
    J. parents, and, siblings

5. **A.** NO CHANGE
    B. Barnard but as she began to receive critical
            success for her writing; she
    C. Barnard, but as she began to receive critical
            success for her writing, she
    D. Barnard; but as she began to receive critical
            success for her writing she

6. Which of the following would NOT be an
    acceptable alternative to the underlined portion?

    F. 1868, in that year,
    G. 1868; at that time,
    H. 1868, the year when
    J. 1868. That was the year when

7. **A.** NO CHANGE
    B. received, and is
    C. received, and it is
    D. received, this is

73

5. Since the second half of the twentieth century, computers have been programmed to play chess with increasing success. They can now play chess at an extremely high level.

A turning point in the development of artificial intelligence came in 1996. When world chess champion Garry Kasparov faced off against a specially-programmed IBM computer known as Deep Blue. The project, originally named ChipTest, was founded at Carnegie Mellon University. After graduation, the three students, who had run the project, were hired by IBM Research to continue their quest to build a machine capable of defeating the world champion.

In 1989, Kasparov was enlisted to participate in an initial match, against the computer. He won the match easily, however the IBM team was persistent. Finally, in 1996, another match was scheduled. Kasparov referred to the new, more sophisticated computer as "the monster" and, in the days before the match, spent much of his time scowling in frustration as he sat across from Deep Blue while a computer technician fine-tuned the program, that controlled the machine's moves.

1. Which of the following would NOT be an acceptable alternative to the underlined portion?
   A. success, and they
   B. success; they
   C. success, they
   D. success. In fact, they

2. F. NO CHANGE
   G. 1996; when
   H. 1996, this was when
   J. 1996, when

3. A. NO CHANGE
   B. project originally,
   C. project, originally
   D. project, originally,

4. F. NO CHANGE
   G. students who had run the project
   H. students who had run the project,
   J. students, who had run the project

5. A. NO CHANGE
   B. match against,
   C. match; against
   D. match against

6. F. NO CHANGE
   G. easily; however,
   H. easily, however,
   J. easily however,

7. A. NO CHANGE
   B. and, in the days before the match
   C. and in the days, before the match,
   D. and in the days. Before the match

8. F. NO CHANGE
   G. program that,
   H. program that
   J. program. Which

74

6. Colons

Colons have two major uses:

1) Introduce a list

2) Introduce an explanation

Important: A colon must follow a full sentence that can stand on its own as a complete thought. A colon does not, however, have to be followed by a complete sentence.

Colon before a list

Incorrect: The Great Bear Rainforest contains: Western Red Cedar, Sitka Spruce, and Douglas Fir trees.

Correct: The Great Bear Rainforest contains three main tree species: Western Red Cedar, Sitka Spruce, and Douglas Fir

Although *The Great Bear Rainforest contains* is a full sentence because it contains a subject and a verb, it does not make sense on its own.

Colon before an explanation

Incorrect: The Amazon parrot does not make an ideal pet for most people **because: it** requires much more attention and entertainment than many other animals do.

Correct: The Amazon parrot does not make an ideal pet for most people **for one major reason: it** requires much more attention and affection than many other animals do.

When a colon precedes an explanation, a complete sentence typically follows the colon. For this reason, there are instances in which a colon, a semicolon/period, or a dash (see next page) is grammatically acceptable:

Correct: The Amazon parrot does not make an ideal pet for most **people: it** requires much more attention and affection than many other animals do.

Correct: The Amazon parrot does not make an ideal pet for most **people; it** requires much more attention and affection than many other animals do.

Correct: The Amazon parrot does not make an ideal pet for most **people. It** requires much more attention and affection than many other animals do.

When either a colon or a semicolon is acceptable, the ACT will never ask you to choose between them.

7. Dashes

While dashes are typically the most unfamiliar punctuation mark for many test-takers, mostly because they are used more frequently in British English than in American English, they are fairly straightforward to master.

Dashes have three major uses:

1) Set off a non-essential clause

2) Introduce a list or explanation

3) Create a deliberate pause

The vast majority of ACT questions that test dashes test the first usage. Questions testing the second usage appear occasionally, and questions testing the third appear only rarely.

A. Set Off a Non-Essential Clause: 2 dashes = 2 commas

When used this way, two dashes are exactly equivalent to two commas. If one dash appears, so must the other. Another punctuation mark such as a comma cannot be used in place of the dash.

    Incorrect: London **– which is a very old city,** has many new buildings.

    Correct: London **– which is a very old city –** has many new buildings.

The choice to use two dashes rather than two commas is purely a stylistic one, and the ACT will never require you to choose between the two. The only rule is that dashes must go with dashes and commas with commas. One of the ACT's favorite errors is to mix and match commas and dashes.

For example:

The Norman Conquest – which occurred in

1066, marked an important step in the

development of the English language.

1. **A.** NO CHANGE
   B. 1066 – marked
   C. 1066. Marked
   D. 1066: marked

If you know that a dash must only be paired with another dash, you can immediately choose (B).

B. Before a List or Explanation: Dash = Colon

When used this way, a dash is the exact equivalent of a colon and must come after a full, stand-alone statement.

List: The Great Bear Rainforest contains three main tree **species – Western Red Cedar**, Sitka Spruce, and Douglas Fir.

Explanation: The Amazon parrot does not make an ideal pet for most **people – it** requires much more attention and affection than many other animals do.

The dash vs. colon distinction is purely stylistic; the ACT will never ask you to choose between them.

C. Create a Pause

A dash can also be used for stylistic reasons: to deliberately interrupt a statement or to create a dramatic pause or sense of suspense.

Create a pause: After eight hours of driving, we finally arrived **home – and** that was when we discovered that we had forgotten to close all of the windows.

Because questions testing this use of dashes appear very rarely, you do not need to spend a lot of time focusing on it; you should simply be aware that it exists. Moreover, when this construction does appear in an answer choice, the focus of the question will often be content or style rather than grammar. In such cases, you are simply responsible for recognizing that it is acceptable to use a dash this way and will not be required to make a correction.

list / description *complete sentence*

Combined Drill: Colons and Dashes (answers p. 252)

1. Fish have the wildest <u>names: fangtooth,</u>
    ₁
    blobfish, stargazer, and even snakehead. The

    northern snakehead, an invasive and predatory

    species, is a fish that undoubtedly lives up to its

    name. Its head tapers to a point, making it look as

    if <u>someone, perhaps</u> a mad scientist— had grafted
    ₂
    a snake's head and several inches of scaly body

    onto a fish. Its fins hang unevenly from its body, as

    if they were tacked on as an afterthought. Given

    the fish's wild appearance, it's hardly a surprise that

    scientists have given it a <u>nickname: Frankenfish.</u>
    ₃

1. **A.** NO CHANGE
    B. names, fangtooth
    C. names. Fangtooth
    D. names fangtooth

2. **F.** NO CHANGE
    G. someone perhaps
    H. someone: perhaps
    J. someone – perhaps

3. Which of the following would be an acceptable
    alternative to the underlined portion?

    A. nickname. Frankenfish
    B. nickname Frankenfish
    C. nickname – Frankenfish
    D. nickname; Frankenfish

2. Wrangell-St. Elias National Park, the largest

    national park in the United States, represents

    everything compelling about Alaska. It is

    <u>immense – larger,</u> in fact, than Belgium. It
    ₁
    showcases towering mountains – Mount St. Elias

    stands over 18,000 feet <u>tall as well as</u> glaciers.
    ₂
    Alaska's human history is also displayed in the

    mining towns of McCarthy and Kennicott. And,

    appropriate for Alaska, just getting there is an

    <u>adventure: it's a long day's</u> drive just to reach the
    ₃
    long, rough road leading to the park.

1. **A.** NO CHANGE
    B. immense. Larger,
    C. immense larger,
    D. immense; larger,

2. **F.** NO CHANGE
    G. tall – as well as
    H. tall, as well as
    J. tall; as well as

3. Which of the following would NOT be an
    acceptable alternative to the underlined portion?

    A. adventure; it's a long day's
    B. adventure, it's a long day's
    C. adventure. It's a long day's
    D. adventure – it's a long day's

78

3. The appearance of mosaic murals, pictures made of many small pieces – has remained unchanged for thousands of years. However, the last few decades have seen the emergence of a new style. Colorful three-dimensional stone wall murals. One such mural was produced by Janna Morrison in 2005. She combined the piecework of mosaic murals with traditional soap stone slab carving to produce: lifelike tropical plants, flowers, and sea life scenes ranging in size from a few inches to life size plants inlaid along entire walls.

4. Frank Lloyd Wright (June 8, 1867 – April 9, 1959) was many things: in addition to being a architect who designed more than 1,000 buildings, he was also an interior designer and writer. His architectural philosophy held that: buildings should be designed in harmony with people and their surrounding environments. This idea, which became known as organic architecture – was best exemplified by his design for the Fallingwater home (1935): a house built into the side of a hill and balanced over a waterfall. Used as Wright's summer residence, it is considered a masterpiece of American architecture.

1. A. NO CHANGE
   B. murals pictures
   C. murals – pictures
   D. murals: pictures

2. F. NO CHANGE
   G. style: colorful
   H. style, colorful
   J. style; colorful

3. A. NO CHANGE — Needs to be complete sentence b4 colon
   B. produce lifelike tropical plants – flowers,
   C. produce lifelike tropical plants: flowers,
   D. produce lifelike tropical plants, flowers,

1. Which of the following would be the LEAST acceptable alternative to the underlined portion?
   A. things – in addition
   B. things and in addition
   C. things; in addition
   D. things. In addition

2. F. NO CHANGE
   G. that buildings: should
   H. that buildings should
   J. that, buildings should

3. A. NO CHANGE
   B. architecture was
   C. architecture: was
   D. architecture, was

4. F. NO CHANGE
   G. home (1935). A house
   H. home (1935); a house
   J. home (1935), and a house

79

5. When it came to food, a pirate's life could be

difficult, living at sea, far from major seaports,
1
meant that hunger was a normal part of daily

living. The absence of warm, dry storage spaces put

normal pantry staples such as: flour and dried
2
beans at a high risk of mold. Climate also presented

preservation problems – keeping fresh fruits and
3
meats was next to impossible in warmer waters.

Fresh water was also difficult to keep during long

sea voyages because it could easily be contaminated

by algae and microbes. In contrast, dried meats and

hardtack, a relatively sturdy biscuit – were regular
4
parts of a pirate's diet, although the latter was often

infested with ants.

1. A. NO CHANGE
   B. difficult living at sea
   C. difficult: living at sea,
   D. difficult; living, at sea

2. F. NO CHANGE
   G. such as flour, and
   H. such as – flour and
   J. such as flour and

3. All of the following would be acceptable
   alternatives to the underlined portion EXCEPT

   A. problems: keeping
   B. problems, but keeping
   C. problems. Keeping
   D. problems; keeping

4. F. NO CHANGE
   G. hardtack a relatively
   H. hardtack – a relatively
   J. hardtack. A relatively

Cumulative Review: All Punctuation, Chapters 1-7 (Answers p. 252)

1. The first time I went to the beach was last

summer, but I wasn't on a vacation. I am a member
   1
of a navy sea-training program, and I went to the

beach for orientation. My trip didn't involve

typical beach activities like: sunbathing, playing
                              2
volleyball, and building sandcastles. It was,
   2

however, one of the most challenging, yet
                              3

rewarding experiences I have ever had.
   3

2. The killer whale, also referred to as the orca is
                                         1
actually a member of the dolphin family. Killer

whales are found in every ocean. They inhabit the
                              2
frigid Arctic and Antarctic regions as well as the

tropical seas. As a species, killer whales have a

diverse diet, although individual populations often
         3

specialize in particular types of prey, some feed

exclusively on fish, while other's hunt marine
                              4
mammals such as sea lions, seals, walruses, and

even large whales.

---

1. Which of the following would NOT be an
   acceptable alternative to the underlined portion?

   A. NO CHANGE
   B. summer but I wasn't
   C. summer; however, I wasn't
   D. summer. I wasn't

2. F. NO CHANGE
   G. like sunbathing, playing volleyball, and,
   H. like sunbathing playing volleyball, and
   J. like sunbathing, playing volleyball, and

3. A. NO CHANGE
   B. challenging; yet rewarding
   C. challenging yet rewarding
   D. challenging, yet, rewarding

1. A. NO CHANGE
   B. orca, is
   C. orca - is
   D. orca; is

2. Which of the following would NOT be an
   acceptable correction to the underlined portion

   F. ocean, they inhabit
   G. ocean; in fact, they inhabit
   H. ocean, and they inhabit
   J. ocean; they inhabit

3. A. NO CHANGE
   B. diet. Although individual populations
   C. diet, but individual populations
   D. diet, individual populations

4. F. NO CHANGE
   G. others' hunt
   H. others hunt
   J. others, which hunt

81

3. Located on the 103rd floor of the Willis <u>Tower,</u>
1

<u>(formerly known as the Sears Tower), the</u>
1

observation deck is 1,353 feet above the building's

mezzanine <u>level, and is</u> one of the most famous
2

attractions in Chicago. Elevators take tourists to

the top in about 60 <u>seconds, letting them</u> feel the
3

pressure change as they rise. They can also

experience how the building sways on a windy day.

Clear glass windows allow them to see far over the

plains of Illinois and across Lake <u>Michigan, to</u>
4

<u>Indiana,</u> Michigan, and Wisconsin on a sunny day.
4

1. **A.** NO CHANGE
   B. Tower (formerly known as the Sears Tower), the
   C. Tower, (formerly known as the Sears Tower) the
   D. Tower (formerly known as the Sears Tower); the

2. **F.** NO CHANGE
   G. level and is
   H. level, it is
   J. level; and it is

3. **A.** NO CHANGE
   B. seconds, this lets them
   C. seconds; letting them
   D. seconds and letting them

4. **F.** NO CHANGE
   G. Michigan to: Indiana,
   H. Michigan, to Indiana
   J. Michigan to Indiana,

4. The Ancient Olympic Games were held every

four <u>years, at the sanctuary</u> of Zeus in Olympia,
1

Greece. They involved a series of athletic festivals

in which <u>representatives of various</u> city-states
2

competed among themselves in sports such as

<u>wrestling, and chariot racing.</u> Artistic competitions
3

were held during the Games as well. It was once

widely <u>believed, all</u> conflicts among the
4

participating city-states were postponed until the

Games were finished, but that idea is only a

modern myth.

1. **A.** NO CHANGE
   B. years at: the sanctuary
   C. years at the sanctuary
   D. years at the sanctuary,

2. **F.** NO CHANGE
   G. representatives, of
   H. representatives of,
   J. representatives; of

3. **A.** NO CHANGE
   B. wrestling and chariot racing
   C. wrestling and, chariot racing
   D. wrestling; and chariot racing

4. **F.** NO CHANGE
   G. believed: all
   H. believed all
   J. believed, that all

82

5. Do elephants really have good memories, or is that just a saying? In fact, a study of elephant memory shows, having a strong memory helps
<u>shows, having</u>
1
elephants survive in the wild. Scientists studying elephants in Tanzania's Tarangire National Park <u>knew that, some</u> elephants had lived through
2
a terrible drought in the late 1950s. When a second drought occurred in <u>1993; the</u> only
3
elephant groups that left the park were those with members old enough to remember the earlier drought. The other <u>group which stayed</u> in the park,
4
was composed of elephants <u>who's members</u> were
5
too young to have experienced the first drought.

1. **A.** NO CHANGE
   B. shows: having
   C. shows having
   D. shows – having

2. **F.** NO CHANGE
   G. knew, that some
   H. knew, some
   J. knew some

3. **A.** NO CHANGE
   B. 1993. The
   C. 1993, the
   D. 1993, and the

4. **F.** NO CHANGE
   G. group that stayed
   H. group it stayed
   J. group, which stayed

5. **A.** NO CHANGE
   B. whose members'
   C. who's member's
   D. whose members

6. <u>Track star, Jesse Owens</u> was one of the most
1
famous runners of the twentieth century. What not many people <u>realize; however,</u> is that that "Jesse"
2
was not his real name. Owens' parents named him James <u>Cleveland. Which was</u> then shortened to
3
"J.C." At the age of nine, he moved from Alabama to Ohio, and when his new teacher asked his name, he said his <u>nickname because</u> of his Southern
4
accent, she mistakenly thought he had said "Jesse." The name stuck and he was known as Jesse Owens for the rest of his life.

1. **A.** NO CHANGE
   B. Track star Jesse Owens,
   C. Track star, Jesse Owens,
   D. Track star Jesse Owens

2. **F.** NO CHANGE
   G. realize, however
   H. realize, however,
   J. realize though,

3. **A.** NO CHANGE
   B. Cleveland, this
   C. Cleveland, it
   D. Cleveland, which

4. **F.** NO CHANGE
   G. nickname. Because
   H. nickname, because
   J. nickname; but because

7.   A commemorative stamp is a <u>stamp</u>

<u>issued</u> on a significant date such as an anniversary
1

to honor or <u>commemorate: a place, event, person,</u>
2
or object. The subject of the commemorative

stamp – typically, a well-known historical <u>figure, is</u>
3
usually spelled out in print. In contrast, regular

stamps, officially known as definitive <u>stamps,</u>
4

<u>which normally depict</u> the subject along with the
4
denomination and country name only. Many postal

services issue several commemorative stamps each

<u>year, they sometimes hold issuing ceremonies, at</u>
5
locations connected with the subjects.

Commemorative stamps can be used alongside

ordinary <u>stamps, but</u> unlike definitive stamps,
6
which are often reprinted and sold over a

long period of time for general <u>usage</u>
7

<u>commemorative</u> stamps are usually printed in
7

limited <u>quantities, and sold</u> for a much shorter
8

period of time, usually until supplies run out.

1. **A.** NO CHANGE
   B. stamp; issued
   C. stamp, issued
   D. stamp and issued

2. **F.** NO CHANGE
   G. commemorate – a place, event
   H. commemorate. A place, event,
   J. commemorate a place, event,

3. **A.** NO CHANGE
   B. figure is
   C. figure, and it is
   D. figure – is

4. **F.** NO CHANGE
   G. stamps, normally depict
   H. stamps, and they normally depict
   J. stamps that normally depict

5. **A.** NO CHANGE
   B. year, they sometimes hold issuing ceremonies at
   C. year, sometimes holding issuing ceremonies at
   D. year; sometimes holding issuing ceremonies at

6. **F.** NO CHANGE
   G. stamps but
   H. stamps; but
   J. stamps, however

7. **A.** NO CHANGE
   B. usage; commemorative
   C. usage – commemorative
   D. usage, commemorative

8. **F.** NO CHANGE
   G. quantities and sold,
   H. quantities and sold
   J. quantities, they are sold

8. Singing and percussion are the most important

aspects of traditional, Native American music.
    1

Vocalization takes many forms, however from solo
                                2

and choral song to call-and-response. Percussion

instruments, especially drums, and rattles are
                    3

common accompaniments they help keep the
               4

rhythm steady for the singers, who generally use
                           5

their native language. Traditional music usually

begins with slow and steady beats that grow

gradually faster and more emphatic, while various

flourishes like: drum and rattle tremolos, shouts,
                6

and accented patterns add variety and signal
 6

changes in performance for singers and dancers.

1. **A.** NO CHANGE
    B. aspects of traditional
    C. aspects, of traditional
    D. aspects, of traditional,

2. **F.** NO CHANGE
    G. forms however,
    H. forms however
    J. forms, however,

3. **A.** NO CHANGE
    B. instruments, especially drums and rattles,
    C. instruments especially drums, and rattles,
    D. instruments – especially drums and rattles,

4. **F.** NO CHANGE
    G. accompaniments, and help
    H. accompaniments; helping
    J. accompaniments that help

5. **A.** NO CHANGE
    B. singers. Who
    C. singer's, who
    D. singers and who

6. **F.** NO CHANGE
    G. like drum and rattle tremolos, shouts, and
    H. like drum and rattle tremolos; shouts, and,
    J. like drum, and rattle tremolos shouts and

9. The Crystal palace, an enormous modular
                       1

wood, glass, and iron structure designed, by
                       1

Joseph Paxton was originally erected in
    1
Hyde Park in London to house The Great

Exhibition of 1851, it showcased the products of
                2

countries around the world. The building was a

1. **A.** NO CHANGE
    B. an enormous modular wood, glass, and
            iron structure designed by Joseph Paxton –
    C. an enormous modular wood, glass, and
            iron structure designed by, Joseph Paxton,
    D. an enormous modular wood, glass, and
            iron structure designed by Joseph Paxton,

2. **F.** NO CHANGE
    G. 1851, and showcased
    H. 1851 it showcased,
    J. 1851, which showcased

85

classic example of form following <u>function. Its</u>
₃

<u>shape</u> and size were based on the size of the panes
₃
of glass, which measured 10 inches wide

by 49 inches long. Because the entire building

was scaled around those <u>dimensions, the</u>
₄
entire outer surface could quickly be glazed

with millions of identical panes.

Paxton's design reflected his practical brilliance

as a <u>designer, and</u> problem-solver. It incorporated
₅

many breakthroughs, offered <u>practical advantages,</u>
₆

<u>no</u> conventional building could match and, above
₆

<u>all embodied</u> the spirit of innovation the
₇

Great Exhibition was intended to celebrate.

3. All of the following are acceptable alternatives
to the underlined portion EXCEPT

A. function: its shape
B. function – its shape
C. function, its shape
D. function; its shape

4. F. NO CHANGE
   G. dimensions. The
   H. dimensions the
   J. dimensions; the

5. A. NO CHANGE
   B. designer and
   C. designer, and,
   D. designer and,

6. F. NO CHANGE
   G. practical advantages no
   H. practical, advantages no
   J. practical advantages. No

7. A. NO CHANGE
   B. all, embodied
   C. all; embodied
   D. all embodied,

10. When Margarete Bagshaw was growing up she
had no desire to become a painter. Bagshaw – a
———
1

member of the Pueblo Indian tribe, was the
———
2

daughter of renowned artist, Helen Hardin, but she
———
3
was more interested in studying medicine. That

changed however, when Bagshaw was 26 years
—————
4
old. On a whim, she decided to try her hand at

drawing. To her surprise, she found she enjoyed it.
———
5
She decided to enter some local competitions. She
———
5

made sure only to enter ones that were judged

anonymously, though, because she
—————
6
did not want the judges to be unfairly influenced by

her family history, of artistic achievement.
———
7

Bagshaw was not expecting to have much

success, however she quickly gained local
—————
8

recognition. And soon began exhibiting nationally.
—————
8

She initially avoided using pastels because they

1. **A.** NO CHANGE
   B. up. She
   C. up, she
   D. up; she

2. **F.** NO CHANGE
   G. tribe, was
   H. tribe was
   J. tribe – was

3. **A.** NO CHANGE
   B. artist, Helen Hardin
   C. artist Helen Hardin,
   D. artist Helen Hardin

4. **F.** NO CHANGE
   G. changed; however,
   H. changed, although
   J. changed, however,

5. Which choice is NOT an acceptable alternative
   to the underlined portion?

   A. enjoyed it; she decided
   B. enjoyed it, she decided
   C. enjoyed it; therefore, she decided
   D. enjoyed it and so decided

6. **F.** NO CHANGE
   G. anonymously; though
   H. anonymously, though
   J. anonymously; though

7. **A.** NO CHANGE
   B. history of artistic
   C. history, of artistic,
   D. history of artistic,

8. **F.** NO CHANGE
   G. success, however, she quickly gained
      local and recognition; and soon began
   H. success; however, she quickly gained
      local recognition, and soon began
   J. success; however, she quickly gained
      local recognition and soon began

87

were her mother's favorite <u>medium instead,</u> she
9

decided to work with oil paints. Almost

immediately, she began to produce <u>creations,</u>
10

<u>characterized by</u> abstract shapes, and bold
10
colors. Although her works, ~~which hang in~~

<u>galleries throughout Santa Fe, are frequently</u>
11

compared to those of Picasso, Bagshaw says her

<u>paintings, and</u> other creations are inspired by both
12
legends and her observations of the natural world

surrounding her home in New Mexico.

Now, ~~as an established artist, herself,~~ Bagshaw
13
is beginning to experiment with other forms of

<u>media such as: bronze, wood and clay.</u> Most
14
recently, she has created a series of pieces out of

New Mexico clay. Because the pieces are very

shallow, they cannot hold any objects. Bagshaw

decorates them, however, so that they resemble her

paintings. They also recall the creations of Lucy

<u>Lewis; a master</u> Pueblo potter whom Bagshaw
15
counts among her influences.

9. A. NO CHANGE
   B. medium, instead
   C. medium. Instead,
   D. medium, instead

10. F. NO CHANGE
    G. creations characterized by
    H. creations, that are characterized by
    J. creations characterized, by

11. A. NO CHANGE
    B. Santa Fe are frequently
    C. Santa Fe and are frequently
    D. Santa Fe are frequently,

12. F. NO CHANGE
    G. paintings, and,
    H. paintings and
    J. paintings; and

13. A. NO CHANGE
    B. artist herself,
    C. artist, herself
    D. artist herself

14. F. NO CHANGE
    G. such as bronze wood and
    H. such as bronze, wood, and,
    J. such as bronze, wood, and

15. A. NO CHANGE
    B. Lewis. A master
    C. Lewis a master
    D. Lewis, a master

8. Verbs: Agreement and Tense

Although many ACT questions test – or appear to test – both agreement/number and tense simultaneously, it is important to understand that the two concepts are entirely distinct.

1) **Number** answers the question "how many" – it indicates whether a verb is **singular** or **plural**. Verbs must **agree** with their subjects: singular subjects take singular verbs, and plural subjects take plural verbs.

2) **Tense** answers the question "when" – it indicates past, present, or future.

Let's consider the following sentence:

> **The feathers** of the black-backed woodpecker **has** evolved to blend in with charred trees so that they are invisible to predators lurking in the forest.

This sentence contains a **disagreement** between the subject and the verb because the subject (*feathers*) is plural and the verb (*has*) is singular. The singular noun *woodpecker*, which appears immediately before the verb, is part of the prepositional phrase *of the black-backed woodpecker* and has no effect on the number of the verb.

In order to correct the sentence, it is necessary to change the **number** of the verb, using the plural verb *have* rather than the singular verb *has*.

When many students encounter this type of sentence, however, their first instinct is to change the **tense** of the verb and use the simple past *had*. While this change does make the sentence grammatically acceptable, there is no compelling reason for the tense to be altered and, more importantly, the correction does not truly address the actual problem with the sentence: the subject and the verb disagree.

But, you might wonder, why does that matter if using *had* fixes the sentence anyway? Why bother learning all that grammar if you can get the question right without worrying about any of it? Well, because you could very well see a question that looks like this:

The works of artist Alan Chin <u>has included</u>
                                     1

elements inspired by both the California gold rush

and the transcontinental railroad.

1. **A.** NO CHANGE
   B. includes
   C. have included
   D. having included

In this scenario, you don't have the option of changing *has* to *had*. Whether or not you realize it, you're being forced to deal with the actual error. If you can't hear that there's a problem and don't have the grammatical tools to figure it out, you're unfortunately out of luck. You can probably recognize that (D) is awkward and breaks the "*–ing* is bad" rule, but beyond that…you're reduced to guesswork.

Subject-verb agreement errors aren't usually easy to hear, so when they occur in the original version of a passage, many students will quickly glance through the answer choices before picking "NO CHANGE" and then moving on without a second thought. This is not what you want to do.

In reality, the key to dealing with these questions is to work <u>backwards</u>, using the answer choices to determine what the question is testing.

Subject-verb agreement questions can be answered using the following steps:

1) Look at the answer choices.

If you examine the answer choices, you can see that (A) and (B) contain singular verbs, *has*, *includes*, and (C) contains a plural verb, *have*. (You can assume that (D) is incorrect because it contains a gerund.)

When some answer choices contain singular verbs while other answer choices contain plural verbs, a question is almost always testing subject-verb agreement.

2) Identify the subject and determine whether it is singular or plural.

When dealing with a subject-verb agreement question, never assume that the noun right before a verb is the subject. In fact, **the noun right before a verb will almost never be the subject.** If it were, the question would be too easy, and it wouldn't be on the test in the first place.

When an underlined verb is located close to the beginning of a sentence, the subject is virtually always right at the beginning of the sentence. So back up and look at the first words of the sentence: *The works*. That's your subject. *Works* has an *–s* on the end of it, so it's plural.

Alternately, if you really don't want to worry about grammar, you can think about it logically. What "has included elements inspired by both the California gold rush and the transcontinental railroad?" It can only be *the works* of artist Alan Chin. A *person* can't contain elements inspired by both the California gold rush and the transcontinental railroad, at least not under normal circumstances, and your job is to think about what makes the most sense – not to invent wild explanations in order to justify the answer you happen to like.

3) Find the verb that agrees with the subject

Since *works* is plural, you need a plural verb, and only (C) contains a plural verb (*have*). So (C) is the only possible answer.

Notice that although (B) contains a verb in one tense (*includes*), while the verbs in (A) and (C) contain verbs in a different tense (*has*/*have included*), you do not need to worry about tense at all in order to answer the question correctly. The only thing that matters is subject-verb agreement. The fact that different answers contain different tenses is simply a distraction technique, designed to make the question look more complicated than it actually is. **In reality, many questions that appear to be testing both subject-verb agreement and tense are actually testing subject-verb agreement only.** So if you start worrying about tense, you'll probably waste a lot of time and might not even get to the correct answer. If, on the other hand, you start by figuring out the subject and working from that information, you'll go much more quickly and be able to focus on exactly what the question is actually testing.

Subject-Verb Agreement: Common Structures

Subject-verb agreement questions typically appear two or three times per ACT. While they are less common than questions involving commas or other types of punctuation, they are also virtually guaranteed to appear, and learning to recognize disagreements can easily boost your score a point or two.

To reiterate: every sentence must contain a subject and a verb that agrees with it in number:

- Singular subjects must take singular verbs.

- Plural subjects must take plural verbs.

Virtually all ACT questions that deal with number ask about verbs in the 3rd person singular (*she/he/it/one*) and 3rd person plural (*they*) forms.

The most important thing to remember about the singular vs. plural forms of a verb is as follows:

- 3rd person singular verbs end in –*s*.

- 3rd person plural verbs do **not** end in –*s*.

Note that this is the opposite of nouns, which take an –*s* in the plural (e.g. *the book* is singular and *the books* is plural, whereas *she talks* is singular and *they talk* is plural).

	Correct	Incorrect
Singular subject:	The artist paints.	The artist paint.
Plural subject:	The artists paint.	The artists paints.
	The artist and her helper paint.	The artist and her helper paints.

To be and *to have* are two of the most commonly tested verbs on the ACT. Because they are irregular, it is important that you be able to recognize their singular and plural forms.

		To be	To have
Present:	**singular**	is	has
	plural	are	have
Past:	**singular**	was	had
	plural	were	had

To reiterate: When you encounter a set of answer choices that contains both singular and plural options, you should immediately back up and attempt to identify the subject; it is very easy to become confused if you try to rely on your ear!

To be

is   91

present: S
          P   are

To have

has
have

past.   S   was
         P   were

had
had

Unfortunately, questions that test subject-verb agreement rarely place the subject and the verb next to one another. That would be too easy. They do, however, fall into several predictable structures.

A. Subject – Prepositional Phrase – Verb

Subject – prepositional phrase – verb is the most common type of subject-verb agreement structure; often, it will be the only type of subject-verb agreement question that appears on a given test.

To reiterate: a preposition is a time or location word that can be placed before a noun. For an extended list, you can see p. 10, but the most common prepositions include *of, to, at, with, for, from, in, on,* and *by.*

A prepositional phrase is simply a phrase that begins with a preposition (e.g. *at the museum, by the author, of the experiment*). In a sentence, a prepositional phrase always ends right before the verb.

In the examples below, the subject and verb are in bold, and the prepositional phrase is underlined:

1. **The destruction** of coral reefs **is** becoming a major problem worldwide.

2. **The patent** for the first mechanical pencils **was** granted to Sampson Morgan and John Hawkins in the early nineteenth century.

3. **Opposition** to rodeos from animal-rights workers **focuses** primarily on the poor treatment and living conditions of the horses used in competitions.

Prepositional phrases are often placed between subjects and verbs to distract from disagreements. Furthermore, the prepositional phrase often ends with a noun that **does** agree with the verb. If you only look at the noun right before the verb, it is very easy to get fooled. For example:

Incorrect: In recent years, **farmers** in many parts of Brazil **has** succeeded in reducing the acidity of their soil, substantially increasing their production of food.

Correct: In recent years, **farmers** in many parts of Brazil **have** succeeded in reducing the acidity of their soil, substantially increasing their production of food.

Occasionally, the ACT will combine a **compound subject** (two singular nouns connected by *and*) with a prepositional phrase. If you are not careful, this error can be extremely difficult to catch.

Incorrect: **The cultivation and consumption** of the tomato **is** widespread in South America.

Correct: **The cultivation and consumption** of the tomato **are** widespread in South America.

Important: Watch out for "one" as a subject. It's singular but will virtually always appear with a long prepositional phrase ending with a plural noun.

Incorrect: **One** of the world's most famous paintings **are** the *Mona Lisa*, which has hung in the Louvre since 1797.

Correct: **One** of the world's most famous paintings **is** the *Mona Lisa*, which has hung in the Louvre since 1797.

B. Essential and Non-Essential Clauses

Non-essential Clause

In this structure, a non-essential clause is inserted between the subject and the verb to distract from a disagreement. When the information between the commas is crossed out, the error is revealed. For example:

Incorrect: <u>Green tea</u> with mint, (which is) a popular drink in many Middle-Eastern countries, **are** said to have many health benefits.

Cross Out: <u>Green tea</u> with mint, ~~(which is) a popular drink throughout many middle-eastern countries,~~ **are** said to have many health benefits.

Correct: <u>Green tea</u> with mint, which is a popular drink in many Middle-Eastern countries, **is** said to have many health benefits.

Sometimes, the disagreement will occur **within** the non-essential clause:

Incorrect: <u>Green tea</u> with mint, **which are** a popular drink in many Middle-Eastern countries, is said to have many health benefits.

Correct: <u>Green tea</u> with mint, **which is** a popular drink in many Middle-Eastern countries, is said to have many health benefits.

Essential Clause with "That"

Sometimes the disagreement will involve a clause beginning with *that*. As is true for disagreements involving non-essential clauses, the disagreement can be placed around the clause or within it.

Incorrect: **A drink** <u>that is popular in many Middle Eastern countries</u> **are** green tea with mint, said to have many health benefits.

Correct: **A drink** <u>that is popular in many Middle Eastern countries</u> **is** green tea with mint, said to have many health benefits.

Incorrect: Popular in many Middle Eastern countries, **green tea** with mint is a drink <u>that</u> **are** said to have many health benefits.

Correct: Popular in many Middle Eastern countries, **green tea with mint** is a drink <u>that</u> **is** said to have many health benefits.

C. Verb before subject (rare)

In this structure, the verb is placed **after** the subject in order to distract from the disagreement. Sometimes this error is signaled by the presence of a preposition at the beginning of the sentence, but other times there is no tip-off. Although sentences that invert the normal order of subject and verb may sound odd to you, it is important to understand that the error lies in the disagreement between the subject and the verb, not in the unusual syntax (word order). For example, consider the following sentence:

Incorrect: Lush valleys **lies** at the crossroads of the Andes mountains and the Amazon jungle.

This sentence contains a disagreement: the subject (*lush valleys*) is plural while the verb (*lies*) is singular because it ends with an *–s*. When the sentence is written this way, it's fairly easy to hear the error. But if the sentence is rearranged to begin with a preposition, the error suddenly becomes much harder to hear.

Incorrect: *At* the crossroads of the Andes and the Amazon jungle **lies** <u>lush hillsides and valleys.</u>

Correct: *At* the crossroads of the Andes and the Amazon jungle **lie** <u>lush hillsides and valleys.</u>

Other sentences with this error will not contain a preposition at the beginning of the sentence:

Incorrect: Radioactivity is generally not considered harmful when people are exposed to it for brief periods, but less clear **is** <u>its long-term effects.</u>

Correct: Radioactivity is generally not considered harmful when people are exposed to it for brief periods, but less clear **are** <u>its long-term effects.</u>

When there is no preposition at the start of the sentence, there are unfortunately no real tip-offs for this error besides the presence of both singular and plural verb forms in the answer choices. The easiest way to identify the subject is simply to ask yourself *what* is "less clear" – the plural noun *long-term effects* is the only option that makes sense, so the plural verb *are* must be required.

Verb Tense

The most important thing to understand about verb tense on the ACT is that correct answers to tense questions are largely **based on context**. Two or three verbs may be grammatically correct when a sentence is read independently, but only one answer will be correct when it is considered in the context of a paragraph. **As a result, you must typically read from a sentence or two before to a sentence or two after in order to obtain enough information to answer verb tense questions.**

As is true for agreement questions, you should plan to work from the answer choices. The presence of answer choices containing the same verb in different tenses indicates that a question is testing tense. **Unlike answers to agreement questions, however, answers to tense questions do not usually include both singular and plural verbs.** The focus is only on **when** an action occurred, not on how many people/things performed it.

For example, compare the follow two sets of hypothetical answer choices. We don't even need a passage; the answer choices themselves allow us to make an educated guess about what each question is testing.

1. **A.** NO CHANGE
   B. is gone
   C. were gone
   D. was gone

2. **F.** NO CHANGE
   G. has gone
   H. went
   J. goes

Although the answer choices to these two questions might at first glance seem interchangeable, there are actually some important differences between them.

That mix of singular and plural verbs suggests that the **first question is testing agreement**; the fact that there are verbs in different tenses is most likely an irrelevant distraction. In contrast, **the second set of answers focuses on tense**. (G), (H), and (J) could all agree with a singular subject, so there is no problem of singular vs. plural. The real question is whether the action happened in the past or present.

So how, then, do you go about deciding what tense a verb belongs in? On the ACT, the vast majority of tense questions follow one simple rule: **unless there is a clear reason for a verb to change tense, a verb should be consistent with (or "parallel to") the other verbs in sentence or paragraph.** That is why you must make sure to read the surrounding sentences whenever you encounter a question testing tense.

For example:

> The tomato **is** consumed in many different ways, including raw, as an ingredient in many dishes and sauces, and in drinks. Botanically a fruit, it **is** considered a vegetable for culinary purposes. It **is** also rich in lycopene, which **may** have beneficial health effects. It **belongs** to the nightshade family, and its plants typically **grow** from three to ten feet high and **have** a weak stem that often **sprawls** over the ground.

In the above passage, the verb tense remains consistent because all of the verbs are in the **present tense** – they are describing something that is true *now*. But what if you were to see something like this?

> The tomato **is** consumed in many different ways, including raw, as an ingredient in many dishes and sauces, and in drinks. Botanically a fruit, it **was** considered a vegetable for culinary purposes.

Now the last verb is in the **past tense**. It no longer matches the verbs in the preceding sentence. But if you just looked at the second sentence by itself, you would have no way of knowing that there was a problem.

Overview of Major Tenses

While there are many tenses that could in theory be tested on the ACT, the reality is that only a handful of common tenses are tested on a regular basis. Again, the focus is on testing your ability to recognize when common tenses are and are not used correctly in context – not on complex rules that you are unlikely to encounter in everyday reading and writing.

A. Present

The present tense indicates that an action is occurring now.

Correct:	Tomatoes **grow** in greenhouses around the world.
Correct:	Masks **play** an important role for members of the Hopi tribe.
Correct:	The novel *Robinson Crusoe* **tells** the story of a man who must survive after he **is** shipwrecked on a desert island.

The last sentence contains an example of the **literary present**. It is conventional to use the present tense to discuss books, even when they are set in the past. Although you may not remember to do this in your own writing, you should know that the present tense will not be considered wrong when used this way on the ACT.

The **present progressive** is used to emphasize that an action is happening right at the moment. It is formed by adding the present participle (*–ing*) to *is* or *are*.

Correct:	The tomatoes that we planted last spring **are becoming** very large.

While the present progressive is not a main focus of the ACT, it does appear occasionally. You should know that it is a form of the present and **is considered parallel to another verb in the regular present tense**.

For example:

As far back as I can remember, I have helped my family grow vegetables in the garden in back of our house. We plant tomatoes every spring and <u>are attempting</u> to sell this year's crop at a local farmers market.
1

1. **A.** NO CHANGE
   B. will have attempted
   C. attempting
   D. would attempt

When you first look at the answer choices, you might think that there's no good answer. (C) obviously doesn't work since it omits the verb. (Even if you can't identify the grammatical problem, you can probably hear that something sounds very off). But (A), (B), and (D) might seem equally weird. The only way to answer this question with certainty is to look back at the other verb in the sentence: *plant*. It's in the present tense, which means that you need to put this verb in the present tense as well. Even if you don't like the way *are attempting* sounds, you can recognize that *are* is in the present tense, whereas *will* and *would* are not. So (A) is correct.

B. Present Perfect vs. Simple Past

Present perfect = *has/have + past participle*

For **regular** verbs, the past participle is formed by adding *–ed*. For **irregular** verbs ending in *–ow*, the past participle usually ends in *–own*. For irregular verbs ending in *–ing* or *–ink*, it usually ends in *–ung* or *–unk*.

paint	→	painted	grow	→	grown	sing	→	sung
stay	→	stayed	throw	→	thrown	ring	→	rung
seem	→	seemed	blow	→	blown	drink	→	drunk

Still other irregular verbs do not follow one of these patterns (e.g. *bring → brought, come → came, think → thought*). If you cannot hear when one of these past participles is incorrect, you must memorize them. (See list on p. 89).

The **most important irregular verb** to know is *to be*, which becomes *has been* (singular) and *have been* (plural) in the present perfect.

The present perfect is used for actions that **began in the past** and that are still **continuing in the present**. The words *for, since, over,* and *during* usually act as tip-offs that the present perfect is required.

> Correct: Masks **have played** a sacred role in Hopi culture <u>for</u> thousands of years.

This sentence means that masks began playing a sacred role in Hopi culture thousands of years ago, and that they are still playing a sacred role in Hopi culture today.

> Correct: <u>Since</u> around 500 B.C., people **have cultivated** tomatoes in Mesoamerica.

This sentence means that people began cultivating tomatoes around 500 B.C. in Mesoamerica and are still cultivating tomatoes there today.

> Correct: <u>Over/During the last 150 years</u>, the tomato **has gone** from being a relatively obscure fruit grown by only a handful of farmers to one of the most popular salad ingredients.

This sentence means that 150 years ago, the tomato was a relatively obscure fruit; that between 150 years ago and now, it became one of the most popular salad ingredients; and that it remains one of the most popular salad ingredients today.

When a tip-off word is not present, the present perfect is also commonly used to describe an action that occurred very recently. For example:

> Correct: Scientists **have reported** that the breakthrough may result in the development of new technologies.

In different contexts, however, this sentence could contain a verb in many different tenses and still be correct; in the absence of a word such as *for* or *since*, there is no absolute reason that the verb must appear in the present perfect. **To reiterate:** on the ACT, the correct answer will always be a question of context. If the surrounding verbs are in the present perfect, the verb in question should be in the present perfect unless there is a clear-cut reason that a different tense is required.

The **simple past** is called "simple" because, unlike the present perfect, it consists of only one word: the simple past form of the verb (otherwise known as the **preterit**).

For regular verbs, the **simple past** is formed exactly the same way the present perfect is formed: by adding *–ed*. In fact, the verbs are identical in both tenses. The only difference is that present perfect verbs follow *has* or *have* (not *had*), while simple past verbs do not.

For irregular verbs ending in *–ing* or *-ink*, the simple past usually ends in *–ang* or *–ank*. For irregular verbs ending in *–ow*, it usually ends in *–ew*.

paint →	painted	grow →	grew	sing →	sang
stay →	stayed	throw →	threw	ring →	rang
seem →	seemed	blow →	blew	drink →	drank

As is true for the present perfect, many common verbs do not follow this pattern in the simple past (e.g. *think → thought, go → went*), and if you cannot hear when they are used incorrectly, you must memorize them.

The **most important irregular verb** is *to be*, which becomes *was* (singular) and *were* (plural) in the simple past.

Whereas the present perfect is used to refer to actions that are still occurring, the simple past is used to describe a **finished action in the past**. Very often, it will be accompanied by a **date** or **time period** that clearly indicates that a particular event or action occurred a long time ago. For example:

Correct: Members of the nobility often **lived** in castles during the Middle Ages.

This sentence means that members of the nobility often lived in castles during the Middle Ages but provides no information about whether they lived in castles after that period.

Correct: Sometime around 500 B.C., the inhabitants of Central and South America **began** to cultivate the first tomatoes.

In this sentence, the simple past verb *began* indicates that sentence is describing a one-time action that ended in the past. The sentence indicates the first cultivation of tomatoes occurred in 500 B.C. only, not after that time.

Some sentences can be written using either the present perfect or the simple past. Compare:

Correct: Maria Fernanda Cardoso's work **has appeared** in museums around the world.

This version of the sentence indicates that the artist's work is *still* appearing in museums around the world and may continue to do so in the future.

Correct: Maria Fernanda Cardoso's work **appeared** in museums around the world.

This version of the sentence indicates that the artist's work appeared in museums around the world in the past but is *no longer* doing so.

Again, in cases in which either the present perfect or the simple past is acceptable, the correct answer will usually depend on the tense of the verbs in surrounding sentences.

C. Past Perfect

Past Perfect = *had* + *past participle*

- She had gone.
- It had rung.
- They had insisted.

Although many students believe that the past perfect and simple past are interchangeable (e.g. *had said* and *said*), that is not the case. In fact, the past perfect is only used in a specific situation: **when a sentence describes two finished events or actions in the past, the past perfect is used to refer to the action that came <u>first</u>.**

In some sentences, either the past perfect or the simple past can be used. For example:

Correct: Before a complete version of Louisa May Alcott's novel *Little Women* was published in 1880, the book **had appeared** in two separate volumes.

Correct: Before a complete version of Louisa May Alcott's novel *Little Women* was published in 1880, the book **appeared** in two separate volumes.

In the first version of the sentence, the past perfect (*had appeared*) is used to emphasize that a particular event occurred **before** a second event: *Little Women* appeared in two separate volumes (event #1), and later it appeared as complete volume (event #2).

In the second version of the sentence, the simple past (*appeared*) keeps the verb parallel to the other verb in the sentence, *was*, which is also in the simple past.

What we cannot do, however, is put the first verb in the past perfect because that verb clearly refers to an event that occurred **after** another event:

Incorrect: Before a complete version of Louisa May Alcott's novel *Little Women* **had been** published in 1880, the book appeared in two separate volumes.

When the phrase "by the time" appears, the past perfect is <u>required</u>.

Incorrect: <u>By the time</u> Martha Graham retired from the stage in 1970, she **gave** hundreds of performances.

Correct: <u>By the time</u> Martha Graham retired from the stage in 1970, she **had given** hundreds of performances.

Logically, Martha Graham gave hundreds of performances (action #1) before she retired (action #2).

When both the simple past and the past perfect are acceptable, the ACT will never ask you to choose between them. If both tenses appear in answer choices, one of them will typically be formed incorrectly, eliminating it as a possible answer. Otherwise, both tenses will be incorrect based on context.

D. Formation Errors: Past Participle and Simple Past

As mentioned earlier, the ACT is generally less concerned with your understanding the nuances of using complex tenses than it is with ensuring that you can recognize serious and glaring errors in verb usage. As a result, verb questions focus as much as on the proper **formation** of tenses as they do on the proper **use** of tenses. Errors in tense formation typically fall into several categories:

i. Past participle replaces simple past

The past participle can **only** be used after a form of *to have* or *to be*; it cannot stand alone. Only the simple past can stand alone. Some ACT questions, however, will incorrectly replace the simple past with the past participle:

Incorrect:	Sometime around 500 B.C., the inhabitants of Central and South America **begun** to grow tomatoes.
Correct:	Sometime around 500 B.C., the inhabitants of Central and South America **began** to grow tomatoes.

ii. Past participle without "to have" or "to be"

In this error, a sentence will clearly require the past participle but omit the necessary verb before it.

Incorrect:	Since around 500 B.C., tomatoes **grown** in Central and South America.
Correct:	Since around 500 B.C., tomatoes **have grown** in Central and South America.

Incorrect:	Beginning in around 500 B.C. tomatoes **grown** in Central and South America.
Correct:	Beginning in around 500 B.C. tomatoes **were grown** in Central and South America.

iii. Simple past replaces past participle

Sometimes, however, this error is tested in a slightly subtler form. In this case, the simple past rather than the past participle will appear after a form of *to have* or *to be*.

Incorrect:	Since the first millennium B.C., tomatoes **have grew** in Central and South America.
Correct:	Since the first millennium B.C., tomatoes **have grown** in Central and South America.

Incorrect:	Today, tomatoes **are grew** in many varieties in greenhouses around the world.
Correct:	Today, tomatoes **are grown** in many varieties in greenhouses around the world.

iv. Past participle without "–ed"

Incorrect:	The sculpture was **fashion** from clay, wood, and bronze.
Correct:	The sculpture was **fashioned** from clay, wood, and bronze.

Infinitive	Simple Past	Past Participle
To (a)rise	(A)rose	(A)risen
To (a)waken	(A)woke	(A)woken
To be	Was	Been
To become	Became	Become
To begin	Began	Begun
To blow	Blew	Blown
To break	Broke	Broken
To choose	Chose	Chosen
To do	Did	Done
To draw	Drew	Drawn
To drink	Drank	Drunk
To drive	Drove	Driven
To fling	Flung	Flung
To fly	Flew	Flown
To freeze	Froze	Frozen
To get	Got	Gotten
To give	Gave	Given
To go	Went	Gone
To grow	Grew	Grown
To hide	Hid	Hidden
To know	Knew	Known
To ride	Rode	Ridden
To ring	Rang	Rung
To run	Ran	Run
To see	Saw	Seen
To sew	Sewed	Sewn
To shrink	Shrank	Shrunk/shrunken
To sing	Sang	Sung
To sink	Sank	Sunk/sunken
To speak	Spoke	Spoken
To spring	Sprang	Sprung
To steal	Stole	Stolen
To stink	Stank	Stunk
To swim	Swam	Swum
To take	Took	Taken
To tear	Tore	Torn
To throw	Threw	Thrown
To wear	Wore	Worn
To write	Wrote	Written

101

E. Would and Will

Questions testing *will* (future) and *would* (conditional) appear infrequently, and you should not worry about them until you are fully comfortable with the various past tense errors already discussed.

Future = *will + verb*

The future is used to describe actions that have not yet occurred.

> Correct: Undoubtedly, works choreographed by Martha Graham **will continue** to be performed for many years to come.

Conditional = *would + verb*

The conditional is used to describe **hypothetical** situations: ones that *could* occur but have not *actually* occurred.

> Correct: Many people who think of the tomato as a vegetable **would be** surprised to learn that it is actually a fruit.

When a sentence describes a situation in the past, *would* can also refer to an action that, from the perspective of the past, has not yet occurred – even if from today's perspective, that action occurred a long time ago.

> Incorrect: When Martha Graham began dancing in the early twentieth century, no one knew that she **will** become one of the greatest choreographers of all time.

> Correct: When Martha Graham began dancing in the early twentieth century, no one knew that she **would** become one of the greatest choreographers of all time.

Shortcut: *Will* should not generally appear in the same sentence as a verb or date/time in the past. In the above sentence, the verb *began* and the phrase *early twentieth century* indicate that *would* should be used.

Important: answer choices containing "will have" and "would have" are nearly always <u>incorrect</u> because they create unnecessary tense switches and make sentences wordy and awkward. When you see one of these constructions in an answer choice, you should generally assume the answer is wrong.

Past conditional = *would have + past participle*

The past conditional describes an action that could have happened but that did not actually happen.

> Correct: If we <u>had remembered</u> to close the windows, the paintings **would have been** saved.

Future perfect = *will have + past participle*

The future perfect describes an action in the future that will be finished *before* a second action. As is true for the past perfect, the phrase *by the time* is a tip-off that this tense is required. In nearly all cases, however, you will only be asked to recognize that this tense is being used correctly and will not have to fix errors involving it.

> Correct: <u>By the time</u> the paintings are complete, the artist **will have spent** more than six months working on them

F. To vs. –ING

On the ACT the *to* form of a verb (infinitive) and the *–ing* form (gerund or participle) are sometimes switched with one another. Note that you do <u>not</u> need to worry about the gerund/participle distinction in such cases.

If you see an *–ing* word underlined, plug in the *to* form and vice-versa.

Incorrect: Though she was one of the few women of her time **gaining** international prominence, Clara Barton would not have described herself as a proponent of women's rights.

Correct: Though she was one of the few women of her time **to gain** international prominence, Clara Barton would not have described herself as a proponent of women's rights.

Unfortunately, these questions must be answered by ear. There is no rule and no "trick" to indicate which form should be used in a particular situation.

Important: sometimes, when switching an *–ing* form with a *to* form, you must also place a preposition before the *–ing* form in order for a sentence to make sense.

Incorrect: Deactivated viruses form the basis of many vaccines known for their effectiveness **to prevent** disease.

Incorrect: Deactivated viruses form the basis of many vaccines known for their effectiveness **preventing** disease.

Correct: Deactivated viruses form the basis of many vaccines known for their effectiveness **in preventing** disease.

Sometimes, both a *to* and an *–ing* form are acceptable. In such cases, you will never be asked to choose between the two forms.

Correct: Soon, the members of the dance company will begin **to rehearse** for the performance.

Correct: Soon, the members of the dance company will begin **rehearsing** for the performance.

The list on the following page contains common idioms with *–ing* and *to* forms.

Idioms with –ING	Idioms with TO
Accused of being	Agree to be
Accustomed to being	Allow to be
Admired for being	Appear/seem to be
Admit to being	Arrange to be
After being	Aspire to be
Avoid being	Attempt to be
Banned from being	Choose to be
Before being	Claim to be
Consider being	Consider to be
Deny being	Decide to be
Describe being	Decline to be
Discuss being	Deserve to be
Effective in/at being	Encourage to be
Enjoy being	Expect to be
Famous for being	Fail to be
Imagine being	Have the ability to be
In charge of being	Inclined to be
In the hope(s) of being	Inspire (someone) to be
(In)capable of being	Intend to be
Insist on being	Known to be
Known as/for being	Manage to be
Mind being	Neglect to be
Postpone being	Offer to be
Praised for being	Prepare to be
Prevent from being	Promise to be
Protect from being	Refuse to be
Regarded as being	Reluctant to be
Report being	Require to be
Resent being	Seek to be
Risk being	Shown to be
Seen as being	Strive to be
Stop being	Struggle to be
Succeed in/at being	Tend to be
Used to being	Threaten to be
Viewed as being	Want to be
Without being	Wish to be

Drill: Verb Agreement and Tense (answers p. 253)

1. Kite-flying has a long history in Japan:

according to legend, the first kites <u>were flew</u> nearly
                                        1
1,400 years ago, and since that time, kite-flying

<u>had remained</u> a delightful tradition. Kites are
      2
made from a bamboo framework and

layers of *washi* paper – paper made by hand in the

traditional style. Colorful narrative illustrations and

legendary heroes from Japanese folklore <u>decorate</u>
                                            3
their surfaces. Every region of the country has its

own distinct kite design, with more than 130

varieties in all. For this reason, there is no single

design that <u>are</u> typical of Japanese kites.
              4

singular subject

2. Each July, one of the world's largest folk-art

festivals <u>bring</u> together artists from every corner of
            1
the globe for a vast and colorful international

bazaar. For several weeks, more than 200 artists

from 60 countries gather <u>in offering</u> handmade
                             2
masterworks. The festival is located in Santa Fe, a

destination rich with culture and history. The work

prep of master artists <u>line</u> the walls as market-goers
                              3
are given the opportunity to find one-of-a-kind

treasures and <u>have met</u> their creators.
                  4

1. A. NO CHANGE
   B. flown
   C. were flown
   D. had flew

2. F. NO CHANGE
   G. would have remained
   H. will remain
   J. has remained

3. A. NO CHANGE
   B. decorates
   C. have decorated
   D. has decorated

4. F. NO CHANGE
   G. will be
   H. is
   J. had been

1. A. NO CHANGE
   B. bringing
   C. brought
   D. brings

2. F. NO CHANGE
   G. for offering
   H. to offer
   J. with offering

3. A. NO CHANGE
   B. have lined
   C. were lining
   D. lines

4. F. NO CHANGE
   G. meet
   H. meeting
   J. had met

Singular verbs end in -S
Plural verbs DON'T end in -S

3. In a village at the edge of a rainforest, the
skilled and nimble fingers of an old woman bends
1
fabric and straw into graceful baskets. The baskets
are the perfect size to hold papayas, but they also
held centuries of craft and tribal identity.
2
     Basket weaving is one of the most widespread
crafts in the history of human civilization, but the
preservation of ancient baskets is difficult because
3
natural materials like wood and grass decay rapidly.
As a result, much of the history of basket making
would be lost. On the other hand, weaving
4
techniques, which are often passed along from
generation to generation, has been preserved
5
throughout the centuries and are still being
expanded upon today.

1. A. NO CHANGE
    B. will bend
    C. bend
    D. has bent

2. F. NO CHANGE
    G. would hold
    H. holded
    J. hold

3. A. NO CHANGE
    B. are
    C. was
    D. had been

4. F. NO CHANGE
    G. has been
    H. would have been
    J. have been

5. A. NO CHAGE
    B. have been preserved
    C. was preserved
    D. preserved

4. As the world's first supersonic passenger jet, the
Concorde was regarded as a marvel of engineering.
Most jets fly at maximum speeds of about 550
miles per hour, but the Concorde could have gone
1
more than two times as fast – double the speed of
sound. During its 27 years of service, the world's
fastest commercial aircraft transported passengers
across the Atlantic ocean in only two hours.

1. A. NO CHANGE
    B. gone
    C. will go
    D. went

In 2003, the Concorde was retired from flight. Now, however, a plane that is capable to fly halfway around the world in a mere four hours may soon exist.

For engineers, the elimination of sonic booms have been one of the biggest challenges involved in building a new supersonic plane. Airplanes that break the sound barrier are extremely loud, so they must be flew primarily over water. This time around, engineers claim that they have found a way to transform the loud booms into something much softer. The solution involves thinner wings and hidden engines. Moreover, lightweight materials and innovative engine technology allows the plane to fly twice as fast as the Concorde.

5. In North America, cranberries were cultivated by Native Americans long before the first European settlers arrived, but not until the mid-nineteenth century was the first berries marketed and sold. Sometime around the turn of the nineteenth century, Sir Joseph Banks, a British scientist, used seeds from the United States to harvest cranberries in England, but Banks

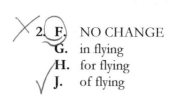

2. **F.** NO CHANGE
   G. in flying
   H. for flying
   J. of flying

3. **A.** NO CHANGE
   B. were
   C. is
   D. are

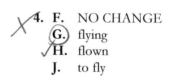

4. **F.** NO CHANGE
   G. flying
   H. flown
   J. to fly

5. **A.** NO CHANGE
   B. has allowed
   C. is allowing
   D. allow

1. **A.** NO CHANGE
   B. were
   C. is
   D. has

never marketed his crop. Then, in 1816,
2
Henry Hall, a veteran of the Revolutionary war,

planted the first-recorded commercial cranberry

bog in Dennis, Massachusetts. By the mid-

nineteenth century, the modern cranberry industry

was in full swing, and competition among growers

were fierce.
3

    The business operated on a small scale at first:

families and community members harvested

wild cranberries and then sold them locally. As the

market grown to include larger cities such as
4
Boston and New York, however, farmers

competed to unload their surplus cranberries

quickly, and what was once a local venture

has become a highly profitable business.
5

2. **F.** NO CHANGE
   G. has never marketed
   H. never markets
   J. had never marketed

3. **A.** NO CHANGE
   B. was
   C. have been
   D. would be

4. **F.** NO CHANGE
   G. has grew
   H. grew
   J. had grown

5. **A.** NO CHANGE
   B. has became
   C. becomes
   D. became

9. Pronouns: Agreement and Case

Pronouns are words that replace nouns. Like verbs, pronouns must agree in **number** with their **antecedents** – the nouns they refer to. **Singular nouns take singular pronouns, and plural nouns take plural pronouns.**

Pronouns are necessary because without them, it would be necessary to repeat a noun each time it was referred to. For example, the following passage does not use any pronouns to refer to the noun *tomato*:

> **The tomato** is consumed in many different ways, including raw, as an ingredient in many dishes and sauces, and in drinks. While **the tomato** is botanically a fruit, **the tomato** is considered a vegetable for culinary purposes. **The tomato** is also rich in lycopene, which may have beneficial health effects. **The tomato** belongs to the nightshade family, and **the tomato's** plants typically grow from three to ten feet high and have a weak stem that often sprawls over the ground. **The tomato** is a perennial in **the tomato's** native habitat, and **the tomato** is often grown outdoors in temperate climates.

Notice how incredibly repetitive this version is, and how awkward it is to read. Now we're going to replace all those repetitions of the singular noun *tomato* with the much shorter singular pronoun *it*:

> **The tomato** is consumed in many different ways, including raw, as an ingredient in many dishes and sauces, and in drinks. While **it** is botanically a fruit, **it** is considered a vegetable for culinary purposes. **It** is also rich in lycopene, which may have beneficial health effects. **It** belongs to the nightshade family, and **its** plants typically grow from three to ten feet high and have a weak stem that often sprawls over the ground. **It** is a perennial in **its** native habitat, and **it** is often grown outdoors in temperate climates.

Notice how much smoother and easier to read this version is.

Here, the antecedent and the pronoun **agree** because *the tomato* is a singular noun, and *it* is a singular pronoun.

The pronoun *it* is also correct because it is used **consistently**: the same singular pronoun is always used to refer to the same singular noun. But what if we were to do this?

> **The tomato** is consumed in many different ways, including raw, as an ingredient in many dishes and sauces, and in drinks. While **it is** botanically a fruit, **it** is considered a vegetable for culinary purposes. **They are** also rich in lycopene, which may have beneficial health effects.

In the last sentence, the noun and pronoun no longer agree because the noun *tomato* is singular and the pronoun *they* is plural. If we only look at the last sentence, though, we have no way of knowing whether the agreement is correct or incorrect – we must look at the surrounding sentences in order to spot the inconsistency. **While a pronoun disagreement may sometimes occur within a sentence, you will very often need to look at the surrounding sentences to determine whether there is an error.**

A. One vs. You

You   →   You
One   →   One

While both *one* and *you* can be used to talk about people in general, the two pronouns cannot be mixed and matched within a sentence or paragraph but must remain consistent throughout. In addition, they should not be paired with any other pronoun.

If you cannot recognize pronoun errors in the original version of the passage, the most efficient way to solve these questions is to start with the answer choices and work backwards from there. In order for this technique to be effective, however, you must be able to recognize common pronouns as well as remember to read the surrounding sentences (before and, if necessary, after) if the error is not apparent from the sentence with the underlined pronoun.

For example:

If you want to avoid insect invasions, you

should avoid leaving crumbs lying on the floor.

You should also avoid leaving dirty dishes in the

sink since ants and mice are attracted to leftovers.

Finally, <u>one</u> should make sure that cracks in the
    1

floor and walls are sealed because pests can often

enter homes by wriggling through tiny spaces.

1. **A.** NO CHANGE
   B. We
   C. They
   D. You

Let's analyze this question. If you were just to read the sentence with the underlined pronoun on its own, you probably wouldn't see anything wrong. This is where are lot of people run into trouble: instead of looking at the surrounding sentences for an error, they simply pick (A) and move on.

But here the answer choices, particularly (D), provide a big clue as to what the sentence is testing. All of the options include pronouns, telling us that we need to look around and see what other pronouns are in the paragraph; the rest of the sentence with the underlined pronoun doesn't help because it contains no other pronouns.

When we look at the other sentences in the paragraph, we can see that they contain the pronoun *you*. That means that the pronoun in this sentence must match. So (D) is the only possible answer.

Bonus points if you caught the pronoun shift in this explanation.

B. People vs. Things

Sometimes different pronouns are used to refer to people and to things.

People (e.g. painters, doctors, musicians):

Singular Nouns		Plural Nouns
She, He	→	They
Her, His	→	Their

On the ACT, questions testing singular and plural pronouns often test *one* and *you* at the same time.

For example:

Mae Jemison became the first African-

American woman to travel into space when she

went into orbit aboard the Space Shuttle

Endeavour on September 12, 1992. After <u>one's</u>

                                           1

medical education and a brief general practice,

Jemison served in the Peace Corps for two years.

1. **A.** NO CHANGE
   B. her
   C. their
   D. your

Since the underlined pronoun can only refer to Mae Jemison, who is clearly female, *her* is the sole possibility, and the answer must be (B). Provided that you actually read the passages and don't just skip from question to question, these tend to be among the most straightforward questions on the English section.

Important: When it is unclear whether a singular noun (e.g. an artist, an architect, a cook) refers to a male or a female, the phrase "he or she" or "his or her" should be used. Although "they" is considered an acceptable gender-neutral alternative in everyday English, the ACT is more concerned with your ability to match singular pronouns to singular nouns, and plural pronouns to plural nouns.

Incorrect:	When <u>an artist</u> works with oil paints, **they** should allow at least a week for paintings to dry.
Correct:	When <u>an artist</u> works with oil paints, **he or she** should allow at least a week for paintings to dry.
Incorrect:	<u>An artist</u> who works with oil paints should allow at least a week for **their** paintings to dry.
Correct:	<u>An artist</u> who works with oil paints should allow at least a week for **his or her** paintings to dry.

111

Things (e.g. cities, books, paintings):

For Singular Nouns		For Plural Nouns
It	→	They/Them
Its	→	Their
This	→	These
That	→	Those

Important: the most commonly tested pronoun pairs are "it vs. they" and "its vs. their."

Questions testing pronoun agreement often include distractor answers that make them seem more complicated than they actually are. While most of these questions are relatively straightforward if you know what to look for, they can also become unnecessarily tricky and/or time consuming if you don't.

For example:

The cacao bean is the dried and fully

fermented fatty bean of the cacao tree

(Theobroma cacao). <u>Their</u> the source of cocoa
                                1
butter and solids, including chocolate, as well

as an ingredient in many Mesoamerican dishes

such as molé and tejate.

1. **A.** NO CHANGE
   B. It is
   C. One is
   D. They're

Let's start by looking at the answer choices. We have four different pronouns: *their* (don't ever forget the "NO CHANGE" option), *it*, *one*, and *they're*. Since all of the verbs agree with the subjects, agreement isn't important. On the other hand, the presence of both singular and plural pronouns tells you that you need to check pronoun agreement. That means you must ask yourself what noun that pronoun refers to (*what* is the source of cocoa butter and solids…?) and whether that noun is singular or plural.

When you back up to the previous sentence, you can see that the pronoun must refer to *the cacao bean*. Since *cacao bean* is singular, you need a singular pronoun: *it*. That leaves (B) as the only possibility.

Note that it does not matter that the pronoun *they* would logically refer to the plural noun *cacao beans*. The problem is that the words *cacao beans* do not actually appear in the paragraph, and **a pronoun can only refer to a word that actually appears**.

What happens to many students when they encounter a question like this, however, is that they immediately get distracted by (D). They know that *they're = they are*, which makes sense in the original version, and that *there is* possessive and doesn't make sense, so they immediately assume that the question is testing "they're vs. their" and pick (D). It never occurs to them that the question could really be testing "it vs. they." In order to avoid making this error, you must train yourself to notice when both singular and plural pronouns are included among the answer choices.

C. Missing or Ambiguous Antecedent

As mentioned on the previous page, the noun to which a pronoun refers must appear either in the same sentence as the pronoun or in a surrounding sentence. Typically it will appear in an earlier sentence (most often the sentence immediately before), but occasionally it will appear in a later one.

When the noun that a pronoun refers to is missing or unclear, it is necessary to make it clear which noun the pronoun refers to. On the ACT, that often involves adding the specific name of the person, place, or thing that the pronoun refers to. For example:

Daniel Liebeskind and Ken Nakamura are

among the most celebrated architects in the

world. <u>He is</u> known for creating simulated
          1
"cities" in which he seeks to simultaneously

express the physical and virtual worlds.

1. **A.** NO CHANGE
   B. Their
   C. Nakamura is
   D. He would be

Because *Daniel* and *Ken* are both male names, we have no way of knowing which architect *he* refers to. Only (C) makes it clear by supplying the actual name.

Important: although the shortest answer is often correct on the ACT, this pattern does not apply to missing/ambiguous antecedent questions. In fact, the longest answer is often correct. For example:

Some sources claim that Spanish conquistador

Hernán Cortés was the first person to bring the

tomato to Europe in 1521. Others say that

Christopher Columbus, a Genoese working for the

Spanish monarchy, took it back as early as 1493.

Regardless of which version is true, reports from

that time period all agree that <u>they were</u> intensely
                                            2
suspicious when they first encountered the small

yellow fruit.

2. **F.** NO CHANGE
   G. one was
   H. members of the Spanish court were
   J. we were

Since the passage describes how two explorers brought the tomato back to Europe, it makes sense that "they" would refer to the Europeans who first encountered it – but the noun *Europeans* doesn't actually appear. We must therefore insert a noun that clearly indicates who was "intensely suspicious." Only (H) supplies that noun.

Pronoun Case

Pronoun case questions appear rarely on the ACT, but they do show up every so often, so if you're aiming for a 30+ score, you should be prepared for how to handle them.

Case refers to whether a pronoun is being used as a **subject** or an **object**.

Nouns that act as subjects can be replaced by **subject pronouns**:

	Singular	Plural
1st person	I	We
2nd person	You	You
3rd person	She/He/It/One	They

If we replace the subjects in the following sentences with subject pronouns, they become:

1. **Hernán Cortés** was the first explorer to bring the tomato to Europe.
   → **He** was the first explorer to bring the tomato to Europe.

2. **Members of the Spanish Court** were intensely suspicious of the small yellow fruit.
   → **They** were intensely suspicious of the small yellow fruit.

3. Tramping through the woods, **Jane and I** could hear birds singing and leaves crackling.
   → Tramping through the woods, **we** could hear birds singing and leaves crackling.

Nouns that act as objects can be replaced by **object pronouns**:

	Singular	Plural
1st person	Me	Us
2nd person	You	You
3rd person	Her/Him/It/One	Them

If we replace the objects in the following sentences with object pronouns, they become:

1. Members of the Spanish Court greeted Hernán Cortés with surprise.
   → Members of the Spanish courted greeted **him** with surprise.

2. Architect Ken Nakamura is known for designing simulated **"cities."**
   → Architect Ken Nakamura is known for designing **them**.

3. Later on that day, Jane's dog sat with **Jane and me** in the garden.
   → Later on that day, Jane's dog sat with **us** in the garden.

When you look at the charts on the previous page, notice that some pronouns have the same subject and object forms (e.g. *it, one, you*) while others can only be used as subjects or objects (e.g. *me, she, they*).

In contrast, all proper names (*Hernán Cortés, Jane, Ken Ito*) can be either subjects or objects.

So, for example, we can write the following sentence several ways:

Correct: Yesterday evening, Ann went to the museum with Bob.

Correct: Yesterday evening, **she** went to the museum with Bob. (*Ann* replaced with subject pronoun)

Correct: Yesterday evening, Ann went to the museum with **him**. (*Bob* replaced with object pronoun)

What we cannot do, however, is replace a subject pronoun with an object pronoun or vice-versa.

Incorrect: Yesterday evening, **her** went to the museum with Bob.

Incorrect: Yesterday evening, she went to the museum with **he**.

Incorrect: Yesterday evening, **her** went to the museum with **he**.

When subjects and objects are singular, mistakes are pretty easy to catch by ear, regardless of whether you know anything about grammar. But when subjects and objects are plural, things suddenly get trickier. For example:

Correct: Yesterday evening, Ann and Rosita went to the museum with Bob.

But what happens if we want to replace *Ann* with a pronoun. Do we say *She and Rosita went to museum with Bob*, or *Her and Rosita went to the museum with Bob*? The key is to cross out the proper name + *and* in order to make the pronoun singular. When the pronoun is singular, any error can be easily heard.

Incorrect: Yesterday evening, her ~~and Rosita~~ went to the museum with Bob.

Since you wouldn't say *her went to the museum with Bob*, you wouldn't say *her and Rosita went to the museum with Bob* either. You would, however, say *she went to the museum with Bob*. Therefore:

Correct: Yesterday evening, **she** and Rosita went to the museum with Bob.

The same thing is true for object pronouns:

Incorrect: Yesterday evening, Ann went to the museum with **he and Rosita**.

Cross out: Yesterday evening, Ann went to the museum with he ~~and Rosita~~.

Correct: Yesterday evening, Ann went to the museum with **him**.

Correct: Yesterday evening, Ann went to the museum with **him and Rosita**.

Sometimes, though, the underlined pronoun or pronouns will not be paired with a proper name. For example:

At the exhibit, Mark and I stood staring at

the sculpture of a crow. Mark asked if he could

touch it, and slowly, the artist picked the piece

up and handed it to ~~him and~~ I.
1

1. **A.** NO CHANGE
   B. us
   C. we
   D. them

The easiest way to handle these questions is to treat them essentially the same as you would a pronoun paired with a proper name – that is, cross out each pronoun + *and* in turn.

Cross out: …the artist picked up the piece and handed it to **him ~~and I~~**.

It's fine to say *the artist…handed it to him*, but now we need to make sure to check the other side:

Cross out: …the artist picked up the piece and handed it to **~~him and~~ I.**

It's not correct to say *the artist…handed it to I*, so (A) can be eliminated.

Now plug in each of the remaining answers:

(B) …the artist picked up the piece and handed it to **us**.

Yes, that sounds ok, and it makes sense since the writer talks about "Mark and I."

(C) …the artist picked up the piece and handed it to **we**.

No, that's clearly wrong.

(D) … the artist picked up the piece and handed it to **them**.

That sounds ok, but it doesn't make sense. The writer is talking about "Mark and I," not other people.

So the answer is (B).

As a **shortcut** you can also use the following rule: **any pronoun that comes after a preposition must be an object pronoun.**

Given the context of the sentence, (D) clearly does not make any sense and can be eliminated immediately. (A) and (C) can also be eliminated because *to* is a preposition, which must be followed by an object pronoun, and *he, I,* and *we* are all subject pronouns. That leaves (B), which is correct because *us* is an object pronoun.

116

Drill: Pronoun Agreement and Case (answers p. 253)

1. There are over 3,000 lizard species, but the Komodo dragon, a reptile with ancestors that date back more than 100 million years, wins the prize for being the largest living lizard in the world. <u>Its</u>

    name came from rumors of a large dragon-like lizard inhabiting the warm, hilly islands of Indonesia. Indeed, the yellow color of its long, forked tongue reminds people of a mythical fire-spitting dragon. Despite its ancient roots, the Komodo dragon was unknown to <u>them</u> until 1910,

    when it was observed in Komodo National Park.

1. **A.** NO CHANGE
    B. Their
    C. They're
    D. It's

2. **F.** NO CHANGE
    G. those people
    H. us
    J. scientists

2. Along the coast of Florida, where I live with my family, big storms are a common occurrence. Every year from June to October, <u>me and them</u>

    gather around the television, watching anxiously as the forecaster announces whether each new storm will hit our town – and how severe <u>their</u> impact

    will be. Last year, we found ourselves directly in the path of a hurricane. As the storm bore down on us, the lights began to flicker wildly, and only moments later <u>it</u> went out altogether. Three

    hours later, they still hadn't come back on.

1. **A.** NO CHANGE
    B. I and them
    C. me and they
    D. we

2. **F.** NO CHANGE
    G. they're
    H. its
    J. it's

3. **A.** NO CHANGE
    B. this
    C. they
    D. we

3. Space is a dangerous place. You cannot

breathe, scream, or do much of anything without

a spaceship to protect <u>oneself</u>. Even inside the
                         1

spaceship, performing simple tasks can become an

adventure. But what about frying? Believe it or not,

the problem of frying food in space has become

the subject of serious scientific investigation.

Prompted by a Russian cosmonaut who craved

fried potatoes while living at the International

Space Station (ISS), <u>they</u> investigated the "effect of
                        2

increased gravitational acceleration in potato deep-

fat frying" for *International Food Research*.

In order to study this question, the researchers,

John S. Lioumbas and Thodoris D. Karapantsios,

stuck a deep-fryer onto a giant centrifuge at the

European Space Research and Technology Center.

<u>He</u> found that at a force of 3-g, which is three
3

times Earth's gravity, the potatoes formed a perfect

crispy crust in around half the usual time. Making

French fries would be very difficult on the ISS,

though. On Earth, the hot liquid at the base of a

pan rises because <u>their</u> density is lower than that of
                        4

the cooler liquid above. In space, however, the hot

liquid doesn't rise, and the crust never forms. The

result: soggy fries – without a crust.

1. **A.** NO CHANGE
   B. yourself
   C. him or herself
   D. themselves

2. **F.** NO CHANGE
   G. he
   H. someone
   J. two researchers

3. **A.** NO CHANGE
   B. They
   C. One
   D. We

4. **F.** NO CHANGE
   G. its
   H. it's
   J. they're

118

4. Almost immediately, you sense that it isn't

going to be a typical afternoon at the museum.

The first thing <u>one sees</u> is a forty-something man
                    1
astride a saddle, a Manila hemp lariat in his hand,

whooping it up as you watch him try to rope a

wooden calf on the floor. He's missing,

but is clearly under the impression he shouldn't be,

and so <u>they keep</u> trying. That's a theme of the
        2
New Mexico History Museum's exhibit

"Cowboys, Real and Imagined," which is hands-on,

familiar, and full of lessons to be learned.

   Ask a person to describe a cowboy, and

<u>he or she</u> will probably mention a ten-gallon hat,
   3
a pair of boots, and a trusty steed. Those

characteristics have <u>they're</u> roots in the sixteenth
                       4
century. At that time, <u>they</u> brought over horses
                        5
from the Iberian peninsula in Spain. Herders with a

long tradition of managing livestock on the rolling

hills of the Iberian Peninsula, the *vaqueros* set up

shop in New Mexico. As time went on,

<u>our</u> leather boots, stoicism, and devotion to their
  6
horses became synonymous with the American

cowboy.

1. **A.** NO CHANGE
   B. they see
   C. you see
   D. he sees

2. **F.** NO CHANGE
   G. one keeps
   H. you keep
   J. he keeps

3. **A.** NO CHANGE
   B. they
   C. him or her
   D. he or her

4. **F.** NO CHANGE
   G. their
   H. its
   J. it's

5. **A.** NO CHANGE
   B. one
   C. we
   D. a group known as *vaqueros*

6. **F.** NO CHANGE
   G. one's
   H. their
   J. his

5. It's common to hear people complain that

you're just looking for a little peace and quiet.
    1
When they say "quiet," though, they're probably

not thinking of a place like the anechoic chamber

at Orfield Laboratories in Minnesota. The

chamber is considered the quietest place on

earth – so quiet that its noise level is measured in
                      2
negative decibels. According to the lab's founder,

Steven Orfield, "You'll hear your heart beating,

sometimes you can hear your lungs, hear your

stomach gurgling loudly. In the anechoic chamber,

one becomes the sound."
    3
    Because the chamber is so silent, companies

often test its products there to find out just how
            4
much noise they make. NASA has also

sent astronauts to help them adapt to the silence

of space. For most people, however, the room is a

deeply disconcerting place. Auditory cues are

necessary to balance and walk. Without it, people
                                        5
have trouble orienting themselves and even

standing. Despite that, laboratory researchers

compete to see how long he or she can stay in the
                                  6
chamber. The record? Forty-five minutes.

1. A. NO CHANGE
   B. their
   C. they're
   D. one is

2. F. NO CHANGE
   G. their
   H. its' Non exsistant
   J. it's

3. A. NO CHANGE
   B. one would become
   C. they have become
   D. you become

4. F. NO CHANGE
   G. they're
   H. these
   J. their

5. A. NO CHANGE
   B. this
   C. him
   D. them

6. F. NO CHANGE
   G. one
   H. they
   J. we

120

10. Adjectives and Adverbs

Adjectives modify **nouns and pronouns**, and they are typically placed **before** the nouns or pronouns they modify. They can also be used with **verbs of being** (e.g. *to be*, *to become*, and *to seem/appear*), in which case they appear **after** verbs. In the sentences below, the adjective is in bold and the noun it modifies is underlined.

Correct:	Members of the Spanish court were **puzzled** by the small yellow fruit.
Correct:	Ken Nakamura is known for designing **simulated** cities.
Correct:	Martha Graham was one of the **greatest** American choreographers of the twentieth century.

Adverbs modify verbs, adjectives, or other adverbs. They are usually formed by adding *–ly* to the adjective, or *–ily* to adjectives that already end in *–y*. Adverbs can be placed **before or after verbs** and **before adjectives and other adverbs**.

Adjective	Adverb
Quiet	Quietly
Hasty	Hastily

In the sentences below, the adverb below is in bold and the word it modifies is underlined.

Adverb modifies verb:	Jonas Salk worked **diligently** on a cure for polio for many years.
Adverb modifies adjective:	Martha Graham was a **highly** influential choreographer.
Adverb modifies adverb:	The crocodile moved **astonishingly** quickly through the water.

An adjective **cannot** be used to modify a verb:

| Incorrect: | When the curtain rose, the dancer began to move **slow** and **graceful**. |
| Correct: | When the curtain rose, the dancer began to move **slowly** and **gracefully**. |

Likewise, an adverb **cannot** be used to modify a noun.

| Incorrect: | When the curtain rose, the **gracefully** dancer began to move across the stage. |
| Correct: | When the curtain rose, the **graceful** dancer began to move across the stage. |

On the ACT, **adverbs and adjectives are switched with one another**. In the most common version of the adjective vs. adverb error, you will be given a pair of underlined words, **the first of which should be an adverb and the second of which should be an adjective**. The incorrect answer choices will present the words in various combinations of adjective and adverb. If you have a reasonably good knowledge of standard English, however, **you will often be able to answer adjective vs. adverb questions by ear**.

Important: watch out for adjectives that end in –*y* (e.g. *busy, noisy, hungry*). If you don't read carefully, you can easily mistake these adjectives for adverbs.

For example:

Martha Graham was an American modern dancer and choreographer who had an extraordinarily strongly impact on her art form –
her influence on dance has been compared to that of Picasso on the visual arts.

1. **A.** NO CHANGE
   B. extraordinarily strong
   C. extraordinarily strongly
   D. extraordinary strong

Strong modifies the noun *impact*, so *strong* must be an adjective. *Strongly*, which appears in (A) and (C), is an adverb, so those two answer choices can be eliminated.

An adverb is then necessary to modify the adjective *strong*. (D) can be eliminated because *extraordinary* is an adjective, even though it ends in –*y*.

(B) is correct because it is the only option that uses an adverb (*extraordinarily*) to modify an adjective (*strong*), which in turn modifies a noun (*impact*).

Other questions will simply replace an adjective with an adverb or vice-versa in the incorrect version but include answer choices that bring in other concepts, such as commas or semicolons, as well.

The wooden fish is a traditionally percussion instrument used throughout China, Japan, and Korea. The fish is hollow with an exterior ridge and produces a hollow sound when it is struck.

2. **F.** NO CHANGE
   G. traditional; percussion
   H. traditional percussion
   J. traditional, percussion

In this case, the adjective *traditional* must modify *percussion instrument*. No adverb is needed at all, so (F) is out. Don't get distracted by (J); the comma is unnecessary because the adjectives cannot be separated by *and* (you would not say, *The wooden fish is a traditional and percussion instrument*), nor can they be reversed (*The wooden fish is a percussion, traditional instrument*). (H) is correct because the adjective *traditional* is used to modify the adjective *percussion*, and when one adjective modifies another, no comma is needed.

Although the use of adjectives and adverbs may seem fairly straightforward, the ACT does sometimes test these parts of speech in non-straightforward ways – most often by asking you where in a sentence a particular adjective or adverb should be placed. If you cannot answer these questions by ear, you must be able to identify the word in question as an adjective or adverb and recognize what type(s) of word(s) it can be placed next to.

Remember that adjectives and adverbs are modifiers, and modifiers must always be placed next to the words they modify. So in order to decide where a given word belongs, you must be able to 1) identify it as either an adjective or an adverb and 2) recognize the noun or verb that it logically modifies.

Modification with Adjectives

Let's start with the fact that adjectives modify nouns. Somewhere around third grade, you probably learned that a noun referred to a person, place, or thing. You probably understood "thing" to refer to a physical object like a house or a dog or a train.

That's true, but it's only half the story. Nouns can also refer to abstract concepts like "idea" or "effort" or "impact." Very often, these nouns end in *–tion* or *–ment* (e.g. notion, deliberation, agreement).

If you have difficulty recognizing when a word is a noun, you can use the following rule: a noun is a word that can follow "a" or "the."

So, for example, *concept* is a noun because you can say "a concept" or "the concept." And *relationship* is a noun because you can say "a relationship" or "the relationship." On the other hand, *maintain* is not a noun because you cannot say "the maintain."

As mentioned earlier, an adjective that modifies a noun must be placed **before** the noun, not after (e.g. you would always say "the good book," not "the book good"). That rule may seem quite obvious in a short, isolated phrase, but many students panic and do not think to apply it when dealing with longer, more complex sentences. **When you have difficulty hearing where in a sentence a particular word belongs, you must rely on your knowledge of parts of speech and where they are placed relative to one another.**

During his fall from notoriety to obscurity,

engineer Nikola Tesla created a legacy of invention

that still <u>genuine</u> fascinates today.
       1

1. The best place for the underlined word is

   A. where it is now
   B. after the word *engineer*
   C. before the word *legacy*
   D. before the word *that*

The most effective way to answer this type of question is to plug the underlined word into the spot in the sentence indicated by each answer choice and see whether it fits. The steps on the following page outline a strategy for determining the correct placement of words when you cannot automatically hear where they belong.

123

Let's assume that you've tried plugging in all of the options and can't find one that clearly sounds right. In order to avoid guessing, you need to identify what part of speech you're dealing with. If you're not sure, you can figure it out: **when the ACT asks you where a single word belongs, that word is virtually always either an adjective or an adverb.** So the question becomes whether *genuine* modifies a noun or a verb.

To test it out, pick a common noun and verb, and put the word next to it. It sounds fine to say "the genuine book," and since *book* is a noun, that makes *genuine* an adjective. On the other hand, you can't say "he genuine went," with *genuine* modifying the verb *went*, so *genuine* cannot be an adverb.

So now you know that *genuine* is an adjective. That means it must be placed before a noun. Now we check out our options and see which ones put it before a noun.

(A) … engineer Nikola Tesla created a legacy of invention that still **genuine** fascinates today.

No. Adjectives go before nouns, and *fascinates* is a verb.

(B) …engineer **genuine** Nikola Tesla created a legacy of invention that still fascinates today.

No, this places the adjective **after** the noun *engineer* and adjectives go **before** nouns. *Nikola Tesla* is also noun, but the placement of an adjective before his name makes absolutely no sense.

(C) …engineer Nikola Tesla created a **genuine** legacy of invention that still fascinates today.

Yes, this option correctly places the adjective *genuine* before the noun *legacy*. You know that *legacy* is a noun because you can say "the legacy." It doesn't sound great, but it works grammatically.

(D) …engineer Nikola Tesla created a legacy of invention that **genuine** still fascinates today.

No, *still* is not a noun because you cannot say "the still."

So grammatically, the only possibility is (C).

Modification with Adverbs

You can also expect to see questions that require you to determine where an adverb should be placed. These questions are frequently easier than questions testing adjectives since the –*ly* on the end of the word tells you immediately that you're dealing with an adverb.

For example:

Unlike other mountain ranges that run along fault lines, the Adirondacks resemble a dome. They were formed by a surge in the Earth that exposed buried rocks <u>previously</u> more than a billion years old.

2. The best place for the underlined word is

    F. NO CHANGE
    G. before the word *surge*
    H. before the word *buried*
    J. before the word *years*

In this question, the –*ly* on the end of *previously* indicates that it's an adverb. That means that it most likely belongs next to a verb, although it could modify an adjective or another adverb as well.

So next we're going to see which options place it next to those parts of speech.

(F) …exposed buried rocks **previously** more than a billion years old.

No. That doesn't make sense – the rocks weren't *previously* more than a billion years old. Their age hasn't changed. It's just that they're no longer buried.

(G) …They were formed by a **previously** surge

No. Neither *a* nor *surge* is a verb. So there's absolutely no way that (G) can be right.

(H) …a surge in the Earth that exposed **previously** buried rocks more than billion years old.

Yes, that makes sense. The rocks were buried *previously*, and when the surge occurred, they were exposed. In addition, the adverb is correctly placed next to a verb, *buried*.

(J) …exposed buried rocks more than a billion **previously** years old.

No. That doesn't make sense. It also puts the adverb after an adjective (adverbs can only go before adjectives) and before a noun, which doesn't work at all. So (J) is out as well.

Which means that the answer is (H).

Comparatives vs. Superlatives

Comparative = –ER or MORE + ADJECTIVE

Superlative = –EST or MOST + ADJECTIVE

Adjective	Comparative	Superlative
Small	Smaller	Smallest
Funny	Funnier	Funniest
Fascinating	More fascinating	Most fascinating

An adjective that takes –er or –est should never take more or most as well. For example:

Incorrect: Roald Amundsen and four members of his expedition arrived at the South Pole five weeks **more earlier** than Robert Falcon Scott and his team.

Correct: Roald Amundsen and four members of his expedition arrived at the South Pole five weeks **earlier** than Robert Falcon Scott and his team.

Incorrect: When traveling over large distances, many people choose to go by airplane because the airplane is the **most fastest** option available.

Correct: When traveling over large distances, many people choose to go by airplane because the airplane is the **fastest** option available.

Note: In general, one-syllable adjectives and two-syllable adjectives ending in –y take –er and –est in the comparative and superlative forms (e.g. *calm, calmer, calmest; hasty, hastier, hastiest*). All other adjectives take *more* or *most* (e.g. *interesting, more interesting, most interesting*). **The ACT rarely tests this rule in isolation but instead combines it with other errors** (e.g. you will not generally be asked to choose between *busier* and *more busy*).

The comparative is used to compare **two** things.

Incorrect: Roald Amundsen and four members of his expedition arrived at the South Pole five weeks **earliest** than Robert Falcon Scott and his team.

Correct: Roald Amundsen and four members of his expedition arrived at the South Pole five weeks **earlier** than Robert Falcon Scott and his team.

The superlative is used to compare **three or more** things.

Incorrect: Out of all the American choreographers who were active during the twentieth century, Martha Graham is perhaps the **more famous** one.

Correct: Out of all the American choreographers who were active during the twentieth century, Martha Graham is perhaps the **most famous** one.

Even though the above sentence does not include a number, it can very reasonably be assumed that more than three American choreographers were active during the twentieth century.

On the ACT, many questions test both comparatives vs. superlatives, and adjectives vs. adverbs simultaneously – that is, all four forms will be found among the answer choices, as in the examples below.

Because the concepts discussed in this chapter are commonly tested concurrently with the concepts discussed in the following chapter, additional questions can be found in the combined drill at the end of the next chapter. Answers to the questions below can be found on p. 253.

1. Lena Mary Calhoun Horne was an African American singer, actress, civil rights activist and dancer. At the age of sixteen, she became a nightclub performer before moving to Hollywood, where she had small parts in numerous movies and more substantially parts in the films *Cabin in the Sky* and *Stormy Weather*.

    1. **A.** NO CHANGE
          B. most substantial
          C. most substantially
          D. more substantial

2. Although groundhogs can reach the age of fourteen in captivity, they usually live no more than two or three years in the wild. Young groundhogs are particularly vulnerable to attacks by snakes, which can more easily enter the burrow.

    1. **F.** NO CHANGE
          G. more easier
          H. easily
          J. easy

3. You've probable seen calculators with solar cells – tiny devices that never need batteries and that sometimes don't even have an "off" button. As long as there's enough light, they seem to work forever. You may also have seen more larger solar panels, perhaps on emergency road signs or in parking lots to power the lights.

    1. **A.** NO CHANGE
          B. more probably
          C. most probable
          D. probably

    2. **F.** NO CHANGE
          G. larger
          H. more largely
          J. largely

11. Word Pairs and Comparisons

Word Pairs

There are two main kinds of comparisons: those that indicate **similarity**, and those that indicate **difference**. Both kinds of comparisons are formed using **word pairs**, which are listed below. These words must always appear together; they cannot be mixed and matched with each other or paired with other words.

A. As…as

As…as is used to indicate that two people or things are equal.

Incorrect:	Among pioneers of modern dance, Isadora Duncan is **as** renowned a dancer and choreographer **than** Martha Graham.
Correct:	Among pioneers of modern dance, Isadora Duncan is **as** renowned a dancer and choreographer **as** Martha Graham.

B. Not only…but (also)

Saying that something is **not only** x **but (also)** y means that it is x **as well as** y.

Incorrect:	Martha Graham was **not only** a great dancer **and** she was (also) a great choreographer.
Correct:	Martha Graham was **not only** a great dancer **but** she was (also) a great choreographer.

C. Comparative (more/less)…than

Incorrect:	Measuring 25 feet, a python named Medusa is **longer as** any other snake in the world.
Correct:	Measuring 25 feet, a python named Medusa is **longer than** any other snake in the world.

D. (N)either…(N)or

Incorrect:	In the United States, **neither** Nikolai Tesla **or** James Joule is as famous as Thomas Edison.
Correct:	In the United States, **neither** Nikolai Tesla **nor** James Joule is as famous as Thomas Edison.

E. From…to

Incorrect:	Great White sharks have been known to consume everything **from** whales **and** car tires.
Correct:	Great White sharks have been known to consume everything **from** whales **to** car tires.

128

Comparing Amounts: Fewer vs. Less, Much vs. Many

Fewer and *many* are used for things that are **quantifiable** – things that <u>can</u> be counted.

They are used with **plural** nouns.

Incorrect: There are **less** types of animals in Antarctica than anywhere else in the world.

Correct: There are **fewer** types of animals in Antarctica than anywhere else in the world.

Incorrect: There are **much** types of animals that inhabit the African savannah.

Correct: There are **many** types of animals that inhabit the African savannah.

Since "types of animals" is plural and can be counted, *fewer* and *many* and should be used respectively.

Less and *much* are used for things are **not quantifiable** – things that <u>cannot</u> be counted.

They are used with **singular** nouns.

Incorrect: There is **fewer** animal life in Antarctica than anywhere else in the world.

Correct   There is **less** animal life in Antarctica than anywhere else in the world.

Incorrect: There is **many** more animal life in Africa than anywhere else in the world.

Correct   There is **much** more animal life in Africa than anywhere else in the world.

Since "animal life" is singular and cannot be counted, *less* and *much* should be used respectively.

Important: only *than*, not *then*, should be used to form a comparison.

Incorrect: Measuring 25 feet, a python named Medusa is **longer then** any other snake in the world.

Correct: Measuring 25 feet, a python named Medusa is **longer than** any other snake in the world.

129

"That of" and "Those of"

When two nouns are compared, one noun can also be replaced with the words *that of* or *those of.*

Singular Comparison

Correct: In the 1950s, most people in the United States were more familiar with Norman Rockwell's **art** than with Wassily Kandinsky's **art.**

Correct: In the 1950s, most people in the United States were more familiar with Norman Rockwell's **art** than with **that of** Wassily Kandinsky.

In the above sentence, the singular pronoun *that* replaces the singular noun *art. That of = the art of.* A plural pronoun cannot be used.

Incorrect: In the 1950s, most people in the United States were more familiar with Norman Rockwell's **art** than with **those of** Wassily Kandinsky.

Plural Comparison

Correct: In the 1950s, most people in the United States were more familiar with Norman Rockwell's **paintings** than with Wassily Kandinsky's **paintings.**

Correct: In the 1950s, most people in the United States were more familiar with Norman Rockwell's **paintings** than with **those of** Wassily Kandinsky.

In the above sentence, the plural pronoun *those* replaces the plural noun *paintings. Those of = the paintings of.* A singular pronoun cannot be used.

Incorrect: In the 1950s, most people in the United States were more familiar with Norman Rockwell's **paintings** than with **that of** Wassily Kandinsky.

Although *that of* and *those of* may sound strange to you, they are both acceptable, provided that the pronoun and the noun agree. You will not, however, be asked to choose between *that of/ those of* and a noun. Rather, you will typically only be responsible for recognizing that *that of/ / those of* is an acceptable alternative to the noun.

Combined Drill: Adjectives, Adverbs, Comparisons, Word Pairs (answers p. 253)

1. Meteoroids are the smallest members of the

solar system, ranging from large chunks of rock

and metal to minuscule fragments no <u>larger then</u> a
1

grain of sand. Whenever a meteoroid plows into

the Earth's atmosphere, it creates a meteor: an

<u>extremely briefly</u> flash of light in the sky.
2

    Millions of meteors occur in the Earth's

atmosphere daily. Just as many meteoroids appear

in the atmosphere during daylight <u>as appear</u>
3

at night; however, meteors are usually observed

after dark, when <u>faintly objects can more</u>
4

<u>easily</u> be identified. The light produced by a meteor
4

may come in a variety of shades, depending on

<u>visible</u> the chemical composition of the meteoroid
5

and the speed of its movement through

the atmosphere.

1.
  A. NO CHANGE
  B. larger than
  C. largest then
  D. largely than

2.
  F. NO CHANGE
  G. extreme brief
  H. extremely brief
  J. extreme briefly

3.
  A. NO CHANGE
  B. that appear
  C. they appeared
  D. than appear

4.
  F. NO CHANGE
  G. faintly objects can more easy
  H. faint objects can most easy
  J. faint objects can more easily

5. The best placement for the underlined word is

  A. where it is now
  B. before the word *light*
  C. before the word *may*
  D. before the word *composition*

2. Julia Child might have been one of the <u>more</u>
1

<u>prominently</u> American chefs of the twentieth
1

century, but unlike many other well-known cooks,

she never stopped relying on recipes. Famous for

the <u>exceptional</u> amount of detail she put into her
2

cookbooks, Child often went through multiple

1.
  A. NO CHANGE
  B. mostly prominently
  C. most prominent
  D. most prominently

2. The best placement for the underlined word is

  F. where it is now
  G. after the word *amount*
  H. after the word *detail*
  J. after the word *cookbooks*

versions of her recipes as she perfected them for

publication. For example, her recipe for white

sandwich bread was one of her <u>most simplest</u>
                                        3
recipes, but she revised it throughout her

<u>repeatedly</u> long career. It was first published
    4
in *Mastering the Art of French Cooking*,

which appeared in 1961. <u>Less than</u> a decade later,
                              5
she re-published a <u>slightly differently</u> version of the
                            6
recipe in a companion volume devoted exclusively

to French breads. Finally, in 2000, the recipe

appeared yet again in one of her last books, *Julia's*

Kitchen Wisdom.

3. When steel magnate Andrew Carnegie

purchased the land for his New York City house

in 1898, he purposely bought property as far north

<u>than</u> possible. The <u>relative spaciously grounds</u>
  1   2
were large enough for a private garden –

one of the few in Manhattan. Completed three

years later, the house boasted <u>much</u> modern
                                        3
features. It was the first private residence in the

United States to be built on a steel frame and one

of the first in New York to have a passenger

3. **A.** NO CHANGE
   B. more simpler
   C. more simply
   D. simplest

4. The best placement for the underlined word is

   F. where it is now
   G. before the word *revised*
   H. after the word *throughout*
   J. after the word *long*

5. **A.** NO CHANGE
   B. Lesser then
   C. Less then
   D. Fewer then

6. **F.** NO CHANGE
   G. slight differently
   H. slightly different
   J. slight different

1. **A.** NO CHANGE
   B. as
   C. from
   D. OMIT the underlined portion

2. **F.** NO CHANGE
   G. relatively spaciously
   H. relatively spacious
   J. relative spacious

3. **A.** NO CHANGE
   B. most
   C. more
   D. many

elevator. Furthermore, the house contained both a central heating system and an early form of air-conditioning. In the basement, a miniature railroad car ran between a storage bin and the furnace, where it was heated <u>immense</u> in a pair of boilers.
4

4. During World War II, a gasoline shortage forced many drivers to install clunky power generators that converted wood into gas, a process known as gasification. Despite their popularity, the generators were <u>quickly tossed aside once</u>
1
<u>fossil fuels became ready available</u> again.
1
Now, however, gasification has been rediscovered 6,000 miles away as a <u>potential</u>
2
source of alternative power. In a California warehouse, All Power Labs has slowly begun resurrecting this <u>more then</u> century-old technology.
3
In five years, the company has sold hundreds of generators known the "Power Pallet." Each pallet is approximately as <u>largely as</u> a refrigerator and can
4
produce clean fuel for about fifteen percent of the usual cost. For countries with <u>less</u> resources, the
5
the pallets open up a whole new world of possibilities.

4. The best placement for the underlined word is

   F. where it is now
   G. after the word *where*
   H. after the word *was*
   J. after the word *of*

1. A. NO CHANGE
   B. quick tossed aside once fossil fuels were ready available
   C. quickly tossed aside once fossil fuels were readily available
   D. quick tossed aside once fossil fuels were readily available

2. The best placement for the underlined word is

   F. where it is now
   G. before the word *rediscovered*
   H. before the word *miles*
   J. before the word *power*

3. A. NO CHANGE
   B. more than
   C. mostly as
   D. most

4. F. NO CHANGE
   G. larger than
   H. large than
   J. large as

5. A. NO CHANGE
   B. lesser
   C. few
   D. fewest

5. In the early nineteenth century, popcorn

exploded into <u>literally</u> popularity in the United
      1

States. Watching dried corn kernels pop was

considered a <u>wildly amusingly</u> form of
                  2

entertainment, and by 1850, popcorn had become

sufficiently widespread to be mentioned in books

and newspapers. Suddenly, the snack was

available everywhere, and nowhere was it <u>more</u>
                                              3

<u>common as</u> at entertainment sites such as circuses.
   3
    Then, in 1855, the first steam-powered popcorn

maker was invented by Charles Cretor. The

<u>lightly portable</u> machine eliminated the need
   4

for a kitchen. As a result, popcorn could

now be served far <u>more easier than</u> potato chips at
                        5
outdoor sporting events and fairs. Furthermore,

popcorn soon came to dominate the

snack market because its aroma was more

appealing than <u>that of</u> any other snack food. Still,
                  6
movie theaters refused to allow popcorn into their

auditoriums.

1. The best place for the underlined word is

    A. where it is now
    B. after the word *early*
    C. after the word *popcorn*
    D. after the word *United States* (placing a
        period afterward)

2. F. NO CHANGE
    G. wilder amusing
    H. wild amusingly
    J. wildly amusing

3. A. NO CHANGE
    B. more common than
    C. commoner then
    D. more commonly than

4. F. NO CHANGE
    G. light, portable
    H. light portable,
    J. lightly and portable

5. A. NO CHANGE
    B. easier then
    C. more easy then
    D. more easily than

6. F. NO CHANGE
    G. one of
    H. that on
    J. that which

12. Modification

In any given sentence, modifiers should be placed as close as possible to the nouns, pronouns, or phrases they modify. When modifiers are separated from the words or phrases they modify, the result is often unclear and awkward, and sometimes completely absurd.

Two kinds of modification errors are tested on the ACT:

1) Dangling Modifiers

2) Misplaced Modifiers

Dangling Modifiers

While dangling modifiers are not a major focus of the ACT, you can expect to see one or two on every test.

Sentences that include dangling modifiers are characterized by an introductory clause that describes the subject but does not name it. This clause is always set off from the rest of the sentence by a comma.

Whenever a sentence contains such an introductory clause, the subject must appear immediately after the comma. If the subject does not appear there, the modifier is said to be dangling, and the sentence is incorrect.

> Incorrect: An elementary school teacher from Arkansas, increased funding and support
> for public libraries were what Bessie Boehm Moore advocated for.

The first thing we can note about the above sentence is that it contains an introductory clause (*An elementary school teacher from Arkansas*) that does not name the subject – it does not tell us who the elementary school teacher from Arkansas *is*.

We must therefore ask ourselves whom that introductory clause describes. When we look at the rest of the sentence, it is clear that this description can only refer to Bessie Boehm Moore.

The words *Bessie Boehm Moore* do not appear immediately after the comma, so the modifier is dangling.

In order to fix the sentence, we must place Bessie Boehm Moore's name after the comma.

> Correct: An elementary school teacher from Arkansas, **Bessie Boehm Moore**
> advocated for increased funding and support for public libraries.

135

Watch out for the possessive version of the subject placed immediately after the introductory clause. In general, any possessive noun placed immediately after an introductory clause will be incorrect.

Incorrect: An elementary school teacher from Arkansas, **Bessie Boehm Moore's goal** was to achieve increased funding and support for public libraries.

At first glance, this sentence looks and sounds correct. But who is the elementary school teacher from Arkansas? *Bessie Boehm Moore*, not her *goal*. And here, the *goal* is the subject – not *Bessie Boehm Moore*. The modifier is therefore dangling.

Correct: An elementary school teacher from Arkansas, **Bessie Boehm Moore** had the goal of achieving increased funding and support for public libraries.

When fixing dangling modifiers, it is most important that you identify the subject because when you look at the answer choices, you are looking for an option that places the subject right after the introductory clause. If the subject is not placed there, you can immediately eliminate the answer.

Important: it is acceptable to begin the main clause with a modifier describing the subject because that description is considered part of the <u>complete subject</u>.

Correct: A native of Arkansas, **elementary school teacher Bessie Boehm Moore** had the goal of achieving increased funding and support for public libraries.

In addition, the presence of a participle, particularly a present participle, at the beginning of a sentence often signals a dangling modifier.

Present Participle

Incorrect: **Stretching** from one end of the city to the other, the efficiency of <u>Frankfurt's tram system</u> often surprises both tourists and city residents.

Correct: **Stretching** from one end of the city to the other, <u>Frankfurt's tram system</u> often surprises both tourists and city residents with its efficiency.

Past Participle

Incorrect: **Born** in a small town in Missouri, the majority of <u>singer and actress Josephine Baker</u>'s career was spent performing throughout Europe.

Correct: **Born** in a small town in Missouri, <u>singer and actress Josephine Baker</u> spent the majority of her career performing throughout Europe.

Occasionally, however, you will have no choice but to rearrange the entire sentence. For example:

Correct: The train system stretches from one end of the city to the other and often surprises tourists and city residents with its efficiency.

Correct: The train system, which stretches from one end of the city to the other, often surprises tourists and city residents with its efficiency.

Misplaced Modifiers

Unlike dangling modifiers, misplaced modifiers do not necessarily involve introductory clauses and can occur anywhere in a sentence. They do, however, also involve modifiers separated from the words or phrases they are intended to modify and often result in sentences whose meanings are unintentionally ridiculous.

Incorrect: Claude McKay was one of the most important poets of the Harlem Renaissance that moved to New York City after studying agronomy in Kansas.

Read literally, the above sentence indicates that the Harlem Renaissance moved to New York City when it was obviously Claude McKay who did so. In order to correct the sentence, we need to make it clear that McKay, not the Harlem Renaissance, was the one who moved to New York City.

There are usually several ways to correct a misplaced modifier. Any rearrangement that places the modifier next to the correct noun or phrase is acceptable.

Correct: One of the most important poets of the Harlem Renaissance, Claude McKay moved to New York after studying agronomy in Kansas.

Correct: Claude McKay, one of the most important poets of the Harlem Renaissance, moved to New York after studying agronomy in Kansas.

Correct: Claude McKay was one of the most important poets of the Harlem Renaissance; he moved to New York City after studying agronomy in Kansas.

Let's look at an ACT-style example:

Pigeons have long played an important role as messengers, as a result of their homing ability, speed, and altitude. <u>During the Franco-Prussian War in 1871, the French military used pigeons to transport messages to Paris,</u>¹ a time when the city was surrounded by Prussian troops.

1. **A.** NO CHANGE
   B. During the Franco-Prussian War in 1871, pigeons were used by the French military to transport messages to Paris,
   C. Pigeons were used to transport messages to Paris during the Franco-Prussian War in 1871,
   D. In 1871, during the Franco-Prussian War, the French military using pigeons to transport messages to Paris,

Questions like this can be very tricky because the information you need to answer them is <u>not</u> in the underlined phrase but rather placed afterwards. Because the words *a time* appear after the comma, the information immediately before the comma must refer to that time. It is therefore only necessary to look at the <u>end</u> of each answer choice. Only (C) ends with a time (1871), so it is the only possibility.

Another common way that the ACT tests misplaced modifiers is to ask where in a sentence an underlined phrase should and should NOT be placed. Although these questions test modification, you can often answer them by ear because the sentence will sound so clearly wrong when the underlined phrase is placed in the indicated spot.

For example:

One of the most important African

American poets <u>in the 1920s</u> was Claude McKay,
1
who moved to New York City after studying

agronomy in Kansas.

1. The underlined phrase could be placed in all of the following EXCEPT

   A. The beginning of the sentence (capitalizing the word *in* and adding a comma after 1920s)
   B. After the word *who*
   C. After the word *important*
   D. After the words *New York City*

In order to answer the question, you should plug the underlined phrase into the spot indicated in each answer choice and read the sentence silently to yourself. Be aware that although there will be one place where the phrase in question will indisputably not work, there may be another one where the phrase sounds less than wonderful.

As a result, **you should only choose your answer after you have plugged every answer in and read it in context of the full sentence.**

(A) <u>In the 1920s</u>, one of the most important African American poets was Claude McKay, who moved to New York City after studying agronomy in Kansas.

That sounds fine. The phrase *In the 1920s* modifies the entire sentence.

(B) One of the most important African American poets was Claude McKay, who <u>in the 1920s</u> moved to New York City after studying agronomy in Kansas.

That does sound weird. You don't usually just stick a prepositional phrase between a subject and a verb, so at this point you might be tempted to just pick (B) and move on. But wait: that construction, weird as it may sound to you, is still acceptable. The question is whether there's something worse.

(C) One of the most important <u>in the 1920s</u> African American poets was Claude McKay, who moved to New York City after studying agronomy in Kansas.

That sounds *really* bad. You absolutely can't put a prepositional phrase between an adjective and a noun. It completely interrupts the sentence. So even though (B) sounds bad, (C) sounds worse. But just to be on the safe side, we're going to check D.

(D) One of the most important African American poets was Claude McKay, who moved to New York City <u>in the 1920s</u> after studying agronomy in Kansas.

Ok, that's fine.

So the answer is (C).

Drill: Modification (answers p. 254)

1. In 1876, 23-year-old Maria Spelterini became the only woman ever to cross the Niagara Gorge <u>over a period of eighteen days on a tightrope.</u>[1] Balancing on a two and a quarter inch wire, <u>she crossed just north of the lower suspension bridge.</u>[2] On July 12, she made her first attempt while wearing peach baskets strapped to her feet; on July 19, the second crossing occurred <u>while blind-folded;</u>[3] three days later, she crossed with her ankles and wrists bound; and on July 26, she crossed for the fourth and last time. <u>Never again performing at Niagara, the story of her</u>[4] <u>life remains a mystery.</u>[4]

---

1. **A.** NO CHANGE
   B. on a tightrope, accomplishing that feat over a period of eighteen days
   C. over a period of eighteen days, she did this on a tightrope
   D. on a tightrope, and, in furthermore, its occurrence over a period of eighteen days

2. **F.** NO CHANGE
   G. just north of the lower suspension bridge is where her crossings took place
   H. her crossings took place just north of the lower suspension bridge
   J. and crossing just north of the lower suspension bridge

3. **A.** NO CHANGE
   B. being blindfolded
   C. while Spelterini was blindfolded
   D. a blindfold was worn

4. **F.** NO CHANGE
   G. She never performed at Niagara again, her life story remains a mystery.
   H. Having never again performed at Niagara, the story of her life, therefore, is a mystery.
   J. She never again performed at Niagara, and the story of her life remains a mystery.

---

2. When President James Polk officially confirmed <u>the discovery by James Marshall</u>[1] <u>of gold at Sutter's Mill</u>[1] in Coloma, California in 1848, hopeful prospectors immediately began planning for the trip out west.

---

1. **A.** NO CHANGE
   B. discovering gold at Sutter's Mill by James Marshall
   C. that James Marshall had discovered gold at Sutter's Mill
   D. James Marshall's discovery of gold, it was at Sutter's Mill

Beginning their journey in spring of 1849,

these prospectors took an overland route, known
                                                    2
as "forty-niners," that was risky and mostly
              2
unknown. Some forty-niners traveled alone, but

most formed companies that enabled them with
                                                    3
other miners to share expenses and supplies during
       3
the long journey. Seagoing travelers went south to

Panama by boat. After disembarking, they began
                                            4
a several-day mule ride to the Pacific coast, then
              4
boarded a ship bound for San Francisco.

3. For decades, plastic bags have been a favorite

around the world of store owners because of their
                      1
low price: two cents per bag, in contrast to five

cents for a paper bag. Used widely since the 1970s,
                                              2
environmentalists now estimate nearly a trillion
                                              2
plastic bags are produced worldwide each year. The
     2
problems that these bags cause are well known.

Unable to break down in landfills, animals are
                                              3
harmed when they consume them. They also
          3
contain toxic dyes that contaminate water and soil.

As a result, an increasing number of cities are

banning their use.

---

2. A. NO CHANGE
    B. these prospectors (known as "forty-niners") took an overland route
    C. an overland route was taken by these prospectors, known as "forty-niners"
    D. these prospectors, who were known as "forty-niners," they took an overland route

3. The best placement for the underlined portion of the sentence is

    A. where it is now
    B. after the word *formed*
    C. after the word *supplies*
    D. after the word *long*

4. F. NO CHANGE
    G. After disembarking, a several-day mule ride was begun by them
    H. When they disembarked, beginning a several-day mule ride
    J. They disembarked, and, then, would begin a mule ride lasting for several days

1. The best placement for the underlined phrase is

    A. where it is now
    B. after the word *decades*
    C. after the *bags*
    D. after the word *favorite*

2. F. NO CHANGE
    G. The bags have been used widely since the 1970s, with environmentalists now estimating that nearly a trillion plastic bags
    H. Having been used widely since the 1970s, environmentalists now estimate nearly a trillion plastic bags
    J. The bags, which have been widely used since the 1970s, but environmentalists estimate nearly a trillion plastic bags

3. A. NO CHANGE
    B. harm is caused to animals which consume
    C. animals are harmed by consuming
    D. the bags harm animals that consume

4. Bioluminescence is light produced within a
                                    1
living organism that is created by a chemical
                          1
reaction. Most bioluminescent organisms are found
       1
in the ocean, although a few – including fireflies

and certain fungi – live on land. Dwelling almost
                                              2
exclusively in saltwater habitats, some form of
                    2
bioluminescence is produced by approximately

90% of deep-sea creatures, including fish, bacteria,

and jellies.

1. **A.** NO CHANGE
    B. created by a chemical reaction and
            produced within a living organism.
    C. produced within a living organism, it is
            created by a chemical reaction.
    D. produced within a living organism, which is
            created by a chemical reaction.

2. **F.** NO CHANGE
    G. They dwell almost exclusively within
            saltwater habitats,
    H. Saltwater habitats being dwelled in almost
            exclusively by them,
    J. Bioluminescent organisms dwell almost
            exclusively in saltwater habitats, and

5. Guerilla films are typically made by

independent producers who lack the budget to

obtain permits, rent locations, and build expensive

sets. Consisting mostly of scenes shot in real time,

small casts and simple props typically characterize
                                      1
these films. In the past, guerilla films were often
      1
poorly made; however, their quality has improved

significantly in recent years. While it was once

difficult for filmmakers to obtain the necessary

equipment, professional quality digital cameras are
                                        2
now widely available to filmmakers that are
                    2
inexpensive. Furthermore, filmmakers can now
     2
edit their work from virtually anywhere, eliminating

the need for editing studios and technicians.

1. **A.** NO CHANGE
    B. small casts and simple props typically
            characterizing these films
    C. these films are typically characterized by
            small casts and simple props
    D. and small casts as well as simple props
            typically characterize these films

2. **A.** NO CHANGE
    B. professional quality digital cameras are now
            widely available to filmmakers, and these
            are inexpensive.
    C. now, professional quality digital cameras
            are widely available to filmmakers that are
            inexpensive.
    D. inexpensive professional quality digital
            cameras are now widely available to
            filmmakers.

141

13. Parallel Structure: Lists and Prepositions

In any given list of three or more items, or in the case of two items joined by a conjunction (e.g. *and* or *but*), each item should appear in the same format: noun, noun, noun; gerund, gerund, gerund; or infinitive, infinitive, infinitive.

Whenever you see a question involving a list or part of a list, you should start by making sure that the underlined item(s) match the non-underlined items. Because you can only change the underlined items, the non-underlined items provide essential information about what change should be made.

Example #1

Changes in wind circulation patterns, **runoff**

from sewage, and **they accumulate** chemical
$\quad$ 1
fertilizers can lead to the creation of ocean waters

low in oxygen and inhospitable to marine life.

1. **A.** NO CHANGE
   B. accumulating
   C. to accumulate
   D. accumulation of

In this question, the underlined portion of the sentence contains a pronoun + verb (*they accumulate*), whereas the other items in the list are nouns (*changes, runoff*). In order for the underlined item to match the other two items, it must become a noun. Only (D) contains a noun, so it is correct.

Example #2

Because they have a highly developed sense of

vision, most lizards communicate by **using**

clear body language, <u>to change</u> their colors and
$\quad$ 2
displaying their athletic abilities.

2. **F.** NO CHANGE
   G. they change
   H. will change
   J. changing

Here, the non-underlined items in the list are both gerunds (*using, displaying*). The underlined item must be a gerund as well, so (J) is the only possible answer.

In the case of a list with three or more items, *and* or *or* must appear before the last item. No other word should be used. In the example below, only (C) correctly provides the word *and* before the last item.

Changes in wind circulation patterns, **runoff**

from sewage, <u>the use of</u> chemical fertilizers can
                        3

lead to the creation of ocean waters low in oxygen

and inhospitable to marine life.

3. **A.** NO CHANGE
   B. in addition the use of
   C. and the use of
   D. OMIT the underlined portion

Matching Prepositions

Occasionally, the ACT will also test two-part parallel structure involving prepositions. The rule is that a preposition used on one side of a conjunction or word pair (e.g. *and, but, not only...but*) must also appear on the other side of the conjunction or word pair.

To answer this type of question, you must make sure to back up to the beginning of the sentence and find the preposition that appears **before** the conjunction, then select the matching one from among the answer choices.

For example:

As one of the greatest American dancers and

choreographers of the twentieth century, Martha

Graham was praised **not only** <u>for</u> the brilliance of

her technique **but also** <u>in</u> the vividness and
                          1
intensity of her movements.

1. **A.** NO CHANGE
   B. with
   C. for
   D. to

The word pair *not only...but* tells you that the construction must be the same on both sides. Since the preposition *for* is used after *not only*, it must also be used after *but* as well. So (C) is correct.

You can also think of the solution in terms of the verb *praised*, which in idiomatically correct English must be followed by the preposition *for*. Because the verb praised "applies" to *the brilliance of her technique* and *the vividness and intensity of her movements*, the preposition *for* must be used for both.

Note: it is also acceptable to omit the preposition before the second noun (e.g. *Graham was praised not only for the brilliance of her technique but also the vividness and intensity of her movements*). The ACT will never ask you to choose between a version with the preposition and a version without it.

In addition, when two adjectives are paired with a single verb, the verb does not have to be repeated before the second adjective (e.g. both *Critics were dazzled and audiences were amazed*, and *Critics were dazzled and audiences amazed* are correct). This construction appears very rarely on the ACT, but you should be aware that it is acceptable.

Drill: Parallel Structure (answers p. 254)

1. First there was the frostquake. Then there was the firenado. Now, there's thundersnow. Thundersnow is essentially the same as a thunderstorm; the only difference is that snow falls instead of rain <u>falling</u>. It occurs when the layer of
    ₁
    air closest to the ground is cold enough to create snow but <u>being warmer</u> than the air above it. When
    ₂
    thundersnow occurs at night, lightning appears brighter because it is reflected against the snow.

1. **A.** NO CHANGE
    B. that falls
    C. which falls
    (D.) DELETE the underlined word (ending the sentence with a period)

2. **F.** NO CHANGE
    G. and also warmer
    H. but it is warmer
    (J.) but warmer

2. First popularized in Japan, Haiku is a form of poetry that has become appreciated around the world. Haiku poets are challenged to convey a vivid message in only 17 syllables. In Japan these poems are valued for their simplicity, openness, and <u>being</u>
    ₁
    <u>light</u>. Haiku poems can describe anything, but they are seldom complicated or <u>people have difficulty</u>
    ₂
    <u>understanding them</u>. Each Haiku must contain a
    ₂
    kigo, a season word that indicates what season of the year the Haiku is set. For example, blossoms would indicate spring, snow would give the idea of winter, and <u>summertime would be suggested by</u>
    ₃
    <u>mosquitoes</u>.
    ₃

1. **A.** NO CHANGE
    (B.) sense of lightness
    C. having lightness
    D. they are light

2. **F.** NO CHANGE
    G. cause difficulties in understanding
    H. to understand them is difficult
    (J.) difficult to understand

3. **A.** NO CHANGE
    B. a suggestion of summertime is given by mosquitoes
    (C.) mosquitoes would suggest summertime
    D. summertime is suggested by mosquitoes

3. Whether it's with a sympathetic tilt of the head or <u>an excited sweep of the tail</u>, dogs often seem to
1
be saying they can sense exactly what we're feeling. Scientists have long been uncertain whether dogs can read human emotions, but evidence is growing that canines can accurately "read" what people feel. In fact, a recent study found that dogs are able to distinguish between expressions that indicate happiness <u>and those in which anger is indicated</u>.
2

1. **A.** NO CHANGE
   B. sweeping their tails excitedly
   C. their tails sweeping excitedly
   D. they sweep their tails excitedly

2. **F.** NO CHANGE
   G. and those in which anger is indicated for
   H. and ones that indicate anger
   J. with ones where anger is indicated

4. Spiders are predators. In the insect world, they're fearsome animals – the tiny equivalent of wolves, lions, or <u>acting like sharks</u>. Spiders use a
1
wide range of strategies to capture prey, including trapping it in sticky webs, lassoing it with sticky bolas, and <u>to mimic</u> other insects in order to avoid
2
detection. Trap door spiders dig holes, covering them up with doors made of spider silk and lying in wait for passing prey.

1. **A.** NO CHANGE
   B. or sharks
   C. or as sharks
   D. or they act like sharks

2. **F.** NO CHANGE
   G. they mimic
   H. mimicking
   J. mimic

5. For centuries, there have been reports of

strange bright lights in the sky just before, during,

or they occur after an earthquake. When an
           1
earthquake hit New Zealand in 1888, for example,

spectators claimed to see "luminous appearances"

and feeling "an extraordinary glow." Over the
       2
years, however, descriptions have varied widely:

the lights have been described as white flares,

floating orbs, also flickering flames. Sometimes
                 3
the lights appeared for just a few seconds, but

other times they hovered in the sky for minutes or

hours at a time.
  4

6. Throughout the World War II years, the United

States government rationed foods like sugar, milk,

coffee, meat and consuming canned goods. Labor
                   1
and transportation shortages made it hard to

harvest and moving fruits and vegetables to market,
             2
so individual citizens were encouraged to grow

their own fruits and vegetables in "victory

gardens." Millions of gardens in all shapes and

sizes produced abundant food to support the war

effort. Gardens were planted in backyards, empty

lots, and even with window boxes.
              3

1. A. NO CHANGE
   B. occurring after
   C. having occurred after
   D. after

2. F. NO CHANGE
   G. they would feel
   H. having felt
   J. feel

3. A. NO CHANGE
   B. and having flickering flames
   C. flickering flames as well
   D. and flickering flames

4. F. NO CHANGE
   G. lasting for hours
   H. even being hours
   J. in hours

1. A. NO CHANGE
   B. to consume canned goods
   C. with the consumption of canned goods
   D. canned goods

2. F. NO CHANGE
   G. move
   H. they moved
   J. having moved

3. A. NO CHANGE
   B. for
   C. to
   D. DELETE the underlined word

146

Neighbors pooled their resources, planting

different kinds of foods and <u>forming</u> cooperatives.
4

While the gardens themselves are now gone,

posters, seed packets, photos, newspaper articles,

and <u>people's having memories</u> still remain to tell us
5
the story of victory gardens.

4. F. NO CHANGE
   G. that form
   H. they would form
   J. to form

5. A. NO CHANGE
   B. people's memories
   C. remembering
   D. they remember

7. Maria Montessori (1870 – 1952) was an Italian

physician and <u>being an educator</u>. She is best known
1
for the philosophy of education that bears her

name as well as <u>in</u> her writings on scientific
2
pedagogy. Today, her educational method is used

in schools throughout the world.

Montessori, however, did not set out to become

a teacher, only <u>to work</u> as a scientist. At sixteen,
3
she enrolled at the Leonardo da Vinci Technical

Institute, studying Italian, mathematics, history,

physics, chemistry, botany, <u>two foreign languages.</u>
4
She did well in the sciences and especially

mathematics. She initially intended to study

engineering but eventually <u>to settle</u> on medicine.
5

1. A. NO CHANGE
   B. to be an educator
   C. as an educator
   D. educator

2. F. NO CHANGE
   G. for
   H. through
   J. with

3. A. NO CHANGE
   B. working
   C. she worked
   D. worked

4. F. NO CHANGE
   G. with two foreign languages moreover
   H. and two foreign languages
   J. two foreign languages also

5. A. NO CHANGE
   B. will settle on
   C. settled on
   D. settling for

147

14. Relative Pronouns: Who(se), Whom, Which, Where, When & That

As is true for other pronouns such as *it* and *she*, some of the pronouns discussed in this chapter can refer to people; others can refer to things; and still others can refer to both people and things.

People	Things	People & Things
Who Whom	Which	Whose That

Which vs. That

Both *which* and *that* refer to things; however, as discussed earlier, *which* always comes after a comma and sets off a non-essential clause, whereas *that* never comes after a comma and sets off an essential clause.

Incorrect: Farm **animals which** were introduced to the Galapagos Islands by early settlers, have been responsible for the destruction of many native species.

Correct: Farm **animals, which** were introduced to the Galapagos Islands by early settlers, have been responsible for the destruction of many native species.

Incorrect: Farm **animals, that** were introduced to the Galapagos Islands by early settlers have been responsible for the destruction of many native species.

Correct: Farm **animals that** were introduced to the Galapagos Islands by early settlers have been responsible for the destruction of many native species.

Who(m) vs. Which

Use *who* or *whom*, not *which*, when referring to people.

Incorrect: King Henry VIII was a British <u>monarch</u> **which** ruled England during the Tudor period and was known for his many wives.

Correct: King Henry VIII was a British <u>monarch</u> **who** ruled England during the Tudor period and was known for his many wives.

Note: *Who vs. that* is not directly tested on the ACT. If different answer choices contain *who* and *that*, there will be other factors that make one answer correct and the other(s) incorrect.

Who vs. Whom

While the ACT tests a version of the "who vs. whom" rule, it only does so at a relatively superficial level. In fact, **to answer "who vs. whom" questions, you really only need to know two things:**

1) "Whom" should **not** be used before a verb.

2) "Whom" **should** be used after a preposition.

(If you'd like a more thorough explanation of the rule, see Appendix C on p. 281.)

"Whom" Before a Verb

The most common ACT error involves incorrectly placing *whom* rather than *who* immediately before a verb.

For example:

Shortly after the Pilgrims arrived in what would

become Massachusetts, they met a Pawtuxet tribe

Member named Squanto <u>whom befriended them,</u>
1

showed them how to plant crops, and acted as an

interpreter with the Wampanoag tribe.

1. **A.** NO CHANGE
   B. who befriended them
   C. which befriended them
   D. and befriending them

The fact that both *who* and *whom* appear in different answer choices clearly suggests that *who vs. whom* is being tested. Besides, the sentence is clearly referring to a person (Squanto), so *which* can't be the answer, and (D) creates a big mess when it's plugged back into the sentence. So it's between (A) and (B).

If you can't hear that *whom befriends* sounds very awkward, or don't trust yourself to pick (B) without knowing the rule, the easiest way to solve the question is to recognize that. Since *whom* cannot go before a verb, **(B) must be the correct answer.**

Note: In order to apply the "no *whom* before a verb" rule effectively, you must be able to recognize verbs. If you are not sure whether a word is a verb, try putting *to* in front of it. So, for example, *befriend* is a verb because you can say *to befriend*. Otherwise, know that a word that ends in *–ed* is almost always a verb (e.g. *befriended*). Although these "tricks" will not always work for irregular verbs, they will work often enough to make it well worth your while to use them.

"Whom" after a preposition

Whenever you are asked to choose between *who* and *whom* after a preposition, the answer will always be *whom* (provided that the sentence refers to a person rather than a thing).

To reiterate, the prepositions most likely to appear on the ACT include *of, from, for, to, by, in, about,* and *with.*

Shortly after the Pilgrim settlers arrived in what

would become Massachusetts, they met Squanto, a

Pawtuxet tribe member <u>from who</u> they learned
1
about planting crops and surviving in the New

World.

1. **A.** NO CHANGE
   B. from which
   C. from whom
   D. by him

Since the sentence is talking about a person (Squanto), *which* cannot be used. So (B) is automatically out.

(D) can be eliminated as well because the preposition is wrong: the Pilgrim settlers learned *from* Squanto, not *by* Squanto.

That leaves (A) and (C). *Whom* must be used after a preposition, and *from* is a preposition, so *whom* should be used. **The answer is therefore (C).**

Whose

Whose is the possessive form of both *who* and *which.* Although it looks similar to *who,* it can be used to refer to either people or things.

  Correct: Maria Fernanda Cardoso is an artist **whose** installations have appeared in museums in the United States, Great Britain, Colombia, and Australia.

  Correct: Mount Hosmer is an "upside down mountain" **whose** oldest rock formations are found near the top of the mountain and **whose** youngest rock formations are found near the bottom.

Where, When, and "Preposition + Which"

Where refers to places (physical locations) only. It should not be used to refer to stories or times/time periods, even though this usage is common in everyday speech.

When refers to times only.

Preposition + which (e.g. *in which, during which, to which*) can be used instead of *where* or *when*.

Incorrect:	The Middle Ages was a period **where** many farmers were bound to the land they worked.
Correct:	The Middle Ages was a period **when/in which** many farmers were bound to the land they worked.
Incorrect:	*Life of Pi*, written by Yann Martel, is a novel **where** the protagonist survives on a raft in the ocean for nearly a year, accompanied only by a tiger.
Correct:	*Life of Pi*, written by Yann Martel, is a novel **in which** the protagonist survives on a raft in the ocean for nearly a year, accompanied only by a tiger.

Which, however, should be not used without the preposition.

Incorrect:	New York is a city **which** many people travel by subway rather than by car.
Correct:	New York is a city **in which** many people travel by subway rather than by car.
Correct:	New York is a city **where** many people travel by subway rather than by car.

When either *where/when* or *preposition + which* is correct, the ACT will never ask you to choose between them. If both options appear as answer choices, one answer will also contain an additional element (word, phrase, punctuation mark) that is indisputably wrong.

For example:

Although Einstein predicted the presence of black holes, regions of space <u>in which</u> gravity is
_1_
so intense that not even light can escape, he had difficulty believing that they could actually exist.

1. A. NO CHANGE
   B. which
   C. and where
   D. OMIT the underlined portion

While both *in which* and *where* could correctly refer to "regions of space," the addition of the word *and* in choice (C) turns the sentence into a fragment and eliminates (C) as an option. (B) can be eliminated because *which* by itself cannot generally be used to refer to a place, and (D) does not work because the sentence does not make grammatical sense if the pronoun is removed altogether.

Drill: Relative Pronouns (answers p. 254)

1. The tale of Hansel and Gretel, the story of two

young children <u>whom</u> stumble across a cottage

       1

made of gingerbread, played an important role in

the history of sweets. It was published in 1812,

<u>a time where</u> many bakers already knew how to

    2

create elaborate structures from other types of

candy. Inspired by the tale, they began form their

gingerbread into houses. Soon, gingerbread

construction was elevated to an art form <u>whose</u>

                           3

popularity quickly spread through Europe and the

United States.

1. **A.** NO CHANGE
   (B.) who
   C. they
   D. which

2. **F.** NO CHANGE
   G. this was when
   H. a time which
   (J.) when

3. **(A.)** NO CHANGE
   B. its
   C. who's
   D. and whose

2. Shortly after I moved from Chicago to Lincoln,

Nebraska, I attended the eighty-fifth birthday party

of a woman <u>whom</u> was one of the city's original

        1

settlers. The <u>room, that</u> was decorated

        2

with banners and balloons, also held family

photographs – crisp new snapshots of

grandchildren and great-grandchildren, wedding

photographs from the mid-twentieth century, and

worn black-and-white portraits of ancestors <u>whose</u>

                                   3

stoic expressions and sturdy, upright figures

seemed to embody the harshness of life in an

1. **A.** NO CHANGE
   B. for whom
   (C.) who
   D. she

2. **F.** NO CHANGE
   G. room, and which
   H. room that,
   (J.) room, which

3. **(A.)** NO CHANGE
   B. who's
   C. their
   D. which

unforgiving new environment. These people

became immortalized in the works of Willa Cather,

by who they were depicted in novels such as *My*
4

Antonia and *O Pioneers!* Cather, an author which
5

lived in Nebraska during the late nineteenth
5

century, chronicled the lives and hardships of the

settlers, preserving their struggles for generations

to come.

4. F. NO CHANGE
   G. by whom
   H. by which
   J. for which

5. A. NO CHANGE
   B. whom lived
   C. who lived
   D. lived

3. Having played a central role in helping the

United States win its independence from Great

Britain, George Washington quickly became a

celebrity. Not surprisingly, he acquired many

admirers, one of whom was Patience Wright.
1

Wright, a sculptor, was known for her

remarkably realistic portraits, that were made out of
2

tinted wax. She had always amused herself and her

children by molding faces out of putty, dough, and

wax, but thanks to a neighbor whom encouraged
3

her, she turned her hobby into a full-time

occupation in 1769.

Wright loved her work, and those who
4

watched her sculpt often commented on the energy

that she brought to the process. In an era where
5

photographs did not exist, skilled portraitists were

1. A. NO CHANGE
   B. one of them
   C. one of who
   D. one of which

2. F. NO CHANGE
   G. portraits that,
   H. portraits, and that
   J. portraits, which

3. A. NO CHANGE
   B. who encouraged
   C. which encouraged
   D. that has encouraged

4. F. NO CHANGE
   G. that who
   H. them which
   J. those whom

5. A. NO CHANGE
   B. and when
   C. in which
   D. that

153

held in high regard. Despite her lack of formal

training, Wright was widely recognized for her

talents. By 1770, she had become successful

enough to open a waxworks house in New York

City, in which it housed her most important work.
6

When fire ravaged the New York studio in

1771, however, Wright decided to relocate to

London. By that time, she had sculpted many

famous figures and had even earned the support

of the Queen of England, whom admired her work
7

deeply. Still, though, she wasn't satisfied. To sculpt

George Washington, a leader to who so many new
8

Americans owed their deep gratitude, would be the

crowning achievement of Wright's career.

6. **F.**   NO CHANGE
    G.   it housed
    H.   when it housed
    J.   which housed

7. **A.**   NO CHANGE
    B.   who admired
    C.   that admired
    D.   and who admired

8. **F.**   NO CHANGE
    G.   for which
    H.   to whom
    J.   that

Cumulative Review: All Grammar & Punctuation, Chapters 1-14 (answers p. 254)

1. "Mountaineering" is a term that includes not

only mountain-climbing but also hiking, and skiing.

The sport traces its origins to early

<u>mountain-climbers attempts</u> to reach the highest

1
point of unclimbed <u>peaks, but it</u> has branched into

2
specializations that address different aspects of the

mountain and now consists of three <u>areas: rock-</u>

3
<u>craft, snow-craft, and</u> skiing. Successful

3
participation in each area requires experience,

athletic ability, and knowledge of safety procedures.

---

1. **A.** NO CHANGE
   B. mountain climbers' attempts
   C. mountain climbers attempt's
   D. mountain climber's attempts

2. All of the following would be acceptable
   alternatives to the underlined portion EXCEPT

   F. peaks. It
   G. peaks; however, it
   H. peaks; it
   J. peaks, it ,

3. **A.** NO CHANGE
   B. areas, rock-craft, snow-craft and
   C. areas, rock-craft, snow-craft and,
   D. areas; rock-craft, snow-craft, and

---

2. When the British archaeologist Howard Carter

arrived in Egypt in 1891, most of the ancient

Egyptian tombs had been <u>discovered, but the</u>

1
location of the tomb holding the little-known King

Tutankhamen still <u>being</u> unknown. After World

2
War I, Carter began an intensive search for "King

Tut's <u>Tomb," he finally discovered</u> steps to the

3
room hidden in the debris near the entrance of the

nearby tomb of King Ramses VI. On November

26, 1922, Carter and a <u>fellow archaeologist, Lord</u>

4
<u>Carnarvon,</u> entered the interior chambers of the

4
tomb, finding them miraculously intact.

---

1. **A.** NO CHANGE
   B. discovered, however, the
   C. discovered. Yet the
   D. discovered, the

2. **F.** NO CHANGE
   G. were
   H. was
   J. is

3. **A.** NO CHANGE
   B. Tomb," he would finally discover
   C. Tomb." He will finally discover
   D. Tomb," finally discovering

4. **F.** NO CHANGE
   G. fellow archaeologist Lord Carnarvon
   H. fellow archaeologist: Lord Carnarvon
   J. fellow archaeologist – Lord Carnarvon

3. Until I was three years old, my family lived with my grandparents in Montana. My grandfather, who
<u>had grown</u> up on a Chippewa reservation, and my
1
sisters and I loved hearing stories about his

youth. When I was eight and my younger sister

Cheyenne was <u>five, her and I</u> would climb onto
2
Grandpa's lap and listen as he spun <u>long,</u>
3
<u>gripping, tales</u> about wild prairie foxes and deer.
3
Seated in front of an imaginary roaring fire,

Cheyenne and I liked to <u>pretend, we</u> were hunters
4
who had just returned to our village after a long

day of tracking animals.

1.
A. NO CHANGE
B. grandfather, whom had grown
C. grandfather had grown
D. grandfather had grew

2.
F. NO CHANGE
G. five, me and her
H. five, she and me
J. five, we

3.
A. NO CHANGE
B. long gripping, tales
C. long, gripping tales,
D. long, gripping tales

4.
F. NO CHANGE
G. pretend: we
H. pretend we
J. pretend that, we

4. Comedian Will Rogers famously described

the Rio <u>Grande, (Spanish for "Great River")</u> as the
1
only river he had ever seen that needed irrigation.

But the river, located just outside of Albuquerque,

<u>New Mexico, capital</u> of the driest state in the
2

United States – <u>deserving</u> its name. Surrounded
3
by the Sandia Mountains and herds of cattle,

the river is a <u>damp, refreshing, world that</u> remains
4

mysterious to both residents and tourists.

1.
A. NO CHANGE
B. Grande, (Spanish for "Great River"),
C. Grande (Spanish for "Great River")
D. Grande (Spanish for "Great River"),

2.
F. NO CHANGE
G. New Mexico capital
H. New Mexico. Capital
J. New Mexico – capital

3.
A. NO CHANGE
B. will have deserved
C. deserves
D. deserve

4.
F. NO CHANGE
G. damp, refreshing world that
H. damp, refreshingly world that,
J. damply refreshing world

156

5. While most types of diving <u>requires</u> divers to
                                        1

either hold their breath or rely on air pumped

from the <u>surface, scuba</u> divers carry their own
                    2

oxygen in tanks that are small, lightweight, <u>and</u>
                                              3

<u>being portable</u>.
    3

   Modern gas <u>tanks known</u> as Porpoises,
                    4

originated in Australia. <u>It was</u> invented
                            5

by a diver named Ted Eldred, <u>whom</u> believed that
                                  6

the existing two-tank model was <u>unnecessary bulky</u>
                                        7

and difficult <u>to manage</u> underwater. To improve on
                  8

this model, he invented a tank consisting of a single

oxygen tank attached to a hose. <u>They</u> can thus
                                      9

control the air pressure at their mouths, not at

the top of the tank.

1. **A.** NO CHANGE
   B. requiring
   C. require
   D. would have required

2. **F.** NO CHANGE
   G. surface; scuba
   H. surface, but scuba
   J. surface. Scuba

3. **A.** NO CHANGE
   B. and also having portable qualities
   C. with portability as well
   D. and portable

4. **F.** NO CHANGE
   G. tanks – known
   H. tanks, known,
   J. tanks, known

5. **A.** NO CHANGE
   B. It had been
   C. They were
   D. They would be

   – tanks vs plural!!

6. **F.** NO CHANGE
   G. who
   H. he
   J. which

7. **A.** NO CHANGE
   B. unnecessarily bulky
   C. unnecessary bulkily
   D. unnecessarily bulkily

8. **F.** NO CHANGE
   G. in managing
   H. for managing
   J. managing

9. **A.** NO CHANGE
   B. One
   C. Divers
   D. It

6. The predator waits patiently while its prey wanders about, unaware that danger lurks just inches away. As it stops on a leaf to taste some fragment <u>sap. The unsuspecting</u> prey is
₁
unaware of its mistake. Suddenly, the <u>predators jaws</u> snap shut. The struggle is quickly
₂
over, and soon the plant settles down to digest its tasty meal.

Plants that eat other creatures? It sounds like a science fiction novel. But there's <u>actually</u>
₃
<u>nothing unnaturally</u> about it; carnivorous plants
₃
have always existed. There are hundreds of <u>varieties; their diets range</u> from microscopic
₄
organisms to spiders. One of these plants <u>has</u>
₅
captured the public's imagination: the Venus Flytrap. Many people who encounter the plant, which was featured in the <u>movie, *Little Shop of*</u>
₆
<u>Horrors,</u> become fascinated by its
₆
<u>strangely dietary habits and unique</u> appearance.
₇
Although the Venus Flytrap has captivated people across the <u>world; it only grows</u> in a very
₈
small geographic area along the coast of the southern United States. Within this area, the plants are further limited to living in humid, wet, and

1. A. NO CHANGE
   B. sap, the unsuspecting prey
   C. sap; the unsuspecting prey
   D. sap, and the unsuspecting prey

2. F. NO CHANGE
   G. predator's jaws
   H. predators jaws that
   J. predators' jaws

3. A. NO CHANGE
   B. actual nothing unnaturally
   C. actually nothing unnatural
   D. actual nothing unnatural

4. Which of the following would NOT be an acceptable alternative to the underlined portion?

   F. NO CHANGE
   G. varieties, their diets range
   H. varieties whose diets range
   J. varieties, their diets ranging

5. A. NO CHANGE
   B. having
   C. have
   D. would have

6. F. NO CHANGE
   G. movie, *Little Shop of Horrors*
   H. movie *Little Shop of Horrors,*
   J. movie *Little Shop of Horrors*

7. A. NO CHANGE
   B. strange dietarily habits and uniquely
   C. strange dietary habits and unique
   D. strangely dietary habits and uniquely

8. F. NO CHANGE
   G. world. This only grows
   H. world, it only grows
   J. world and only grows

158

sunny bogs and wetlands. The flytrap has been

endangered in the wild as a result of over-collection

by Flytrap enthusiasts and <u>destroying</u> the
                                    9
natural wetlands where the plants grow; there

is now a hefty fine for taking a Flytrap from

<u>their</u> native habitat. You can, however, buy one
 10
at any number of nurseries. Just remember not

to get too close to it at feeding time!

9. **A.** NO CHANGE
    B. destroyed
    C. they destroy
    D. the destruction of

10. **F.** NO CHANGE
    G. it's
    H. they're
    J. its

7. You open your eyes to the soft, pale light of

dawn. Ice is <u>everywhere – some of it</u> is carved into
                              1
furniture and sculptures, and some of it is shaped

into huge blocks that form the walls, the ceiling,

and even <u>on the floor</u>. But even though the room is
              2
beautiful, you have to start moving. After all, the

temperature in <u>one's</u> room is below freezing, and
                  3
you've just spent the night sleeping on a slab of ice

while wrapped up in blankets like a mummy. The

beauty, the cold, and the quick morning escape are

all part of the typical ice hotel experience.

    Although they have modern amenities, ice

hotels are <u>essentially largely</u> igloos. Solid blocks
              4

1. Which of the following would NOT be an
    acceptable alternative to the underlined portion?

    A. everywhere, some of it
    B. everywhere. Some of it
    C. everywhere; some of it
    D. everywhere: some of it ✓

2. **F.** NO CHANGE
    G. on the floor as well
    H. being on the floor
    J. the floor

3. **A.** NO CHANGE
    B. their
    C. your
    D. our

4. **F.** NO CHANGE
    G. essential large
    H. essentially large
    J. essential largely

of ice <u>makes</u> up their imposing, barrel-shaped
   5
exteriors. Inside, they <u>gleamed</u> with elaborate ice
                          6
furniture, ice windows, and ice glasses. Colorful

lights make the structures seem more like magical

snow castles than frigid arctic dwellings. The hotels

are built near rivers so that <u>they have</u> easy access to
                                   7
water. The water is then frozen and cut into large

<u>blocks, which are</u> hauled into place with ropes.
      8
From start to finish, the whole process takes about

six weeks. When spring <u>comes, though</u> all the hard
                              9
work melts away, and the hotels cannot be rebuilt

until the following winter.

5. **A.** NO CHANGE
   B. make
   C. would make
   D. making

6. **F.** NO CHANGE
   G. had gleamed
   H. gleam
   J. will gleam

7. **A.** NO CHANGE
   B. one has
   C. you have
   D. workers have

8. **F.** NO CHANGE
   G. blocks that,
   H. blocks, they are
   J. blocks. Which are

9. **A.** NO CHANGE
   B. comes though,
   C. comes, though,
   D. comes while

8. In the 1930s, Marjorie Latimer was the curator

of a tiny museum in the port town of East London,

South Africa. She <u>befriends</u> a local sailor, Captain
                       1
Hendrick Goosen, <u>who's</u> boat, *The Nerine*, fished
                       2
the nearby coastal waters of the Indian Ocean.

When he arrived in <u>port; Captain Goosen</u> often
                       3
called Latimer to pick up any unusual specimens

she might want for her museum.

On December 23rd, 1938, *The Nerine*

returned from a trip to the mouth of the Chalumna

1. **A.** NO CHANGE
   B. will have befriended
   C. had befriended
   D. is befriending

2. **F.** NO CHANGE
   G. whose
   H. his
   J. they're

3. **A.** NO CHANGE
   B. port. Captain Goosen
   C. port, and Captain Goosen
   D. port, Captain Goosen

River. Latimer, who was busy mounting a reptile

collection but felt she ought at least go down to the
    4

docks. She took a taxi, delivered her greetings, and

was about to leave when as she later recounted, she
    5

noticed a blue fin protruding on the deck. Pushing
  5

them aside, she revealed a long, blue fish with
  6

iridescent silver markings. Latimer had no idea

what type of fish it was, but she did know, it had to
    7

go back to the museum immediately. At first, the

taxi driver refused allowing the fish in his cab, but
    8

after a heated discussion, he drove Marjorie and

her specimen back to the museum.

Looking through the few reference books on

hand, Latimer found a picture that stunned her.

With its snake-like head and three-lobed tail, her

specimen was remarkably similarly in appearance
  9

to a prehistoric fish. Further research revealed that

it was a coelacanth – a species believed to have
  10
been extinct for millions of years.

4. F. NO CHANGE
   G. collection, and felt
   H. collections, when she felt
   J. collection, felt

5. A. NO CHANGE
   B. when, as she later recounted, she noticed
   C. when, as she later recounted. She noticed
   D. when as she later recounted, she noticed

6. F. NO CHANGE
   G. the other fish
   H. one
   J. some

7. A. NO CHANGE
   B. know: it
   C. know it
   D. know that, it

8. F. NO CHANGE
   G. refused and allowed
   H. refused to allow
   J. refused in allowing

9. A. NO CHANGE
   B. remarkably similar
   C. remarkable similarly
   D. remarkable similar

10. A. NO CHANGE
    B. coelacanth. A species
    C. coelacanth; a species
    D. coelacanth a species

9. It use to be that every person, who wanted to
   become a clown, dreamed of attending the Ringling
   Brothers and Barnum & Bailey Clown College.

For three decades, Clown College taught the basics:
how to apply clown makeup, how to take a pie in
the nose, and falling down without getting hurt.

   Clown College was the brainchild of Irvin Feld.
   The owner of the Ringling Brothers and Barnum &
   Bailey circus. In 1968, the clown profession seemed
   to be dwindling. Ringling Brothers had only a
   dozen clowns, most of who were in their fifties.

Because there were few suitable replacements, Feld
decided to create a school to train new clowns.

   Feld and the schools' other directors decided to
   hold auditions at universities and theaters around
   the United States. To their surprise, hundreds of
   would-be clowns showed up. The competition was
   intense, only thirty students were selected. When
   the inaugural class members arrived, they
   donned large shoes and baggy pants to learn about
   juggling, stilt-walking, and the fine art of making
   audiences laugh. The classes were free, and Barnum
   and Bailey, itself selected the best graduates to go
   on the road with the troupe.

1. A. NO CHANGE
   B. person; who wanted to become a clown
   C. person who wanted to become a clown
   D. person who wanted to become a clown,

2. F. NO CHANGE
   G. and how to fall down without getting
   H. and how to fall down without to get
   J. falling down without getting

3. A. NO CHANGE
   B. Irvin Field, the owner,
   C. Irvin Field, the owner
   D. Irvin Field: the owner,

4. Which of the following would NOT be an
   acceptable alternative to the underlined portion?

   F. dwindling; Ringling Brothers
   G. dwindling – Ringling Brothers
   H. dwindling; and Ringling Brothers
   J. dwindling: Ringling Brothers

5. A. NO CHANGE
   B. most of whom
   C. most of them
   D. most of which

6. F. NO CHANGE
   G. schools's
   H. schools
   J. school's

7. A. NO CHANGE
   B. intense and only
   C. intense because only
   D. intense. Only

8. F. NO CHANGE
   G. free and Barnum and Bailey, itself,
   H. free, and Barnum and Bailey itself
   J. free; Barnum and Bailey itself,

162

Unfortunately, Clown College became a victim

of it's own success. In 1998, there were about over
9

a thousand trained clowns and little danger of the

profession dying out; therefore, Ringling Brothers
10

has decided to stop offering introductory
11

classes at its permanent residence in Sarasota,

Florida. Today, Clown College continues to reach

students through educational programs for aspiring

clowns as well as with those employees already
12

fortunate enough to tour with The Greatest Show

On Earth®.

9. A. NO CHANGE
    B. its
    C. they're
    D. our

10. F. NO CHANGE
    G. out. So
    H. out, meanwhile
    J. out, as a result

11. A. NO CHANGE
    B. had decided
    C. decides
    D. decided

12. F. NO CHANGE
    G. by
    H. for
    J. to

10. Growing up in Manila's Chinatown was a

noisily and colorful experience. Throughout my
1

childhood, my life revolved around a fascinating

two-block radius in the neighborhood of Bay

Tubig. Although "Bay Tubig" means "bay water"

in Tagalog, the language spoke in the Philipines,
2

we lived in a commercial and residential area

located away from the water. In front of our shop

was Li Fong's stall. It was full of perfectly cut fruit
3

and crates of drinks.

If I ventured a little further, I could lean

against the gates of Changsho Primary School, and

1. A. NO CHANGE
    B. noisy, and colorful
    C. noisy, colorful,
    D. noisy and colorful

2. F. NO CHANGE
    G. speaking
    H. spoken
    J. to speak

3. Which of the following would be the LEAST acceptable alternative to the underlined portion?

    A. stall, it was full
    B. stall, which was full
    C. stall; it was full
    D. stall, full

163

admire the seven-story building, the <u>most tallest</u>
4

structure I had ever encountered. Across from the

school was a temple, which drew many tourists. I

will never forget the giant buses carrying men and

women <u>in strange hats that had giant black boxes</u>
5
<u>around their necks</u>. They often stopped by Li
5
Fong's shop, where they paid his tourist price for a

drink – fifty cents.

    To the right of our shop was the focal point

of the <u>neighborhood: a coffee shop</u> with an
6
amazing food stall that sold fried chicken and

pansit (noodles with seafood and hard boiled eggs).

The shop also housed a delicious rice <u>stall who's</u>
7
owner served rice heaped with the customer's

choice of meat, vegetables, <u>in addition to tofu</u>.
8
    Across from our shop was Bay Tubig's Green.

It might have been the smallest park in Manila,

but crossing <u>them</u> was a thrilling excursion that
9
brought me to the edge of my childhood world.

I thought I would live in Bay Tubig forever.

When I was a <u>teenager, though</u> my family
10
was relocated to another part of the city as a result

4. **F.** NO CHANGE
   G. more taller
   H. mostly taller
   J. tallest

5. **A.** NO CHANGE
   B. who wore strange hats and carried giant black boxes around their necks
   C. wearing strange hats with giant black boxes around their necks
   D. wearing strange hats with boxes around their necks

6. **F.** NO CHANGE
   G. neighborhood. A coffee shop
   H. neighborhood a coffee shop
   J. neighborhood; a coffee shop

7. **A.** NO CHANGE
   B. stall whose
   C. stall thats
   D. stall, the

8. **F.** NO CHANGE
   G. also tofu
   H. tofu as well
   J. and tofu

9. **A.** NO CHANGE
   B. these
   C. their
   D. it

10. **F.** NO CHANGE
   G. teenager, though,
   H. teenager; though
   J. teenager though,

164

of urban renewal <u>plans at that time,</u> I was eager to
11

see a new world. I told <u>myself, I could</u> always
12

come back to visit. Years passed, and I went on to

live in <u>much</u> different neighborhoods around the
13

Philipines and the United States. During that time,

Bay Tubig underwent a massive transformation.

When I last visited, my beloved shop <u>had become</u> a
14

food court. Office workers from the nearby

<u>skyscrapers pouring</u> onto the street during the
15

lunch hour, fighting for space alongside the many

tourists. Despite those changes, Bay Tubig

remains the place that most influenced the person I

am today.

11. **A.** NO CHANGE
   B. plans, at that time
   C. plans. At that time
   D. plans at that time

12. **F.** NO CHANGE
   G. myself: I could
   H. myself I could
   J. myself; I could

13. **A.** NO CHANGE
   B. many
   C. lots
   D. more

14. **F.** NO CHANGE
   G. had became
   H. has become
   J. became

15. **A.** NO CHANGE
   B. skyscrapers, who poured
   C. skyscrapers poured,
   D. skyscrapers poured

Part II:
Rhetoric

15. Shorter is Better: Redundancy and Wordiness

Redundancy and wordiness are two of the most frequently tested concepts on ACT English. Luckily, they're also among the most straightforward. In order to answer questions testing these concepts correctly, you must simply keep one rule in mind: **shorter is better**.

When all of the answer choices are grammatically acceptable and express the same essential information, the shortest option will usually be correct. In fact, you should always **check the shortest answer first** and only look at the longer options if the shortest one is clearly incorrect.

A. Redundancy

Never use two synonyms to describe something when you can use only one word.

For example:

Located in Midland County, Michigan, the

Chippewa Nature Center is one of the most

<u>prominent and well-known</u> nature centers in the
1

United States.

1. **A.** NO CHANGE
   B. prominently well-known
   C. prominent in addition to well-known
   D. prominent

Since *prominent* and *well-known* mean the same thing, only one of them should be used. (D) is thus correct.

In addition, you must sometimes look at the non-underlined portion of the sentence to identify the redundancy. While the original version may be acceptable by itself, it will not be acceptable in context of the sentence.

Located in Midland County, Michigan, the

Chippewa Nature Center is one of the most

prominent American nature centers <u>that is</u>
2
<u>known by many people in the United States.</u>
2

2. **F.** NO CHANGE
   G. being known by many Americans
   H. known by many people there
   J. OMIT the underlined portion (inserting a period after "centers)

Since *prominent* means "known by many people," the underlined portion is unnecessary and (J) is correct.

168

B. Wordiness

Wordiness questions do not always include multiple words with the same meaning. Sometimes they simply add in extra words for no other reason than to make the sentence longer. As a result, **when you have multiple answer choices that express the same information and differ only in length, the shortest answer is generally correct.** You should, however, make sure to plug it back into the sentence to make sure that it does not eliminate important information.

For example:

During the Nimrod Expedition to the South

Pole in 1907, Ernest Shackleton led a group of

explorers on <u>a voyage that was dangerous in</u>
                   1

<u>nature.</u>
 1

1. **A.** NO CHANGE
   B. a voyage of a dangerous sort
   C. a dangerous voyage
   D. a voyage that was dangerous in itself

While all of the answers express the same information, (C) does so in the fewest words and is thus correct.

C. Passive Voice

In a passive construction, the subject and the object are flipped so that the person or thing performing the action becomes the object, and the person or thing on the receiving end of the action becomes the subject. In other words, *x does y* (active) becomes *y is done by x* (passive).

Although it is not absolutely necessary that you master passive constructions since they are by definition longer than active ones, it can be helpful to be able to recognize them because the ACT frequently uses them to make sentences or phrases unnecessarily long and wordy. When the original version of the sentence is passive, it can be difficult to compare its length to the length of the other answer choices simply by looking.

For example:

During the Nimrod Expedition to the South

Pole in 1907, <u>a group of explorers **were** led on a</u>
                   1

<u>dangerous voyage **by** Ernest Shackleton.</u>
            1

1. **A.** NO CHANGE
   B. a group of explorers being led on a dangerous voyage by Ernest Shackleton
   C. Ernest Shackleton led a group of explorers on a dangerous voyage
   D. a dangerous voyage that Ernest Shackleton led a group of explorers on

It's pretty easy to eliminate (B) and (D). If you're using your ear, though, you might think that (A) and (C) sound equally correct, and it isn't immediately obvious which answer is shorter. If you can recognize that (A) is passive and thus longer, however, the question becomes much more straightforward. (C) is active, shorter, and correct.

169

Drill: Shorter is Better (answers p. 255)

1. The issue of free speech as it relates to the First Amendment of the United States Constitution has been a center of controversy <u>about free speech</u>
₁
since the 1950s. In the <u>importantly significant</u>
₂
decision Tinker v. Des Moines Independent Community School District (1965), the United States Supreme Court <u>formally recognized</u> that
₃
freedom of speech and expression do not "end at the schoolyard gate." Unsurprisingly, though, students and school administrators do not always

<u>agree and concur</u> with one another about what
₄
constitutes speech.

1. **A.** NO CHANGE
    B. concerning free speech
    C. in regards to the issue of free speech
    D. DELETE the underlined portion

2. **F.** NO CHANGE
    G. important and significant
    H. important while being significant
    J. significant

3. **A.** NO CHANGE
    B. recognized in a formal manner
    C. undertook formal recognition
    D. recognized, doing so formally,

4. **F.** NO CHANGE
    G. agree in a manner involving concurrence
    H. agree while also concurring
    J. concur

2. When Jordan Romero was in elementary school, he became <u>intrigued and fascinated</u> by a
₁
painting that hung in the hallway of his elementary school. The painting showed seven of the world's highest mountains – one for each continent – and Jordan made up his mind to climb them all.

Remarkably, <u>he achieved an attainment of</u> that
₂
goal when he reached the top of the Vinson Massif at the age of fifteen years, five months, and twelve

1. **A.** NO CHANGE
    B. intrigued in a fascinated way
    C. intriguingly fascinated
    D. fascinated

2. **F.** NO CHANGE
    G. he achieved as well as attaining
    H. he attained
    J. he has attained

days, breaking George Atkinson's record to become the youngest climber ever to summit the tallest mountain on each continent. In the process, Romero also became the youngest person to scale Mt. Everest, reaching the top when he was not even fourteen years old <u>and earning the title of the</u>
₃
<u>youngest person to climb Mt. Everest</u>. Because
₃
licenses to climb Mt. Everest are no longer issued to anyone under the age of sixteen, Romero's record is likely to stand for the foreseeable future.

3. **A.** NO CHANGE
   B. and he earned the title of the youngest person to climb Mt. Everest
   C. and earning the title that he was the youngest person to climb Mt. Everest
   D. DELETE the underlined portion

3. Above a hole in the ice, a polar bear lies waiting for a seal to emerge. In the frozen Arctic landscape, food is <u>scarce and not plentiful</u>, and this large,
₁
white, shaggy hunter must seize every opportunity to pursue its prey.

   The polar bear is one of the largest <u>carnivores</u>
₂
<u>that eats meat</u> in the world, rivaled only by the
₂
Kodiak brown bear of southern Alaska. As its scientific name, *Ursus maritimus* (water-dwelling bear) suggests, the polar bear lives primarily <u>in and</u>
₃
<u>around</u> bodies of water. It is an excellent swimmer
₃
and has been seen as far as 200 miles from land.

1. **A.** NO CHANGE
   B. scarcely not plentiful
   C. scarce while not being plentiful
   D. scarce

2. **F.** NO CHANGE
   G. carnivorous meat-eaters
   H. meat-eating carnivores
   J. carnivores

3. **A.** NO CHANGE
   B. in and also living around
   C. in while being around
   D. DELETE the underlined portion

171

Numerous adaptations make the polar bear

uniquely suited to life in icy habitats. Fur covers

even its feet, allowing for traction on ice. A thick

layer of blubber beneath its fur provides

insulation, <u>which keeps it warm</u>. Its long neck and
4

narrow skull help it glide through the water, and its

front feet are large, flat, and oarlike.

4. **F.** NO CHANGE
   G. this keeps it warm
   H. keeping it warm
   J. DELETE the underlined portion (placing a period after *insulation*)

16. Diction and Register

Diction

The term *diction* simply refers to an author's choice of words. Diction errors involve words that are incorrect for a particular situation, either because they have the wrong meaning or because they are not **idiomatic** – that is, they do not obey the rules of standard written English.

A. Commonly Confused Words

On most ACTs, you will encounter at least one question testing the following pairs of words:

Then vs. Than*

Then = Next

Than = Comparison

Incorrect:	The peacock's feathers are more brightly colored **then** those of any other bird.
Correct:	The peacock's feathers are more brightly colored **than** those of any other bird.

Have vs. Of

Could, should, would, and *might* should always be followed by *have*, **NOT** *of*. This error plays on the fact that when these verbs are contracted with *have* (*might've, could've, would've*), the ending is pronounced like *of*.

Incorrect:	If we had closed the windows before we left, the paintings ~~might of~~ been saved.
Correct:	If we had closed the windows before we left, the paintings **might have** been saved.

Other commonly confused words that could potentially appear on the ACT:

Accept vs. Except	Desert vs. Dessert
Addition vs. Edition	Emit vs. Omit
Allusion vs. Illusion	Lie vs. Lay
Assure vs. Ensure	Perspective vs. Prospective
Averse vs. Adverse	Precedent vs. President
Capital vs. Capitol	Precede vs. Proceed
Council vs. Counsel	Principal vs. Principle
Decent vs. Descent	Used to, NOT Use to

*Also discussed in Chapter 11.

B. Prepositions

Certain verbs and nouns must be followed by specific prepositions.

Incorrect: Anyone who is considering buying a parrot should have a familiarity **in** bird behavior.

Correct: Anyone who is considering buying a parrot should have a familiarity **with** bird behavior.

The phrase *a familiarity* always requires the preposition *with*. Any other preposition is incorrect.

One more:

Incorrect: The unusually large size of the komodo dragon, the largest species of lizard, which has been attributed **toward** their ancient ancestor, the immense varanid lizard.

Correct: The unusually large size of the komodo dragon, the largest species of lizard, which has been attributed **to** their ancient ancestor, the immense varanid lizard.

The verb *attribute* must always be followed by the preposition *to*. Any other preposition is incorrect.

Unfortunately, diction questions are among the most difficult to study for because there are thousands of possible errors and no real pattern to the prepositions tested. The knowledge necessary to answer these questions can really only be gained from extensive, long-term exposure to correct written English. There is no way to prepare in the short term beyond simply being aware that this error exist.

It is therefore not terribly constructive to spend your time memorizing long lists of phrases, especially since questions testing prepositions typically appear no more than once or twice per test.

In general, though, if a given preposition sounds somewhat odd, it's probably wrong. This is one case that requires you to trust your ear. That said, I am including a list of common idioms.

Be curious about
Be particular about
Bring about
Complain about
Set (ab)out**
Wonder about
Worry about
Think about

Known as/to be
Recognized as
Serve as
Translate as**

Accompanied by
Amazed by
Assisted by
Awed by
Confused by
Encouraged by
Followed by
Impressed by
Obscured by**
Outraged by
Shocked by
Stunned by
Surprised by
Perplexed by
Puzzled by

Celebrated for
Compensate for
Criticize for
Endure for
Famous for
Known for
Last for
Look (out) for
Named for/after
Necessary for
Prized for
Responsible for**
Recognized for
Strive for
Wait for
Watch for

Across from**
Apparent from
Defend from/against
Differ(ent) from
Protect from/against
Refrain from

In itself**

Adept in/at
Confident in
Engage in/with
Firm in**
Interested in
Involved in
Succeed in/at
Take pride in

Enter into
Insight into

Appreciation of
Characteristic of
Command of
Composed of
Comprised of
Consist of
Convinced of
Devoid of
(Dis)approve of
Family of**
In recognition of
In the hope(s) of
(In)capable of
Knowledge of
Mastery of
A native of
Offer of
Principles of**
Proponent of
Source of
Suspicious of
Take advantage of
Typical of
Understanding of
Use of

Based on
Depend on
Draw (up)on
Dwell on
Focus on
Insist on
Reflect on
Rely on

Control over
Power over

Central to
Critical to**
Devoted to
Explain to
Exposed/exposure to**
In contrast to
Listen to
Native to
Point to**
Prefer x to y
Recommend x to y
Relate to
Similar to
Threat(en) to
Unique to

Biased toward
Have a tendency toward

Take up**

Contrast with
Correlate with
(In)consistent with
Identify with
(Pre)occupied with
Sympathize with
(Un)familiar with

175

C. Other Parts of Speech

In addition to testing the correct and incorrect use of prepositions, the ACT also tests the correct and incorrect use of other parts of speech – often, but not always, verbs. Unlike prepositions, which are part of fixed phrases, the idiomatic use of other parts of speech is more dependent on context.

Correct Meaning

Questions testing usage ask you to identify which word has the correct meaning or implication in context of the sentence in which it appears.

For example:

As she moved slowly and gracefully across the

stage, the dancer <u>reduced</u> her body to the ground.
                1

1. **A.** NO CHANGE
   B. lowered
   C. decreased
   D. minimized

(A), (C) and (D) all mean "to make smaller," and the sentence does not indicate that the dancer was making her body smaller, only that she was putting it closer to the ground (i.e. making it lower). While *lower* can be used as a synonym for *reduce* in some situations (e.g. one can *reduce* or *lower* a volume), in this case the two verbs are not interchangeable. *Lower* is the verb whose meaning is both consistent with the meaning of the sentence and idiomatically correct.

Many questions testing verb usage are also asked in either "NOT" or "All of the following EXCEPT" form.

For example:

We only realized that the radio was playing

so loudly when our next door neighbor came

and asked us to <u>turn down</u> the volume.
                2

2. Which of the following would NOT be an acceptable alternative to the underlined word?

    F. reduce
    G. decrease
    H. lower
    J. subside

Reduce, *decrease*, and *lower* are all synonyms for "turn down" and are idiomatically correct when plugged into the sentence. Although *subside* means "decrease," it cannot be followed by a noun – a noise can subside, but one cannot subside a noise. So although its meaning is close to that of the other words, it is not idiomatically correct and thus should not be used in the sentence.

Register

Register refers to how **formal** or **informal** an author's language is. Most ACT passages are written in a straightforward, moderately serious tone and are unlikely to contain extremely formal or casual language.

For example:

During the Nimrod Expedition to the South Pole in 1907, Ernest Shackleton led a group of explorers on a dangerous voyage to the South Pole. When Shackleton and the members of his expedition finally arrived, however, they saw a bunch of cool stuff.

1.
   A. NO CHANGE
   B. perceived a multitude of captivating visuals
   C. were greeted by many fascinating sights
   D. noticed interesting things and all that jazz

(A) and (D) are both far more casual and slangy than the rest of the sentence, and (B) is too formal, while (C) correctly matches its neutral, moderately serious tone.

Like diction questions, register questions are difficult to study for because they require you to be familiar with linguistic conventions and to distinguish between informal, moderately formal, and extremely formal writing – skills that can only be acquired from consistent, long-term exposure to a variety of styles and types of writing.

Drill: Diction and Register (answers p. 255)

1. I've never been a light traveler. For most of my life, I prepared for trips by <u>cramming</u> everything I could think of into my luggage. If my backpack

   could hold 50 lbs., I <u>relied on</u> including every last ounce. My bag was inevitably heavy, but I was happy to have all my favorite possessions – whether or not I actually used them.

   Carrying so much weight also gave me a sense of power and security. I felt as if I was prepared <u>with</u> anything. Moreover, I looked suspiciously on people who packed systematically. Something about organized travelers <u>made me feel kind of weird</u>; their methods seemed to destroy the spontaneity that drew me to traveling in the first place.

2. Some people call the durian "the king of fruit." Others can't stand to be within a mile of it. <u>Grown</u> throughout Southeast Asia, the durian resembles a cross between a porcupine and a pineapple, and it can weigh as much as seven pounds.

1. Which of the following would NOT be an acceptable alternative to the underlined word?

   A. tossing
   B. shoving
   C. jamming
   D. gorging

2. Which of the following would most effectively emphasize the writer's determination to fill the backpack completely?

   F. NO CHANGE
   G. wondered about
   H. inquired about
   J. insisted on

3. **A.** NO CHANGE
   B. on
   C. for
   D. to

4. **F.** NO CHANGE
   G. left a highly disconcerting impression
   H. gave me this queasy feeling
   J. bothered me

1. Which of the following alternatives to the underlined word would NOT be acceptable?

   A. Cultivated
   B. Harvested
   C. Elevated
   D. Planted

Its most striking feature, however, is its odor.

The flesh emits <u>a pungent</u> smell that is strong
                        2
and penetrating, even when the husk is intact.

While durian fans regard the fruit as having a

pleasantly sweet fragrance, others find the aroma

overpowering and even revolting. The smell

<u>elicits</u> reactions from deep appreciation to
   3
intense disgust: people claim that it is similar to

rotten onions, turpentine, and sewage. On the

other hand, the durian's taste has been compared

to that of custard or caramel. Some people even

<u>claim</u> to call it sublime.
   4

3. Since 2006, thousands of honey bees have

disappeared without a trace, and no one knows just

why. The phenomenon, known as Colony Collapse

Disorder (CCD), has occurred many times, but this

time it has turned <u>on</u> a global epidemic.
                      1
  David Hackenberg, a Pennsylvania beekeeper,

was the first person to <u>call attention to</u>
                           2
the problem. For years, Hackenberg had lent

his bees to farmers, who used them to pollinate

their crops. In the spring of 2006, he delivered 400

2. Which of the following choices most effectively
   emphasizes the unique nature of the durian's
   scent?

   F. NO CHANGE
   G. a bizarre
   H. a distinctive
   J. an intriguing

3. A. NO CHANGE
    B. invests
    C. controls
    D. maintains

4. The writer of this essay would like to call
   attention to the fact that praising the durian
   can have negative consequences. Which of
   the following best accomplishes that goal?

   F. NO CHANGE
   G. dare
   H. pretend
   J. desire

1. A. NO CHANGE
    B. into
    C. around
    D. toward

2. Which of the following choices is the LEAST
   acceptable alternative to the underlined phrase?

   F. exaggerate
   G. announce
   H. report
   J. publicize

bee colonies to a Florida farm, but when he went to collect them, the bees had <u>gotten the heck out of there</u>.
3

Hackenberg was <u>elated</u>. In the end, he lost
4
about two-third of his hives. He considers himself

lucky, however: some beekeepers have lost 90%

of their bees.

Now, scientists are <u>curious</u> to figure out just
5
what is making so many bees disappear. The causes

of CCD and the reasons for its increasing

occurrence remain unclear, but many possibilities

have been proposed: pesticides, infections,

genetics, loss of habitat, radiation from electronic

devices – or a combination of all these factors.

3. **A.** NO CHANGE
   B. pulled a disappearing act
   C. moved away
   D. vanished

4. The writer would like to convey that Hackenberg was extremely puzzled by the bees' disappearance. Which of the following choices would accomplish that most effectively?

   A. NO CHANGE
   B. devastated
   C. perplexed
   D. galvanized

5. The writer would like to draw attention to the extreme sense of urgency felt by the scientists. Which of the following choices best accomplishes that goal?

   F. NO CHANGE
   G. desperate
   H. determined
   J. hesitant

17. Transitions

Transition questions are among the most common rhetoric questions that appear on the ACT. It is not uncommon for a single English test to include four or five of them, if not more.

Transition questions fall into three general categories:

1) Transitions within sentences

2) Transitions between sentences

3) Transitions between paragraphs

Transitions consist of either single words or several-word phrases, and they are used to show relationships between parts of a sentence, separate sentences, and paragraphs. At the simplest level, they indicate whether ideas are similar or different. ACT transition questions thus test your ability to recognize connections between ideas, and to choose the word or words (if any) that logically reflect those connections.

Sometimes transition questions also test grammar and punctuation, but in general the focus is on meaning. You should, however, make sure to consider whether a given transition works grammatically as well as logically.

There are three major types of transitions, shown in the chart below.

Continuers	Contradictors	Cause and Effect
And	(Al)though	Accordingly
Also	But	As a result
Finally	Despite	As such
Furthermore	Even so	Because
In addition	Even though	Consequently
In conclusion	However	For
In fact	In contrast	So
Indeed	In spite of	Therefore
Likewise	Instead	Thus
Moreover	Meanwhile	
Next	Nevertheless	
Of course	On the contrary	
Similarly	On the other hand	
That is	Otherwise	
Then	Rather	
	Still	
	Whereas	
	While	
	Yet	

Continuers indicate that two sentences are expressing similar ideas.

Correct: The tomato is one of the most popular salad ingredients. **Moreover**, it is also used in many hot dishes, including soups and stews.

They can also be used to **emphasize** an idea presented earlier, usually in the previous sentence.

Correct: Tomatoes are among the oldest crops grown in the New World. **In fact**, they were cultivated as far back as 500 B.C.

Contradictors indicate that two sentences are expressing different ideas.

Correct: Martha Graham retired from dancing when she was 70 years old. **However,** she continued to choreograph for many years after that.

Correct: Martha Graham retired from dancing when she was 70 years old. **Nevertheless,** she continued to choreograph for many years after that.

Cause-and-Effect words indicate that one action is the **result** of another.

Correct: The tomato is one of the most popular salad ingredients. **Therefore/Consequently**, many people believe that it is a vegetable.

For definitions of some less common transitions, see the glossary on p. 198.

Important: The first thing to do when you encounter a transition question is to pick up your pencil and physically cross out the transition in the original sentence. Again: take your hand, pick up your pencil, and draw an actual line through the transition. Do not just draw a line in your imagination. If you need to erase the line later… well, that's why you work in pencil.

Here's why:

The simple fact that you are looking at a particular transition in the original version of the sentence means that you are likely to be unconsciously biased toward that transition. If you read the original sentence and nothing strikes you as particularly odd, there's a decent chance you'll assume the transition that's already there is okay.

The problem, however, is that **transition questions are primarily about what words mean, not how they sound**. A word that sounds completely fine to you might in reality create a completely **illogical** relationship. In order to actually determine the relationship between two ideas, you need to look at them objectively, back-to-back, and see whether they're saying similar things or different things. (Yes, this actually requires you to think.)

Crossing out the transition makes it a lot easier for you to focus on what each sentence is saying. You're a lot less likely to try to see a relationship that isn't there. When words aren't directly in your line of vision, it's a lot harder to get distracted by them.

Let's look at some examples.

Transitions Within Sentences

These questions ask you to identify the relationship between two parts of a sentence. Usually there will only be two clauses involved, but sometimes there will be more. Regardless of how long the sentence is, you need to re-read all of it and obtain a clear understanding of what it is saying before you look at the answer choices. You should also separate the sentence clearly in two – the division will always occur right where the information is underlined – and consider each part separately.

For example:

Conditions in the interior of Antarctica are

inhospitable to many forms of life: sub-zero

temperatures, high winds, and extreme dryness

make it impossible for most animals to survive.

The Antarctic Peninsula and the surrounding

islands have milder temperatures and liquid

water, whereas more animals can thrive.
1

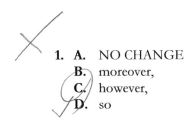

1. A. NO CHANGE
   B. moreover,
   C. however,
   D. so

The first thing we need to do is cross out the underlined transition so that we don't get distracted by it:

The Antarctic Peninsula and the surrounding

islands have milder temperatures and liquid

water, whereas more animals can thrive.
1

1. A. NO CHANGE
   B. moreover,
   C. however,
   D. so

Now, we need to consider what each half of the sentence is saying, looking at the full paragraph for context:

1) Weather conditions on the Antarctic Peninsula are milder than those in the Antarctic interior.

2) More animals can thrive on the Antarctic Peninsula.

The second statement is the **result** of the first: because temperatures are milder on the Antarctic Peninsula than they are in the interior, it is logical that animals can live more easily on the Peninsula.

The only transition that conveys the cause/effect relationship is *so*. The answer is therefore (D).

Notice that although the question appeared to ask about only one word, it actually involved the entire paragraph.

Transitions Between Sentences

Now let's reconsider our passage, this time from a slightly different angle:

Conditions in the interior of Antarctica are

inhospitable to many forms of life: sub-zero

temperatures, high winds, and extreme dryness

make it impossible for most animals to survive.

Therefore, the Antarctic Peninsula as well as the
1
surrounding islands have milder temperatures

and liquid water, so more animals can thrive.

1. A. NO CHANGE
   B. In contrast
   C. As such
   D. Despite

The fact that the first (underlined) word is a transition indicates that you must consider the relationship between this sentence and the previous sentence. Cross out the original transition and consider what the two sentences are saying.

1) Antarctica has a very extreme climate, so animals can't live there.

2) The Antarctic Peninsula and islands have a milder climate, so animals can live there.

Those are opposing ideas, so a contradictor is required. (D) does not work grammatically, leaving (B).

Transitions indicating relationships between sentences can also appear in the middle of a sentence. When this is the case, the transition will be surrounded by commas (i.e. it will be a non-essential word or phrase).

Conditions in the interior of Antarctica are

inhospitable to many forms of life: sub-zero

temperatures, high winds, and extreme dryness

make it impossible for most animals to survive.

The Antarctic Peninsula as well as the

surrounding islands have milder temperatures

and liquid water, therefore, so more animals can
1
thrive.

1. A. NO CHANGE
   B. however
   C. moreover
   D. accordingly

184

As is true when the transition appears at the beginning of the sentence, the easiest way to approach this type of question is to **cross out the transition**.

You must, however, remember to back up and consider the previous sentence; there is no way to determine the answer from only the sentence in which the transition appears.

Again, these two sentences express opposing ideas, making *however* the only option. (B) is therefore correct.

Important: You will also encounter answer choices that do not include a transition. In some cases, the sentence will simply begin without a transition, while in others, "DELETE the underlined word/phrase" will appear as an answer choice. You should always make sure to check these options first because they are usually correct.

For example:

Conditions in the interior of Antarctica are

inhospitable to many forms of life. Therefore,
1

sub-zero temperatures, high winds, and extreme
1

dryness make it impossible for most animals to

survive.

1. A. NO CHANGE
    B. On the other hand, sub-zero temperatures
    C. Nevertheless, sub-zero temperatures
    D. Sub-zero temperatures

Since (D) contains no transition, it is especially important to cross out *therefore* in the original version and examine the two statements without any transition

1) Conditions in the interior of Antarctica are inhospitable to many forms of life.

2) Subzero temperatures, high winds, and extreme dryness make survival impossible for most animals.

The two sentences are definitely discussing similar ideas, but the second sentence is simply providing more detailed information to support the first sentence. The fact that Antarctica has sub-zero temperatures, high winds, and extreme dryness **elaborates on** the original statement that conditions in Antarctica are inhospitable. **It is not, however, a result** of the fact that conditions in Antarctica are inhospitable. So (A) is not the answer.

(B) and (C) can be automatically eliminated because *on the other hand* and *nevertheless* are contradictors, and the two sentences express similar ideas.

In fact, no transition is required here at all, making the answer (D).

Drill 1: Transitions (answers p. 255)

1. In the past, coffees were blended to suit a homogenous popular taste, _____ many different coffee flavors are now being produced.

Step 1: Continue (Contrast) Cause-and-Effect

Step 2:

A. for
B. but
C. and
D. because

2. _____ researchers are unable to drill into the Earth's core, its chemical composition remains a mystery.

Step 1: Continue   Contrast   Cause-and-Effect

Step 2:

A. While
B. Because
C. Despite
D. Although

3. The Taj Mahal is regarded as one of the eight wonders of the world. _____, some people believe that its architectural beauty has never been surpassed.

Step 1: Continue   Contrast   Cause-and-Effect

Step 2:

A. On the other hand
B. For example
C. Indeed
D. However

4. Music serves no obvious purpose. It has, _____, played a role in every known civilization on earth.

Step 1: Continue   Contrast   Cause-and-Effect

Step 2:

A. however
B. therefore
C. in fact
D. moreover

5. _____ modern technology offers remarkable opportunities for self-expression and communication, it also offers many possibilities for distraction.

Step 1: ⟨Continue⟩ Contrast ✓ Cause-and-Effect

Step 2:

    A. Because
    B. Despite
    C. Since
    D. While ⟨circled⟩

6. In order to save an endangered species, preservationists must study it in detail. _____, scientific information about some endangered animals is scarce.

Step 1: Continue ⟨Contrast⟩ Cause-and-Effect

Step 2:

    A. However ⟨circled⟩
    B. Therefore
    C. In fact
    D. Likewise

7. Pyramids are most commonly associated with ancient Egypt. _____, many people are surprised to learn that the Nubians, who lived in modern-day Sudan, constructed a far greater number of pyramids than the Egyptians did.

Step 1: Continue ⟨Contrast⟩ Cause-and-Effect ✓

Step 2:

    A. Consequently ⟨circled⟩
    B. In fact
    C. In addition
    D. For example

8. _____ modern chemistry keeps insects from ravaging crops, removes stains, and saves lives, constant exposure to chemicals is taking a toll on many people's health.

Step 1: Continue ⟨Contrast⟩ — ⟨Cause-and-Effect⟩

Step 2:

    A. Because
    B. Despite
    C. Although ⟨circled⟩
    D. Since

9. In the Middle Ages, fairs often attracted large crowds and led to rioting. _____, authorities were reluctant to grant permission for fairs to be held.

Step 1: Continue Contrast ⟨Cause-and-Effect⟩

Step 2:

    A. In fact
    B. Nevertheless
    C. Furthermore
    D. Therefore ⟨circled⟩

Transitions Between Paragraphs

Unlike questions that ask you to identify transitions between sentences, questions testing transitions between paragraphs deal not with single words but rather with entire sentences. **Although these questions appear to ask about two paragraphs, the answer will usually depend only on the paragraph that the sentence begins.** As a result, you should start by determining the topic of that paragraph and seeing which answer matches. If you cannot determine the answer, you can then back up and read the end of the previous paragraph.

Conditions in the interior of Antarctica are inhospitable to many forms of life: sub-zero temperatures, high winds, and extreme dryness make it impossible for most animals to survive. In contrast, the Antarctic Peninsula and the surrounding islands have milder temperatures and liquid water, so more animals are able to thrive. Most of the penguin species that inhabit Antarctica can only live on the islands, but the Emperor penguin lives on the Antarctic continent itself.

This species <u>has adapted to withstand weather</u>

1
<u>that is both harsh and unpredictable</u>. A thick layer

1
of fat beneath their coats insulates the animals from temperatures that rarely rise above zero degrees Farenheit, and their short, densely packed feathers keep their skin insulated from the cold. They also moult much faster than other species: new feathers emerge even before the old ones fall out so they do not lose heat. They even build their nests higher than the surrounding land so that the nests will not flood if the temperature rises abruptly.

1. Which of the following would provide the most logical transition between the preceding paragraph and the paragraph that follows?

A. NO CHANGE
B. can remain submerged in water for up to eighteen minutes.
C. consumes a diet that consists primarily of fish, with the occasional crustacean or squid.
D. possesses stiff wings that have flattened into flippers for a marine habitat

188

Solution: (A)

Although this question asks you to identify which option would create the most effective transition between paragraphs, you want to start by focusing on the paragraph that the sentence begins.

What does the second paragraph discuss? The various features that allow the Emperor penguin to survive in extremely cold and unpredictable weather. There is no information about the penguin's ability to stay under water for long periods (B), its diet (C), or its flippers (D). On the other hand, (A) logically sets up the topic of the paragraph by presenting the general idea that Emperor penguins have adapted to their extreme weather conditions. (A) is therefore correct.

Important: make sure that you do not pay so much attention to choices (B)-(D) or (G)-(J) that you overlook what's already in the passage. Sometimes the original version will in fact be correct.

Double Transitions

If a transition is used to begin a clause, it should not be repeated in the preceding or the following clause. Only one transition is necessary to indicate the relationship between the two clauses.

For example:

Incorrect: **Although** the Bohemian Waxwing consumes mostly insects when it is a chick, **but** its diet later in life consists primarily of fruit.

Correct: **Although** the Bohemian Waxwing consumes mostly insects when it is a chick, its diet later in life consists primarily of fruit.

Correct: The Bohemian Waxwing consumes mostly insects when it is a chick, **but** its diet later in life consists primarily of fruit.

If two different types of transitions (e.g. a continuer and a contradictor) are incorrectly used within a sentence, you must not only eliminate one of the transitions but also recognize which one creates a logical meaning between the parts of the sentence.

Incorrect: **Although** the Bohemian Waxwing consumes mostly insects when it is a chick, **so** its diet later in life consists primarily of fruit.

Incorrect: The Bohemian Waxwing consumes mostly insects when it is a chick, **so** its diet later in life consists primarily of fruit.

Correct: **Although** the Bohemian Waxwing consumes mostly insects when it is a chick, its diet later in life consists primarily of fruit.

Drill 2: Transitions (answers p. 255)

1. On the screen, three people walk in a garden.

The image is black-and-white, and the figures

move in a jerky way. After a few seconds, they

disappear. Filmed in 1888, *Roundhay Garden Scene*

seems primitive in comparison to the slick, action-

packed movies that are produced today. Therefore,
    1
it is the oldest surviving film in existence.

**1. A. NO CHANGE
    B. In fact,
    C. Nevertheless,
    D. However,**

2. In 1959, Project Mercury became the first

human spaceflight program led by the National

Aeronautics and Space Administration (NASA).

The project was aimed at putting an American into

orbit before the Soviet Union could accomplish

that goal. However, the program ran until 1963 and
    1
involved seven astronauts flying six solo trips.

**1. A. NO CHANGE
    B. In addition, the program
    C. Meanwhile, the program
    D. The program**

3. Chimpanzees and bonobo monkeys

resemble each other physically, but their social

behaviors differ greatly. Chimpanzees have an

omnivorous diet, a troop hunting culture, and

complex social relationships. Bonobo monkeys,

in contrast, eat mostly fruit, rarely hunt, and do
    1
not have a strict social hierarchy.

**1. A. NO CHANGE
    B. therefore
    C. despite
    D. furthermore**

4. A gamelan is a traditional musical ensemble

from Indonesia, typically from the islands of Java

and Bali. Gamelans typically feature a variety of

of instruments, such as xylophones, gongs and

bamboo flutes, and may also include vocalists.

<u>Consequently, gamelan music</u> is an integral part of
     1
Indonesian culture.

1. **A.** NO CHANGE
    B. Thus, gamelan music
    C. Otherwise, gamelan music
    ✓ **D.** Gamelan music

5. The hummingbird is so named because its

beating wings create a humming sound.

Hummingbirds are tiny, with most species

measuring less than five inches. <u>Instead</u>, the
                                    1
smallest known species is the Bee Hummingbird,

which hovers in mid-air by flapping its wings up

to 80 times per second.

1. **A.** NO CHANGE
    B. In contrast
    C. Indeed
    D. Likewise

6. Many people fear or dislike spiders, but spiders

are mostly beneficial because they prey on insects

and other pests. The spiders commonly seen out in

the open during the day are usually harmless and

unlikely to bite people. <u>For instance</u>, poisonous
                          1
spiders generally spend most of their time in

woodpiles, corners, or boxes and rarely come into

contact with human beings.

1. **A.** NO CHANGE
    B. In contrast
    C. Therefore
    D. Nevertheless

7. <u>Although computerized</u> fingerprint scanners
    1
have been a staple of spy movies for decades, but

until recently, they were rarely found in the real

world. Over the last few years, <u>therefore</u>, scanners
2
have become common in many different locations,

including police stations, high-security buildings,

and even computer keyboards. The price of a

scanner has also decreased significantly. <u>However,</u>
3
it is now possible to purchase a USB fingerprint

scanner for under $100.

1. A. NO CHANGE
   B. While computerized
   C. Since computerized
   D. Computerized

2. F. NO CHANGE
   G. in fact
   H. though
   J. for example

3. A. NO CHANGE
   B. Next
   C. In fact
   D. Likewise

8. Straw has been used as a building material for

centuries. Contrary to popular belief, it is not easily

destroyed. <u>In fact</u>, it can actually be quite hardy. In
1
the nineteenth century, settlers in the Nebraska

Sandhills used straw to build houses when wood

and clay were scarce; some of the structures are still

standing today. Builders are hoping such longevity

is a trend, but new homes that use straw do have

some updates. In the updated structures, <u>however,</u>
2
the straw is pressed into panels and framed with

timber for reinforcement. The panels are then

covered in brick so that no straw remains exposed

to the elements.

1. A. NO CHANGE
   B. Nevertheless
   C. For example
   D. However

2. F. NO CHANGE
   G. moreover
   H. for example
   J. on the other hand

193

9. The Silk Road acquired its name from the lucrative trade in Chinese silk carried out along its 4,000 miles, beginning during the Han dynasty (206 BCE – 220 AD). The Chinese took great interest in the safety of their goods, and they extended the
₁
Great Wall of China to ensure the protection of their trade routes.

Trade on the Silk Road was a significant factor in the development of China, India, Persia, Europe, and Arabia, opening long-distance political and economic interactions. Because silk was certainly
₂
the major trade item from China, numerous other types of goods also traveled along the Silk Routes. The Silk Road thus facilitated cultural trade among many different civilizations.

1. **A.** NO CHANGE
   B. goods, they
   C. goods, but they
   D. goods, therefore they

2. **F.** NO CHANGE
   G. While silk
   H. Despite silk
   J. DELETE the underline word (capitalizing the word "silk.")

10. By turning the camera on herself, Cindy Sherman established her reputation as one of the most respected photographers of the late twentieth century. Despite the majority of her photographs
₁
are pictures of herself, these photographs are most definitely not self-portraits. Rather, Sherman uses herself as a vehicle for commentary on a variety of issues of the modern world: the role of the woman,

1. **A.** NO CHANGE
   B. For
   C. Since
   D. Although

194

the role of the artist, and many more. It is through these ambiguous and eclectic photographs that Sherman has developed a distinct signature style. <u>Moreover</u>, she has raised important and
2
challenging questions about the role of women in in society and the media, as well as the nature of artistic creation.

2. **F.** NO CHANGE
   G. Therefore
   H. However
   J. Consequently

11.   For the last two years, I have worked as a naturalist at Olympic National Park in Washington State. Most days, I give talks on wildlife to park visitors and lead nature walks, <u>so</u> sometimes my
1
duties are a little more unusual. Once, I had to crawl around in a cave, trying to catch bats. On a another occasion, I tracked a bear up a mountain.

<u>On the other hand</u>, I waded fully clothed
2
into a lake to rescue a child who couldn't swim.

When I show up for work in the morning, I'm never entirely sure what the day will bring.

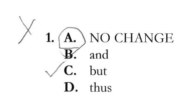

1. **A.** NO CHANGE
   B. and
   C. but
   D. thus

2. **F.** NO CHANGE
   G. Yet another time,
   H. Meanwhile,
   J. That is,

195

3 In the wild, these snakes don't eat very often – sometimes only once a year – but in captivity, they have to be fed frequently. Their diet consists primarily of mice and rats, which are normally kept in a special freezer. A few months ago, though, the electricity in the Visitors' Center failed after a heavy thunderstorm. Nevertheless, I
4
had to store the mice and rats in my own freezer. Before placing them inside, I wrote, "Dead mice, do not eat!" in large, black letters on the box. As you can probably imagine, my roommate wasn't exactly thrilled.

3. Assuming that all of the following are true, which choice provides the most effective transition from the previous paragraph to the paragraph that follows?

A. I usually enjoy my job, but sometimes it can also be stressful.
B. Some of the animals I work with are cute and friendly, others less so.
C. My most memorable experience, however, involved feeding the rattlesnakes that were part of an exhibit in the Visitors' Center.
D. I didn't start out wanting to become a naturalist, but now there's nothing I would rather do

4. F. NO CHANGE
G. However,
H. In fact,
J. As a result,

12. When Merce Cunningham was five years old,
1
he was dancing through the halls of his elementary school in Centralia, Washington. Although his talent and love for the art were already apparent, no one could have foreseen the enormity of his impact on dance in the United States. More than eighty years later, therefore, he was still dancing – and still
2
creating works for Merce Cunningham Dance

1. A. NO CHANGE
B. Despite
C. Whereas
D. DELETE the underlined portion

2. F. NO CHANGE
G. for example
H. however
J. moreover

Company, the company he founded at Black Mountain College in North Carolina. From its inception during the summer of 1953, the company frequently collaborated with visual artists, architects, and musicians. 3

For hundreds of years, dance and music had been considered inseparable: dancers were guided by music, performing their steps in time to its rhythm. Cunningham, however, believed that while dance and music could be performed at the same time and in the same space, they could also exist independently of one another. Nevertheless, his dancers' onstage
4
moves were not dictated by a fixed rhythm but occurred spontaneously and without any influence from the music – even as it played in the background.

3. Which of the following true statements most effectively concludes this paragraph while clearly and specifically connecting it to the paragraph that follows?

A. Cunningham's first name was actually Mercier, "Merce" being a childhood nickname.
B. As a choreographer and teacher, Cunningham had a profound effect on modern dance.
C. It also radically changed the relationship between dance and music.
D. Many dancers who trained with the company eventually formed their own companies.

4. F. NO CHANGE
G. However, his dancers'
H. On the other hand, his dancers'
J. His dancers'

Glossary of Transitions

Accordingly

Consequently ⎱ Therefore, as a result

Correct: Dolphins are social animals. **Consequently,** they live in pods of up to a dozen animals.

Correct: Dolphins are social animals. **Accordingly,** they live in pods of up to a dozen animals.

Furthermore

Moreover ⎱ In addition

Correct: Dolphins are social animals. **Furthermore,** they are highly intelligent.

Correct: Dolphins are social animals. **Moreover,** they are highly intelligent.

In fact

Indeed ⎱ Used to emphasize a preceding statement

Correct: Dolphins are highly intelligent. **In fact,** they are one of the smartest mammals.

Correct: Dolphins are highly intelligent. **Indeed,** they are one of the smartest mammals.

Even so

Still

Nevertheless ⎱ Despite this

Correct: Dolphins are descended from land-dwelling animals. **Nevertheless,** they can only survive in water.

Correct: Dolphins are descended from land-dwelling animals. **Even so,** they can only survive in water.

Correct: Dolphins are descended from land-dwelling animals. **Still,** they can only survive in water.

While
Whereas } Although, but

Correct: **While** dolphins are commonly thought of as fish, they are actually mammals.

Correct: A salmon is a type of fish, **whereas** a dolphin is a type of mammal.

As such – *As a + noun*

As such is one of the trickier transitions, and it's best explained with an example.

Let's start with this sentence:

Correct: Dolphins are social animals, and **because they are social animals**, they live in pods of up to a dozen animals.

We can also write the sentence this way:

Correct: Dolphins are social animals, and **as social animals**, they live in pods of up to a dozen animals.

The sentence is fine as is, but it's a little wordy because the words *social animals* are repeated. To eliminate the repetition, we can replace the phrase *as social animals* with *as such*.

Correct: Dolphins are social animals, and **as such**, they live in pods of up to a dozen animals.

Likewise – Similarly

Correct: As mammals, dolphins are warm blooded. **Likewise,** they nourish their young with milk.

Meanwhile – At the same time, concurrently

Correct: Many people think of dolphins as fish. **Meanwhile,** they ignore scientific research, which long ago established that dolphins are actually mammals.

That is – In other words

That is indicates that the writer is providing a definition or an explanation/clarification.

Correct: Dolphins are mammals – **that is**, they are warm blooded and nourish their young with milk.

199

Maria Tallchief: All-American Ballerina

[1]

"A ballerina takes steps given to her and makes them her own. Each individual brings something different to the same role," the great ballerina Maria Tallchief once said. Tallchief combined great individualism and extraordinary talent, creating a remarkable and vital chapter in American dance.

[2]

Maria Tallchief was born on an Indian reservation in Oklahoma on January 24, 1925. A member of the Osage tribe, she became a trailblazer for Native Americans in the world of ballet. The Osage language is similar to the language spoken by members of the Sioux tribe. When Maria was five years old, she began music lessons and soon discovered that she had perfect pitch. But it was dance that captured the young girl's heart. After five years of study, she joined the Ballet Russe de Monte Carlo, where she quickly became a soloist.

[3]

[1] Balanchine then brought Tallchief home to his Ballet Society, the company that would become New York City Ballet. [2] Her immense popularity with the American public grew in part from the demands the company made on its phenomenally gifted principal dancer: [3] Tallchief was called upon to dance as many as eight performances a week. [4] In fact, many audience members did not realize how technically difficult the part was until much later, when they saw other great ballerinas attempt to perform it. [5] Audiences were awed by her dedication to her art. [6] In *Pas de Six* (1955), Balanchine made use of her subtlety and delicacy to great effect – she danced the lead role radiantly and with apparent ease.

[4]

Throughout her career, Maria Tallchief was known for her collaborations with choreographer George Balanchine. They first worked together in Paris in 1947, and Tallchief eventually inspired a number of his ballets. These included *Orpheus*, *Night Shadow*, and *The Four Temperaments*. In 1954, Tallchief debuted in her most famous role, the Sugar Plum fairy in *The Nutcracker*.

[5]

In 1965, Maria Tallchief surprised the world by announcing her retirement. She still wanted to dance professionally and wanted to pass her love for her art to younger dancers. "New ideas are essential," Tallchief said, "but we must retain respect for the art of ballet, or or else it is no longer an art form."

200

18. Is it Relevant? Inserting, Deleting, and Replacing Information

Most ACT English sections contain at least three or four questions asking you whether sentences or phrases should be changed, inserted, or deleted, and why. Some questions will also ask you to identify what sort of information (e.g. supporting detail) would be provided or lost. These questions essentially test your ability to recognize whether information is **relevant** or **irrelevant** to the focus of a paragraph or passage.

Very often, "insert/delete" questions will take the following form: two answer choices will state that YES, the sentence or phrase in question should be inserted/deleted; and two answer choices will state that NO, the sentence or phrase should NOT be inserted/deleted. Each answer choice will also be accompanied by a short explanation of why the information should be inserted or not (see below for an example).

As a general rule, **you should approach these questions in two parts**: first, determine whether the answer is YES or NO, then cross out the answers that state the opposite so they do not distract you. Then, state **in your own words** why the information should be added or not (e.g. it's off topic). The answer will typically be clear.

Inserting Information

Questions that ask whether information should be inserted typically take the following forms:

Throughout her career, Maria Tallchief was known for her collaborations with choreographer George Balanchine. They first worked together in Paris in 1947, and Tallchief eventually inspired a number of his ballets. These included *Orpheus*, *Night Shadow* and *The Four Temperaments*. In 1954, Tallchief debuted in her most famous role, the Sugar Plum Fairy in *The Nutcracker*. 1

1. At this point in the essay, the author is considering inserting the following sentence:

   Critics called the performance "electrifying" and praised her for the effortless beauty of her movements.

   Should this sentence be inserted?

   A. Yes, because it provides important biographical information about Maria Tallchief.
   B. Yes, because it explains why Maria Tallchief became so famous for her portrayal of the Sugar Plum Fairy.
   C. No, because it distracts from the main focus of the paragraph.
   D. No, because it does not take Maria Tallchief's other roles into account.

Solution: To answer this question, we must look at the previous sentence in order to establish **context**.

What does it tell us? That the Sugar Plum Fairy would become one of Maria Tallchief's most famous roles.

Next, we must determine the relationship between the previous sentence and the sentence in question. The sentence to be inserted describes critics' extremely positive reaction to Tallchief's debut and presents a specific reason for that reaction ("the effortless beauty of her movements").

It therefore **supports** the previous sentence by providing information about why Maria Tallchief became so famous for the role. So the answer is (B).

Replacing Information

Other questions will require you to decide whether existing information should be **changed** in order to be consistent with a particular emphasis or goal. For example, the question on the previous page could also be presented in the following way:

1. Given that all of the following are true, which of the following should be added here to **emphasize the important role** that the Sugar Plum Fairy played in Maria Tallchief's **career as a whole**?

   A. Critics called her performance "electrifying" and praised her for the effortless beauty of her movements.
   B. It was not, however, one of her more technically demanding parts.
   C. Over the next fifteen years, she would go on to dance it hundreds of times.
   D. *The Nutcracker* made George Balanchine a household name in the United States.

When you encounter a question such as this, **underline** the information or point of view that the correct answer must emphasize. Because all of the answers will be grammatically correct and make sense in context, you cannot rely on your ear, nor can you rely only on the surrounding sentences. Instead, you must ask yourself whether the information in each answer choice directly supports the emphasis indicated in the question.

In this case, (A) is no longer the best answer. It still supports the previous sentence by explaining why Maria Tallchief became famous for her portrayal of the Sugar Plum Fairy, but by itself, it does not tell us anything about the importance of that role in her larger career.

(C) does, however, indicate the importance of the role by telling us that Tallchief went on to dance it "hundreds of times." As a result, this option is correct.

(B) is entirely unrelated to the question, and (D) focuses on George Balanchine rather than Maria Tallchief.

Other "replacement" questions will ask you to focus on a single word.

Throughout her career, Maria Tallchief was known for her occasional collaboration with
₁
choreographer George Balanchine. They first worked together in Paris in 1947, and Tallchief eventually inspired a number of his ballets. These included *Orpheus, Night Shadow,* and *The Four Temperaments.* In 1954, Tallchief debuted in her most famous role, the Sugar Plum fairy in *The Nutcracker.*

1. Which of the following best emphasizes the idea that Maria Tallchief and George Balanchine worked together on a regular basis?

   A. NO CHANGE
   B. formal
   C. sporadic
   D. consistent

While all of the answers indicate that Tallchief and Balanchine worked together, only *consistent* means "on a regular basis." (D) is therefore correct.

In a third type of replacement question, no particular focus or emphasis for the information will be given. Instead, you will be presented with four different options and must determine whether the original version is correct based on the context of the passage. Make sure to read the **previous sentence** as well as the **following sentence** in order to determine which answer fits most logically in context.

Throughout her career, Maria Tallchief was known for her collaborations with choreographer George Balanchine. They first worked together in Paris in 1947, and Tallchief learned to keep her
₁
back straight, her head high, and her feet arched.
₁
These included *Orpheus, Night Shadow,* and *The Four Temperaments.* In 1954, Tallchief debuted in her most famous role, the Sugar Plum fairy in *The Nutcracker.*

1. **A.** NO CHANGE
   B. became well known both in France and abroad
   C. grew very fond of him
   D. eventually inspired a number of his ballets

Solution:

-What information is provided in the underlined portion of the sentence?

    Maria Tallchief improved her physical abilities as a ballet dancer while in Paris.

-What information does the following sentence provide?

    A list of ballets.

Even though the first sentence makes perfect sense when it is read out of context, it actually does not connect logically to the sentence that follows. The correct answer must end by introducing the list of ballets. (B) and (C) both work out of context but do nothing to introduce the following sentence. Only the phrase *a number of his ballets* in (D) provides a logical transition to the list of ballets in the next sentence.

One more:

In 1965, Maria Tallchief surprised the world

by announcing her retirement. She <u>still wanted</u>
                                    2

<u>to dance professionally</u> and wanted to pass her
         2

love for her art to younger dancers. "New ideas

are essential," Tallchief said, "but we must

retain respect for the art of ballet, or else it is no

longer an art form."

2. **F.** NO CHANGE
   G. had no intention of dancing past her prime
   H. no longer had anything to offer to the dance world
   J. wanted to maintain her status as a prima ballerina

In this question, both the sentence before and the sentence in question provide crucial information. The previous sentence states that Tallchief decided to retire. (F) and (J), which indicate that she kept dancing, can therefore be eliminated.

(H) is consistent with the previous sentence but not with the information that follows the underlined portion: if *Tallchief no longer had anything to offer the dance world*, then logically she would not want to *pass her art to younger dancers*.

Only (G) makes sense in context of both pieces of information.

Deleting Information

"Delete" questions come in two basic forms:

1) Questions that require you to identify whether information is consistent with the overall focus of the paragraph or passage. These questions are essentially the same as "insert" questions, except that you must determine whether the information is **irrelevant** rather than relevant.

2) Questions that ask *what sort* of information would be lost if a sentence or part of a sentence were deleted. These questions tend to be more challenging because they ask you to go beyond just recognizing whether information belongs in context and identify *how* particular words and phrases contribute to the overall presentation of an idea.

Let's look at some examples:

Maria Tallchief was born on an Indian reservation in Oklahoma on January 24, 1925. A member of the Osage tribe, she was also a trailblazer for Native Americans in the world of ballet. The Osage language is similar to that spoken by members of the Sioux tribe. ⬚1 When she was five years old, she began music lessons and soon discovered that she had perfect pitch. But it was dance that captured the young girl's heart. After five years of study, she joined the Ballet Russe de Monte Carlo, where she was quickly named a soloist.

1. At this point in the essay, the writer is considering deleting the previous sentence. Should it be deleted?

   A. Yes, because Maria Tallchief never mastered the Osage language.
   B. Yes, because it is irrelevant to the focus of the paragraph.
   C. No, because it explains how Maria Tallchief remained connected to her Native American heritage.
   D. No, because it explains the influence of Native American culture on Maria Tallchief's career.

Solution:

What's the focus of the passage?

Maria Tallchief's early life and dance career. Her Native American heritage is mentioned, but there is no other information in the paragraph that relates the Osage tribe, never mind the fact that its members speak a language similar to that of the Sioux. So the sentence should be deleted. Why? It's **off topic**. The answer is therefore (B).

Sometimes the question itself will not directly tell you to consider whether to delete the underlined information. Instead, you'll have to figure it out from the answer choices.

Whenever you see "OMIT the underlined portion" or "DELETE the underlined portion" appear as an answer choice, you must make sure to ask yourself whether the underlined portion is **directly relevant** to the sentence. If it is not, the information should be omitted.

You cannot rely on your ear for these questions: unnecessary information will be presented in a grammatically correct and seemingly logical manner. In order to determine whether the information is truly relevant, you must sometimes stop and reiterate the topic of the sentence/paragraph before deciding whether it should remain.

For example:

Maria Tallchief was born on an Indian reservation in Oklahoma on January 24, 1925. A member of the Osage tribe, she was also a trailblazer for Native Americans in the world of ballet. When she was five years old, <u>an age at which</u> <u>many children first explore their artistic abilities,</u> she began music lessons and soon discovered that she had perfect pitch. But it was dance that captured the young girl's heart. After five years of study, she joined the Ballet Russe de Monte Carlo, where she was quickly named a soloist.

1. A.   NO CHANGE
    B.   around the time that she started kindergarten,
    C.   along with her younger sister, Marjorie,
    D.   DELETE the underlined portion

Solution:

-Who and what do the sentence and paragraph focus on?

The sentence focuses on Maria Tallchief's introduction to music as well as her discovery that she had perfect pitch. The paragraph focuses on Tallchief's early life and introduction to dance.

-Are any of the options *directly* relevant to that topic, and do they and add important/necessary information?

(A)-(C) are generally related to Tallchief, but they're not clearly related to the specific topic of the paragraph – and that's the only part the ACT cares about. So the answer is (D).

Now let's look at something a little harder:

Maria Tallchief was born on an Indian reservation in Oklahoma on January 24, 1925. A member of the Osage tribe, she was also a trailblazer for Native Americans in the world of ballet. The Osage language is similar to that spoken by members of the Sioux tribe. When she was five years old, she began music lessons and soon discovered that she had perfect pitch. It was dance, however, that captured the young girl's heart. 2 After five years of study, she joined the Ballet Russe de Monte Carlo, where she was quickly named a soloist.

2. If the previous sentence were deleted, the passage would primarily lose

F. a necessary transition that explains why Maria Tallchief chose to pursue dance rather than music
G. information describing why Maria Tallchief preferred dance to music
H. irrelevant details that detract from the focus of the paragraph
J. a description of Maria Tallchief's favorite childhood activities

Solution:

In general, you want to approach "primarily lose" questions by focusing on the sentence to be deleted. First, reread the sentence **in context** and ask yourself what information it provides. If you have an accurate understanding, you'll probably come up with something relatively close to the answer. In this case, you might say something like, "it talks about how Maria Tallchief liked dance better than music."

But now you need to be careful. (G) says something very similar, but not *exactly* the same thing. The sentence in question does state that Maria Tallchief preferred dance, but **it does not actually** <u>describe</u> **the reasons** for her preference. And in order to be correct, the sentence must do **exactly** what the answer says.

(F) says something similar to (G), but you might find the wording confusing or be unsure what is meant by "necessary transition." To check it out, we're going to cross it out and read the paragraph without it.

> **When she was five years old, she began music lessons and soon discovered that she had perfect pitch… After five years of study, she joined the Ballet Russe de Monte Carlo, where she was quickly named a soloist.**

When we omit the sentence from the paragraph, we suddenly have a big gap. We jump from a discussion of Maria Tallchief's *music* study to the fact that Maria joined the Ballet Russe as a *dancer*. So the purpose of the missing sentence is to bridge those two ideas by introducing the idea that Maria Tallchief also studied dance, and that she decided to pursue dance rather than music. The answer is therefore (F).

The question on the previous page asked about a sentence that happened to function as a transition, but "primarily lose" questions frequently revolve around **details** and **explanations**. Often, the omitted words are **adjectives** because **the purpose of adjectives is to describe or provide detail**.

For example:

> Balanchine then brought Tallchief home to his
>
> Ballet Society, the company that would become
>
> New York City Ballet. Her ~~immense~~ popularity
>
> with the American public grew in part from the
>
> demands the company made on its ~~phenomenally~~
>
> gifted principal dancer: Tallchief was called upon to
>
> dance as many as eight performances a week. ☐ 1

1. If the words "immense" and "phenomenally" were deleted from the previous sentence, the sentence would primarily lose

   A. an explanation for Maria Tallchief's popularity with the American public
   B. a contrast between Maria Tallchief's reception in Paris and her reception in the United States
   C. information emphasizing Maria Tallchief's talent and enthusiastic reception in New York
   D. nothing, because those words are irrelevant to the meaning of the sentence

Solution: *Immense* and *phenomenally* are both very strong descriptive words; their purpose is to emphasize an idea. What idea? That Maria Tallchief was very popular and very talented. So the answer is (C).

One more:

> In 1965, Maria Tallchief surprised the world by
>
> announcing her retirement. She had no intention of
>
> dancing past her prime and wanted to pass her love
>
> for her art to younger dancers. ☐ 2
>
> "New ideas are essential," Tallchief said, "but we
>
> must retain respect for the art of ballet or else it is
>
> no longer an art form."

2. If the author were to delete the previous sentence, the paragraph would primarily lose

   F. an explanation of why Maria Tallchief chose to retire when she did
   G. a description of how Maria Tallchief helped younger ballet dancers
   H. a discussion of problems that are often faced by older ballet dancers
   J. an analysis of how Maria Tallchief's approach to dance evolved during her career

Solution: What does the sentence discuss? Why Maria Tallchief stopped dancing. In context of the paragraph, it supports the previous sentence by **explaining** why she decided to retire. So the answer is (F).

Drill: Inserting, Deleting Information, and Replacing Information
(answers p. 255)

1. I don't remember when or how it started,

but somewhere along the way, I developed a

fascination with paper: <u>books, photos, and posters,</u>
1
<u>not to mention stationery and greeting cards.</u> I
1
had always been an avid traveler and photographer,

but now paper in the form of memorabilia and

photographic prints started taking over my life.

Brightly colored photographs covered

my bedroom, my living room, and my office.

[2]   Then, about ten years ago, I

discovered the budding world of scrapbooking,

<u>which traces its roots to "commonplace" books in</u>
3

<u>fifteenth century England.</u> Suddenly, paper took on
3

a whole new significance for me.

---

1. If the writer were to delete the underlined information, the sentence would primarily lose

    A. a description of the how the writer used paper in daily life
    B. information explaining why the writer became fascinated with paper
    C. specific examples of the kinds of paper the writer appreciated
    D. an explanation of why the writer preferred certain kinds of paper

2. At this point in the essay, the writer is considering adding the following sentence:

    > At times, I even worried that my walls would collapse under their weight.

    Should this sentence be added?

    A. Yes, because it offers a humorous commentary that emphasizes the main idea of the paragraph.
    B. Yes, because the writer was concerned about the effects of her interest on her family.
    C. No, because it is irrelevant to the description of the writer's house.
    D. No, because it digresses from the idea that the writer enjoyed traveling.

3. **A.** NO CHANGE
    B. which is a popular pastime throughout the United States.
    C. which sometimes makes use of magazine clippings
    D. DELETE the underlined portion

2. Dr. Judith L. Pipher, an astronomer and Seneca Falls, New York resident, has a career that people at the first women's rights convention – held in Seneca Falls in 1848 – could never have imagined. After graduating from the University of Toronto, she began studying for her Ph.D. at Cornell University, <u>which was founded in 1865</u>. Her
1
doctoral work led her to perform groundbreaking research in infrared astronomy, <u>a field devoted to</u>
2
<u>detecting objects in space by measuring the heat</u>
2
<u>energy they emit</u>.
2

   In 1983, Pipher and her colleagues at the University of Rochester mounted a prototype infrared detector onto a campus telescope and took the first telescopic pictures of the moon. Later, she helped design the infrared detectors for the Spitzer Space Telescope, which was launched in 2003 to study brown dwarfs: enormous, planet-like objects too dark to be observed with conventional telescopes. [3]

   Throughout her career, Pipher also chaired national committees that determine funding for NASA and the National Science Foundation. In 2007, she was honored by the National Women's Hall of Fame in – where else? – Seneca Falls, New York.

1. **A.** NO CHANGE
   B. which is located in the Finger Lakes region of New York State
   C. whose campus covers more than 1,000 acres
   D. DELETE the underlined portion

2. The writer is considering deleting the underlined portion of the sentence. Should that change be made?

   F. Yes, because it is irrelevant to the essay's focus on Pipher's groundbreaking achievements.
   G. Yes, because the writer does not explain how heat energy is measured.
   H. No, because it provides a definition that is important to understanding Pipher's work.
   J. No, because it explains why Pipher's research was groundbreaking.

3. At this point in the essay, the author is considering inserting the following sentence

   > Among the telescope's discoveries are four unusually bright galaxies and the deepest image of a galaxy cluster ever obtained.

   Should the sentence be added?

   A. Yes, because Pipher was solely responsible for designing the Spitzer telescope.
   B. Yes, because it supports the point that Pipher made important contributions to astronomy research.
   C. No, because it includes a level of scientific detail that is inconsistent with the rest of the essay.
   D. No, because Pipher did not continue to work on the telescope after helping to design its sensors.

[1]

3. John James Audubon, whose name is today synonymous with wildlife conservation, was a bold entrepreneur, a rugged outdoorsman, and a talented artist. In his own time, however, he was best known as an author and illustrator of wildlife: his masterpiece, *Birds of America*, was published in 1840. ☐ 1

[2]

At the age of 18, Audubon left his home in France
                                                    2
to avoid conscription in Napoleon's army, settling at
                                                    2
a family estate outside of Philadelphia. He filled his house with natural artifacts – animal furs, plants, and his own drawings. In 1820, however, Audubon left his family behind and set out in search of specimens for what would become *Birds of America*. To depict the birds in their natural habitats, he pinned each
                  3
specimen to a wooden grid. Then, using a matching grid, he sketched each bird exactly to scale, reproducing it down to its last feather.

[3]

Audubon then took his portfolio to the Academy of Natural Sciences in Philadelphia, hoping to find a publisher. ☐ 4 Believing that his book would never be printed in the United States, he

1. At this point in the essay, the writer is considering adding the following sentence

   It was comprised of seven volumes of 650 hand-colored prints and took more than ten years to complete.

   Should the sentence be added?

   A. Yes, because it provides specific details supporting the idea that *Birds of America* was a masterpiece.
   B. Yes, because the writer states that Audubon was an outdoorsman as well as an author.
   C. No, because the writer emphasizes Audubon's wide range of skills.
   D. No, because Audubon is primarily known for his conservation efforts today.

2. If the writer were to delete the underlined portion of the sentence, the essay would primarily lose

   F. details supporting the idea that Audubon led an unconventional lifestyle
   G. a piece of historical context necessary to understand the essay
   H. an explanation of why Audubon emigrated to the United States from France
   J. a description of Audubon's upbringing and life in France

3. **A.** NO CHANGE
   B. as quickly as he could
   C. in a completely new way
   D. as realistically as possible

4. Given that all of the following sentences are true, which one should be added to best describe Audubon's experience at the Academy of Natural Sciences?

   F. Unfortunately, his arrogance and disheveled appearance alienated potential investors.
   G. The Academy had been founded by a group of leading American naturalists.
   H. Audubon was impressed by the exhibitions he viewed there.
   J. Dating to 1812, it is the oldest natural science research institution in the Americas.

traveled to England, where he became an instant sensation. His rugged outdoor dress, long hair, and tanned skin seemed like a vision straight out of the Wild West, even though he had not visited Europe in many years. Audubon exhibited his portfolio in London and Paris, the largest cities in Europe, and quickly succeeded in financing his project.

[4]

[A] Turning Audubon's watercolors into book plates was a complex process. [B] Havell and his assistants traced each detail of the original paintings before transferring the images to copper plates. [C] Completed plates were then distributed among dozens of watercolorists, who each filled in a single color. [D] A master colorist then added unique touches to all the plates.

[5]

[E] *Birds of America* was not only an astounding visual achievement but also a remarkable literary triumph. [7] [F] English was Audubon's second language, but he nevertheless described the behaviors of each bird with genuine humor and affection.

5. A. NO CHANGE
   B. had spent years living in the wilderness
   C. was still a relatively young man
   D. was actually quite sophisticated

6. F. NO CHANGE
   G. which were much older than Philadelphia
   H. where he saw many historic sites
   J. OMIT the underlined portion

7. If the words "astounding" and "remarkable" were deleted from the previous sentence, the essay would primarily lose

   A. a description of the images in *Birds of America*.
   B. information emphasizing the extraordinary nature of Audubon's accomplishment.
   C. an observation that contradicts information presented earlier in the essay.
   D. irrelevant details that do not contribute to the development of the paragraph

---

Question 8 asks about the preceding passage as a whole

Upon reviewing the essay, the writer discovers that the following sentence has been left out:

   Robert Havell, one of Britain's most famous engravers, accepted the challenge.

The sentence should best be placed at

   F. Point B in Paragraph 4
   G. Point C in Paragraph 4
   H. Point D in Paragraph 4
   J. Point E in Paragraph 5

212

19. Sentence and Paragraph Order

Sentence and paragraph order questions ask you to identify whether a particular sentence is correctly placed within a paragraph, or whether a particular paragraph is correctly placed within a passage. **The presence of bracketed numbers at the beginnings of sentences signals that a question testing sentence order will appear, and the presence of bracketed numbers at the top of each paragraph signals that a question testing paragraph order will appear.** Whenever you see one of these "clues," try to notice whether anything seems odd or illogical about the order of any sentences or paragraphs as you read.

Sentence Order

When you encounter a sentence order question, you should first determine the topic of the sentence the question is asking about. Then, check whether it follows logically from the previous sentence and connects to the following sentence. If not, back up and reread to see where else that specific topic appears.

[1] Balanchine then brought Tallchief home to his Ballet Society, the company that would become New York City Ballet. [2] Her immense popularity with the American public grew in part from the demands the company made on its phenomenally gifted principal dancer: Tallchief was called upon to dance as many as eight performances a week. [3] In fact, many audience members did not realize how difficult the part was until much later, when they saw other great ballerinas attempt to perform it. [4] Audiences were awed by her dedication to her art. [5] In *Pas de Six* (1955), Balanchine made use of Tallchief's natural subtlety and delicacy to great effect – she danced the lead role radiantly and with apparent ease.

1. The best place for Sentence 3 is

   A. where it is now
   B. after Sentence 1
   C. after Sentence 4
   D. after Sentence 5

Solution:

1) What's the topic of Sentence 3?

The fact that many people who watched Maria Tallchief perform a particular part did not realize how difficult it was until later on. Logically, the particular part that Sentence 3 is talking about must be mentioned in the previous sentence.

2) What's the topic of the previous sentence?

The fact that Maria Tallchief became popular in part because she gave so many performances. The sentence does not mention a specific part.

3) Now, what sentence does mention a specific role?

Sentence 5 mentions that Maria danced the lead role in *Pas de Six*. *Role* and *part* are synonyms, and there is no mention of a specific role elsewhere in the paragraph, so those two sentences must be talking about the same role and should be placed next to each other.

Since Sentence 5 explains just what "the role" refers to, that sentence should come first. In addition, the phrase *apparent ease* in Sentence 5 sets up a contrast with the idea expressed in Sentence 3, namely that the part was actually more difficult than it seemed. The answer is therefore (D).

Drill: Sentence Order* (answers p. 255)

1. [1] Learning to ride a unicycle might seem like a daunting task, but with the right kind of training aids, it doesn't have to be impossible – or even scary. [2] One option is to use a spotter who walks alongside and catches the rider if he or she falls. [3] Another easy way to learn is to find a narrow hallway: riding in a confined space allows the beginning rider to practice balancing from front-to-back and side-to side. [4] Likewise, riding between two chairs placed back-to-back teaches the rider how to find a proper starting position. [5] On the other hand, props such as ski poles should not be used because they hinder balance and create dependence. [6] If a hallway cannot be found, a fence or clothesline can be used as well.   [1]

1. The best place for Sentence 6 is

   A. where it is now
   B. after Sentence 1
   C. after Sentence 2
   D. after Sentence 3

2. [1] For decades, scientists have hoped for a "solar revolution," a shift from relying on natural gas to heat homes and power cars to harnessing electricity from the sun. [2] The conversion of solar heat into usable energy is accomplished through the use of solar panels – also known as modules – which can be installed directly into the ground,

*Paragraph order questions are included with the complete tests beginning on p. 210.

215

mounted on roofs, or built directly into the walls of a building. [3] It's a tantalizing promise: on sunny days, the sun gives off enormous amounts of energy – enough to power houses, office buildings, and schools. [4] Each module is comprised of cells which convert solar radiation into direct current electricity. [5] A single module contains enough cells to power a telephone, but multiple panels must be used for a house or power plant. [1]

1. What is the best placement for Sentence 2?

F.   Where it is now
G.   Before Sentence 1
H.   Before Sentence 4
J.   Before Sentence 5

3. [1] Say the word "sushi," and the first thing that comes to mind is usually an image of raw fish. [2] But sushi is about rice as well as fish. [3] It's the original fast food, dating back to 700 A.D. in Japan. [4] At that time, fish was salted, sandwiched between layers of rice, and pressed with heavy stones, a process that preserved the fish for months or even years. [5] At first, the rice was only used to help start the fermenting process, but food shortages later made the rice too valuable to be thrown away. [6] The curing time was also shortened to three or four weeks, after which both fish and the rice were eaten. [7] As a result, the fish was closer to raw when it was consumed. [1]

1. The best place for Sentence 4 is

A.   where it is now
B.   after Sentence 2
C.   after Sentence 5
D.   after Sentence 6

Paragraph Order

Questions about paragraph order test essentially the same skill as those testing sentence order, only on a larger scale. As is true for sentence order questions, you must determine whether a particular paragraph is logically placed or whether it would make more sense elsewhere in the passage.

While questions testing paragraph order do ask you to deal with more information than most other types of questions do, you do not need to reread the entire passage in order to determine whether a given paragraph is correctly placed; a few key places will usually give you all the information you need.

In general, you should break paragraph order questions into the following steps:

1) Reread the paragraph in question, paying particular attention to the first (topic) sentence, and reiterate the **topic** for yourself in a word or two. Jot it down quickly.

2) Back up and read the **last sentence** of the previous paragraph, and ask whether yourself whether it leads naturally into the topic of the paragraph in question. If yes, it's fine where it is. If not:

3) Skim through the first and last sentence of each paragraph, looking for a mention of that topic. The paragraph in question will almost certainly belong next to that paragraph.

For the following question, please refer to the full passage on p. 200.

The best placement for Paragraph 4 is

   A. where it is now
   B. after Paragraph 1
   C. after Paragraph 2
   D. after Paragraph 5

Solution:

1) What's the topic of Paragraph 4?

Maria Tallchief's collaborations with George Balanchine. More specifically, it is about the beginning of her collaboration with Balanchine – we know this because the second sentence tells us that they **first** worked together in 1947.

2) Back up and read the end of the previous paragraph.

The last sentence of Paragraph 3 discusses a 1955 collaboration with Balanchine. Since 1955 is later than 1947, it would make more sense for that information to come later in the passage. Since the two paragraphs have the same topic, however, they should most likely be located next to one another. (If you want to confirm that no other paragraph mentions Balanchine, you can skim topic sentences of the rest of the paragraph.)

Since Paragraph 4 talks about events that clearly happened before those in Paragraph 3, Paragraph 4 should be placed before it (i.e. after Paragraph 2). So (C) is the answer.

Dividing Paragraphs

Sometimes you will also be asked to identify the point at which a paragraph should be divided in two. These questions essentially test your ability to recognize where a shift in topic or focus occurs. As is true for sentence order questions, paragraph division questions are always accompanied by numbered sentences.

There are two primary ways that you can approach paragraph division questions. You can check the answer choices one by one, looking at each point in the passage and deciding whether it fits in logically with the information that came before it or begins a new idea; or, you can simply read through the paragraph on your own and identify where a break would logically occur. While the first option may seem safer and easier, it can also be time consuming and increase the odds that you'll get stuck between two answers. The second option, on the other hand, requires a bit more thought upfront but is often faster in the end. It also significantly reduces the chances of your second-guessing yourself.

Let's look at a slightly doctored version of our passage for an example:

[1] "A ballerina takes steps given to her and makes them her own. [2] Each individual brings something different to the same role," the great ballerina Maria Tallchief once said. [3] Tallchief combined great individualism and extraordinary talent, creating a remarkable and vital chapter in American dance. [4] Maria Tallchief was born on an Indian reservation in Oklahoma on January 24, 1925. [5] When Maria was five years old, she began music lessons and soon discovered that she had perfect pitch. [6] But it was dance that captured the young girl's heart. [7] After five years of study, she joined the Ballet Russe de Monte Carlo, where she quickly became a soloist. ⬚1

1. The best place to begin a new paragraph is

   A. Sentence 2
   B. Sentence 3
   C. Sentence 4
   D. Sentence 6

In this version, the paragraph has two different focuses: it introduces Maria Tallchief and her career, and it provides biographical information. The shift occurs in Paragraph 4, where the writer first begins to describe Tallchief's early life and background. So the answer is (C).

20. Suppose the Writer's Goal...

"Passage purpose" questions ask you to determine whether a passage accurately reflects the author's goal in writing it. These questions essentially test your ability to recognize **main ideas**, and to distinguish between those ideas and **supporting details**. They are virtually always presented in the following format:

Suppose the writer had intended to write
an essay about... Would this essay fulfill
that goal?

- **A.** Yes, because...
- **B.** Yes, because...
- **C.** No, because...
- **D.** No, because...

An unavoidable difficulty of passage purpose questions is that they always appear as the final question in a set of 15. At that point, the last thing you want to see is another rhetoric question. If you've already encountered a bunch of rhetoric questions in that passage, and if it's the fifth passage and your energy is flagging, you'll be even less inclined to care what the purported "writer" of the passage had actually intended to accomplish.

Furthermore, these questions seem to demand an inordinate amount of work. Chances are, you've been moving mechanically from question to question, taking a few surrounding lines into account when necessary but otherwise more or less ignoring what the passage as a whole is saying. You *really* don't want to go back and read the whole thing again. Uh-uh, not going to happen. You'd rather just try to remember (you sort of do, after all) and take your chances.

Both of these issues tend to hide a larger problem, though. A lot of test-takers aren't really sure how to figure out what a passage is about at all.

How Do You Know What a Passage is "About?"

One of the most common problems that people encounter when answering passage purpose questions is that they're not sure of the different between "talking about" and "being about." In other words, they know that certain pieces of information have been *included* in the passage, but they don't quite know how to tell whether the *entire* passage is about that particular person or thing. And when they do look back at the passage, they get so caught up in the details that they lose sight of the big picture.

Simply put, the topic of the passage is most often the word (or name, title, etc.) that appears most frequently throughout the entire passage. For example, in the full passage on p. 200, Maria Tallchief's name not only appears ten times, but it appears in every single paragraph. Often, you can also simply look at the title of the passage. In this case, the title "Maria Tallchief: All-American Ballerina" tells you everything you need to know.

Specific vs. General

Many passage purpose questions test your understanding of **scope** – that is, whether the topic of a passage is **general** or **specific.**

Passages that are **specific** focus on **a single** person or event (e.g. Maria Tallchief, the opening of the St. Louis Arch) which will be repeatedly mentioned throughout the passage. Other people, events, or ideas may be referred to at various points, but only in relation to the main topic.

Passages that are **general** focus on a **broad topic** or **recurring event** (e.g. pen names, Tejano music, the northern lights); they may use specific people and events as examples, but these references will appear at isolated points in the passage rather than being discussed throughout the entire passage.

Let's look at how this plays out in a question about the Maria Tallchief passage on p. 200.

> Suppose the writer had intended to write an essay
> about how Native American dancers influenced
> ballet in the United States. Would this essay fulfill
> that goal?

Unfortunately, you don't get to look at the answers quite yet. But it doesn't even matter all that much because you already know more or less what they'll say: two will say YES, and two will say NO. **If you can decide on your own whether the answer is yes or no, you won't even have to read two of the answers.**

How do you determine which one it should be? The most important thing to remember is that you don't have to reread the entire passage. In fact, you can simply look at the title: "Maria Tallchief: An American Ballerina." The title tells you that the passage is about one single person, not a group of people (i.e. Native Americans) in general. That might seem suspiciously simple to you – after all, couldn't the passage also talk about other things? Yes, it could, but the **the purpose of a title is to tell you what the passage is about**. If the title says that the passage is about Maria Tallchief, she's going to be the main topic of the passage. Other people might be mentioned, but they will not be the central focus.

The title won't always give you the information you need, though. So if you read the title and you're still not sure, read the first few sentences of the passage. Because ACT English passages are so short, the topic must be presented in the first few sentences by necessity. What do the first two sentences say?

> **"A ballerina takes steps given to her and makes them her own. Each individual brings something different to the same role," the great ballerina Maria Tallchief once said. Tallchief combined great individualism and extraordinary talent, creating a remarkable and vital chapter in American dance.**

The sentence makes it clear that the passage will be about one specific ballet dancer, namely Maria Tallchief. It will not be about Native American dancers in general. The answer to the question is therefore "no," meaning that you can eliminate (A) and (B) without looking at them. As far as you're concerned, they don't exist.

Now the question looks like this:

> Suppose the writer had intended to write an essay about how Native American dancers influenced ballet in the United States. Would this essay fulfill that goal?
>
> A. ~~Yes, because it mentions that Maria Tallchief was a member of the Osage tribe.~~
> B. ~~Yes, because it mentions that Maria Tallchief danced in Paris as well as in the United States.~~
> C. No, because it indicates that Maria Tallchief was the only professional Native American ballerina in the United States in the 1940s and '50s.
> D. No, because the essay focuses on Maria Tallchief and does not discuss other Native American ballet dancers.

Let's consider those remaining answers in terms of general and specific. The question is phrased in a very general way: it asks about Native American dancers, plural. The passage, on the other hand, is specific: it focuses on one single Native American dancer. Which is exactly what (D) says.

You could also play process of elimination and go hunting through the passage to see whether it states that Tallchief was the only professional Native American ballet dancer in the United States during the 1940s and '50s. But that's time consuming and tiring, and you're not really guaranteed to understand why the right answer is right – which increases the chances that you'll second-guess yourself.

Sometimes passage purpose questions are phrased a bit more subtly or confusingly, in ways that don't initially seem as vulnerable to quick shortcuts. For example, the above question could have been phrased this way:

> Suppose the writer had intended to write an essay about how Maria Tallchief influenced the success of Native American dancers in the United States. Would this essay fulfill that goal?
>
> A. Yes, because it mentions that Maria Tallchief was a member of the Osage tribe.
> B. Yes, because it mentions that Maria Tallchief danced in Paris as well as in the United States.
> C. No, because it indicates that Maria Tallchief was the only professional Native American ballerina in the United States in the 1940s and '50s.
> D. No, because it does not provide specific examples of how Maria Tallchief's career affected other Native American dancers.

Now the general vs. specific issue is less clear-cut. But only a little. At first glance, the question does appear to focus on Maria Tallchief; however, if you look carefully, there's that general word *dancers* again.

There are a few ways you can think about the question. First of all, what kind of dance does the passage talk about? Ballet. There is absolutely no mention of another kind of dance. So right there, the writer's goal is too broad for what the passage actually talks about.

Second, if you simply scan the passage, you can see that there are no other Native American dancers mentioned anywhere in the passage. Maria Tallchief and George Balanchine (who is clearly identified as a choreographer) are the only people referred to by name. If no other Native American dancers are mentioned, then the passage can't be about them.

So while the beginning of the passage does indeed *mention* that Maria Tallchief was a "trailblazer" for Native Americans in ballet, that idea is not the *main focus* because the author does not support it by providing specific examples, nor is it mentioned anywhere else in the passage.

To sum up, when answering passage purpose questions:

1) Review the passage briefly before answering it – even if you think you remember what it's about.

    Reread **the title and the introduction,** and if you're still not sure, **the topic sentence of each body paragraph and the conclusion**. Those key places reveal the passage's focus and reveal whether it is specific or general.

2) Ask yourself whether the passage fulfills the writer's intended goal.

    Either way, you can automatically eliminate two answers just by answering "Yes" or "No."

3) Ask yourself why the passage either fulfills or does not fulfill that goal.

    State the reason briefly in your own words. Then, look for the answer that matches.

Test 1 (answers p. 256)

(answers p. 256)

Passage I -b r

Guy Laliberté's Cirque du Soleil

Guy Laliberté is an accordionist, stilt-walker,

and being a fire-eater. He's also the founder of
    1
Cirque du Soleil (French for "Circus of the Sun"),

the Canadian circus, famous for it's spectacular sets
                    2

and amazing acrobats. While it may be unusual,

Laliberte's career choice was hardly surprising:
                        3

when he was a child, his parents took him to watch

the Ringling Brothers and Barnum & Bailey Circus,

an experience that led him to read the biography of
                4

its creator, P. T. Barnum. | 5 |

While still in school, Laliberté produced several

performing arts events. In contrast, he entered the
                        6

world of street performance, playing the

harmonica, and accordion on the streets of
        7

Quebec. He then joined a troupe that

included fire-breathers, jugglers, and acrobats who

hitched around the country from show to show.

1. **A.** NO CHANGE
   B. fire-eater also
   C. fire-eater additionally
   D. fire-eater

2. **F.** NO CHANGE — Dumb mistake
   G. circus famous for its
   H. circus famous, for its
   J. circus; famous for it's

3. **A.** NO CHANGE
   B. hard surprising
   C. hardly surprisingly
   D. hard surprisingly

4. Which of the following best emphasizes Laliberté's enthusiastic response to the circus?

   F. NO CHANGE
   G. allowed
   H. inspired
   J. directed

5. Which of the following provides the most effective transition to the paragraph that follows?

   A. He made up his mind to follow in Barnum's footsteps.
   B. Today, Barnum is remembered mostly as a con artist.
   C. He found the book boring at first, but he persevered and eventually finished it.
   D. In addition to being a showman, Barnum was an author, publisher, and politician.

6. **F.** NO CHANGE
   G. Otherwise, he entered
   H. Afterward, he entered
   J. Therefore, he entered

7. **A.** NO CHANGE
   B. harmonica and accordion,
   C. harmonica and, accordion,
   D. harmonica and accordion

223

He later returned to Quebec, he found a
8

steady job at a hydroelectric dam. Soon after his

employment began, however the company's
9

employees went on strike. Laliberté took the
10

opportunity to return to his life as a street

performer.

In 1984, Laliberté co-founded Cirque du Soleil

with entrepreneur, Gilles Ste-Croix and a small
11

group of colleagues. The name which Laliberté
12
came up with while on vacation in Hawaii, reflects

his idea that "the sun stands for energy and youth,"

and that the circus is about those two words.

Although Cirque du Soleil was originally set
13
up as a one-year project at first, it proved so

popular that its run was extended indefinitely.

Today, the circus, which is active on five

continents, employ approximately
14
4,000 people from over 40 countries. Despite its

mainstream success, Cirque du Soleil remains unique

in one regard: it doesn't have any animals.
15

8. **F.** NO CHANGE
    G. Quebec, where he found
    H. Quebec; finding
    J. Quebec, and he will find

9. **A.** NO CHANGE
    B. began; however,
    C. began, however,
    D. began however,

10. Which of the following would be the LEAST acceptable alternative to the underlined word?

    F. seized
    G. grabbed
    H. jumped at
    J. held

11. **A.** NO CHANGE
    B. entrepreneur, Gilles Ste-Croix,
    C. entrepreneur Gilles Ste-Croix,
    D. entrepreneur Gilles Ste-Croix

12. **F.** NO CHANGE
    G. name – which Laliberté
    H. name, which Laliberté
    J. name. Which Laliberté

13. **A.** NO CHANGE
    B. initially
    C. at once
    D. DELETE the underlined portion

14. **F.** NO CHANGE
    G. employs
    H. would have employed
    J. have employed

15. All of the following would be acceptable alternatives to the underlined portion EXCEPT

    A. regard – it
    B. regard, it
    C. regard. It
    D. regard; it

Passage II

Modular Buildings

Modular buildings, also known as prefabricated buildings, are buildings that consist of multiple sections called modules. The modules, themselves, are six-sided boxes, they are constructed in a remote facility, then delivered to their site of use.

Modular buildings may be used for temporary or permanent facilities such as: construction camps, classrooms, apartment buildings, and industrial facilities. It is used in remote and rural areas where more typical and conventional construction may not be possible. For example, modular accommodation pods being used to house researchers during an Antarctic expedition in 2010.

[1] Modules are usually constructed, on an indoor assembly line. [2] During the first stage, the walls are attached to the floor. [3] As a finishing touch, shingles and siding are added.

[4] Construction of the modules take as little as ten days, but more often several months are needed.

[5]After the walls are firmly in place, drywall ceiling is sprayed on in a booth, and the roof is attached.

[6] Throughout the entire process, building

16. F. NO CHANGE
    G. modules, themselves
    H. modules themselves,
    J. modules themselves

17. A. NO CHANGE
    B. boxes; they
    C. boxes, and
    D. boxes they

18. F. NO CHANGE
    G. such as construction camps; classrooms,
    H. such as construction camps, classrooms,
    J. such as construction camps, classrooms

19. A. NO CHANGE
    B. They are
    C. One is
    D. It would be

20. F. NO CHANGE
    G. typically conventional
    H. typical in addition to conventional
    J. typical

21. A. NO CHANGE
    B. were used
    C. are used
    D. having been used

22. F. NO CHANGE
    G. constructed on
    H. constructed on,
    J. constructed. On

23. A. NO CHANGE
    B. have taken
    C. can take
    D. taking

24. For the sake of logic and coherence of this paragraph, Sentence 5 should be placed

    F. where it is now
    G. before Sentence 2
    H. before Sentence 3
    J. after Sentence 6

225

inspectors are required <u>to supervise</u> the
25
construction and ensure that the company adheres

to all building codes <u>during the whole process.</u>
26

When the modules are <u>final complete</u>, they are
27

transported to the building site. <u>Using a crane, they</u>
28

<u>are set onto the building's foundation by</u>
28
<u>workers</u> where they are joined together; the process
28
can take anywhere from several hours to several

days. The modules can be <u>thrown together</u> side-by-
29
side, end-to-end, or stacked up to six stories in

height, allowing a wide variety of configurations

and styles in the building layout.

25. **A.** NO CHANGE
    B. in supervising
    C. for supervising
    D. they supervise

26. **F.** NO CHANGE
    G. while the whole thing is going on
    H. at the time the process is occurring
    J. OMIT the underlined portion

27. **A.** NO CHANGE
    B. final completely
    C. finally complete
    D. finally completely

28. **F.** NO CHANGE
    G. They are set, by workers, onto the building's foundation, a crane is used
    H. Workers use a crane to set them on the building's foundation,
    J. Workers set them on the building's foundation by crane and

29. **A.** NO CHANGE
    B. tossed around
    C. placed
    D. dropped

Question 30 asks about the preceding passage as a whole

---

30. Suppose the writer's goal had been to write an essay comparing the construction of modular buildings to the construction of traditional buildings. Would this essay fulfill that goal?

    F. Yes, because modular construction is used in areas where traditional construction is impossible.
    G. Yes, because modular buildings take much less time to construct than traditional buildings.
    H. No, because the buildings are so different that their constructions cannot be compared.
    J. No, because the essay focuses only on the construction and use of modular buildings.

Passage III

The Golden Spike

By early 1869, construction on the Transcontinental

Railroid <u>has nearly come</u> to an end. The railroad,
          31

which stretched for 1,907 <u>miles took six years to</u>
                                      32

<u>complete and</u> was intended to connect the Pacific
      32
coast with the existing eastern rail network. It

was primarily built by two <u>companies. The Central</u>
                                          33
Pacific Railroad Company, which built eastward from

California, and the Union Pacific Railroad Company,

which built westward from Iowa.

In January 1869, the companies were working only

miles from each <u>other, and in March, the recently</u>
                                    34
<u>inaugurated president, Ulysses S. Grant,</u> announced
                    34
federal funds would be withheld until the two railroad

companies agreed to meet. After some debate, they

<u>expanded on</u> Promontory Point, Utah, and
      35

telegraph cables were <u>immediately</u> sent to announce
                                  36

that the railroad would be completed there.

Newspaper headlines across the country soon

proudly displayed the news.

31. **A.** NO CHANGE
    B. had nearly come
    C. has nearly came
    D. would nearly come

32. **F.** NO CHANGE
    G. miles, took six years to complete; and
    H. miles took six years to complete, and
    J. miles, took six years to complete and

33. **A.** NO CHANGE
    B. companies: the Central
    C. companies; the Central
    D. companies, and the Central

34. **F.** NO CHANGE
    G. other and in March. The recently
        inaugurated president, Ulysses S. Grant
    H. other, and in March, when the recently
        inaugurated president, Ulysses S. Grant
    J. other, and in March the recently
        inaugurated president; Ulysses S. Grant

35. **A.** NO CHANGE
    B. confirmed that
    C. agreed on
    D. wondered about

36. Which choice would best convey the idea
    that the news of the railroad's impending
    completion was sent as soon as Promontory
    Point was selected as a meeting place?

    A. NO CHANGE
    B. eventually
    C. ultimately
    D. reluctantly

37   David Hewes, a contractor and friend of

Pacific President Leland Stanford, was disappointed

to discover, no one had prepared an item to
         38

commemorate the railroad's completion. He proposed

creating a gold or silver section of rail, but unable to

find a financier, he settled on something

more practical using $400 of his own money, he had
         39

a golden spike cast. The spike was 5 5/8 inches

long, weighed 14.03 ounces, and was made of

17.6 carat gold.   40

Its' top was simply engraved with the words "The Last
41

Spike."

The ceremony was originally scheduled for

May 8th, so poor weather forced it to be rescheduled.
         42

On May 10th, nearly 500 workers, officials, and

onlookers gathered to watch the last tie be hammered

into the track.

37. Assuming that all of the following are true,
    which choice most effectively connects the
    previous paragraph to the paragraph that
    follows?

    A. "The last spike" is usually driven in at
        the completion of a railroad.
    B. Remains of the railroad are still visible.
    C. Not everyone was happy, though.
    D. Hewes was among the railroad's
        most enthusiastic supporters.

38. F. NO CHANGE
    G. discover: no one
    H. discover that, no one
    J. discover no one

39. A. NO CHANGE
    B. practical. Using $400 of his own money,
    C. practical, using $400 of his own money
    D. practical; using $400 of his own money,
        and

40. If the author were to delete the previous
    sentence, the essay would primarily lose

    F. specific information about the spike's
        physical characteristics
    G. an explanation of why the spike was
        cast in gold rather than silver
    H. a description of the materials typically
        used to construct railroad spikes
    J. a comparison between the golden spike
        and the other spikes used on the railroad

41. A. NO CHANGE
    B. It's
    C. Its
    D. There

42. F. NO CHANGE
    G. since
    H. if
    J. but

After <u>an arduously verbose</u> speech by Dr. H. W.
43

Harkness, a Sacramento newspaper publisher and

editor, Leland Stanford took a <u>short, yet mighty</u> swing
44

at the spike – and struck the tie instead! [45]

Not the same thing; read carefully

43. **A.** NO CHANGE
    B. a dull and lengthy
    C. a mind numbing
    D. a totally boring

44. **F.** NO CHANGE
    G. short yet mighty
    H. shortly yet mightily
    J. short, yet mightily

45. As a way to conclude the essay, the writer is considering adding the following true statement:

    > Finally, a rail worker drove in the last spike, and the telegrapher sent the long awaited message: "D-O-N-E."

    Should the writer make this addition here?

    A. Yes, because it logically completes the description of the ceremony.
    B. Yes, because it explains why Stanford was unable to drive in the spike himself.
    C. No, because it omits important information about the rail worker.
    D. No, because it repeats information mentioned earlier in the passage.

Passage IV

Celebrating Tet

[1]

In my house, New Year's starts with a bang –

<u>Vietnamese New Year's, that is.</u> My family came to the
46

United States when I was only five years

old, but each winter, we still welcome the new year

the way we did back home.

46. The author is considering deleting the underlined portion of the sentence. Should it be deleted or kept?

    F. Deleted, because it strays from the essay's focus on the immigration.
    G. Deleted, because the writer left Vietnam too young to remember how New Years was celebrated there.
    H. Kept, because it provides a contrast to the writer's description of American New Years.
    J. Kept, because it specifies which holiday the writer is describing.

229

The holiday – known as <u>Tet begins</u> on the first day of
                                          47
the lunar calendar, which usually falls in late January

or <u>February, celebrations last</u> for at least three days.
                         48

[2]

Before the New Year begins, we clean the house

from top to bottom and dump all the trash <u>because</u>
                                              49
<u>we don't want our fortune to be thrown away during</u>
                          49
<u>the new year.</u> Then, to greet the holiday, we set off
       49
thousands of strings of firecrackers. They make a lively

popping <u>sound, which had put</u> everyone in a festive
              50
mood. Old possessions are packed away in closets.

Children wear new clothes, and adults give out red

envelopes holding freshly-printed money.   51

[3]

Only on the second and third days do my parents

welcome their friends and family. When I was a child,

my father would wake me and my siblings by <u>humming</u>
                                               52
everything from traditional Vietnamese music to

American rock 'n roll. Everyone was cheerful and

excited. The sweet smell of incense throughout the

house made us feel warm and safe.

47. **A.**   NO CHANGE
     B.   Tet, begins
     C.   Tet – begins
     D.   Tet begins,

48. **F.**   NO CHANGE
     G.   February, and celebrations last
     H.   February; celebrations lasting
     J.   February. Otherwise, celebrations last

49. Which of the following true statements, if
     added here, would establish the connection
     between throwing things out on New Years
     and having bad luck?

     A.   NO CHANGE
     B.   we don't want to attract ants and other
               insects
     C.   we're usually too busy to tidy up
     D.   we want our friends and family to feel
               at home

50. **F.**   NO CHANGE
     G.   sound that puts
     H.   sound, this puts
     J.   sound and putting

51. If the writer were to delete the words "new"
     and "freshly printed," the sentence would lose

     A.   a description of a ritual that the writer
               enjoyed
     B.   irrelevant details that detract from the
               development of the paragraph.
     C.   information that develops the idea
               introduced in the previous sentence.
     D.   an indication that Tet is unlike any
               other day of the year.

52. Which of the following choices would indicate
     that the writer's father played the music at
     very high volume?

     F.   NO CHANGE
     G.   wafting
     H.   blaring
     J.   presenting

230

As a child, I could barely contain my excitement when Tet came. As an adult, I've mostly abandoned that tradition.
53

[4]

Like most Vietnamese families, we also have a shrine dedicated to our ancestors. 54
We cook many different kinds of food, and on the third day of our celebration, we place them on the shrine.

[5]

According to tradition, when you visit friends or relatives on the first day of Tet, we become responsible
55
for their luck during the following year: if the people

you visit have bad luck, you will be blamed in their
56

misfortune. However, my family stays at home that
57
day, preparing dozens of rice cakes called *banh chung*.

While they cook, we sit around the fire and listen to

my fathers' stories about his childhood in Vietnam.
58

53. **A.** NO CHANGE
    B. I still find myself thrilled by the celebration
    C. I finally feel at home in the United States
    D. I sometimes feel curiosity about my family's origins

54. At this point in the essay, the writer is considering inserting the following sentence:

    It's covered in bright, shiny red cloth and tall candles.

    Should the sentence be added?

    F. Yes, because it describes a ritual unique to the writer's family.
    G. Yes, because it provides specific details about the shrine's appearance.
    H. No, because the paragraph focuses on the different kinds of food the writer's family prepared.
    J. No, because the writer does not effectively link it to the essay as a whole.

55. **A.** NO CHANGE
    B. they become
    C. you become
    D. he or she becomes

56. **F.** NO CHANGE
    G. to
    H. for
    J. toward

57. **A.** NO CHANGE
    B. Meanwhile
    C. Nevertheless
    D. Consequently

58. **F.** NO CHANGE
    G. father's
    H. fathers
    J. fathers's

[6]

To me, Tet is everything. I wouldn't change that

day for anything in the world. It reminds me not
                                                  59

only of who I am today but also of where I came
                                              59

from.
59

59. Given that all of the following are true, which one best concludes the essay while reinforcing its main idea?

   A. NO CHANGE
   B. Someday, I hope to return to Vietnam and meet my relatives there.
   C. Tet festivities closely resemble those held for Chinese New Year.
   D. Tet is the most important celebration In Vietnamese culture.

Question 60 asks about the passage as a whole.

---

60. For the overall logic and coherence of the essay, Paragraph 5 should be placed

   F. where it is now
   G. before Paragraph 2
   H. before Paragraph 3
   J. before Paragraph 6

Passage V

Bicycle Shares

[1]

A bike sharing service is a system where public
                                          61
bicycles are made available for shared use to individuals

on a very short-term basis. Usually no more than an
                           62
hour. The main goal of bike shares is to create access to

transportation while easing traffic congestion: people

can depart from one location and arrive quickly at

another without worrying about parking, traffic jams,

or whether they are polluting the air.
       63

61. **A.** NO CHANGE
   B. that
   C. in which
   D. when

62. **F.** NO CHANGE
   G. basis usually
   H. basis, usually
   J. basis; usually

63. **A.** NO CHANGE
   B. if they cause air pollution
   C. whether air pollution is caused by them
   D. air pollution

232

[2]

[1] In recent years, the international popularity of bike shares has exploded. [2] Since the first bike

64

share was short-lived, quickly shutting down, it

65

served as an inspiration to cities around the world.

[3] In the United States, bike share programs have

66

largely centered around major cities and universities.

66

[3]

[1] The reasons people participate to bike-shares

67

vary considerably. [2] In some cities, people who might

use their own bicycles don't do so because of concerns

about theft. [3] In addition, many riders find sharing

bikes liberating: a rider can seamlessly transfer to

public transit or to a car without concern about leaving

a bike behind. [4] City residents whom want to take

68

visiting friends or family to local attractions can cover

far more ground than they would of otherwise.

69

---

64. F. NO CHANGE
G. Although
H. Despite
J. When

65. A. NO CHANGE
B. not lasting very long,
C. and didn't make it,
D. OMIT the underlined portion

66. The writer would like to describe the remarkable growth of bike sharing programs. Assuming that all of the following are true, which choice best fulfills that goal?

F. NO CHANGE
G. Some bike share programs have encountered financial difficulties, though.
H. Furthermore, a new type of wheel may improve the bikes' ability to travel in bad weather.
J. Today, there are around 535 bike share programs, with an estimated fleet of 517,000 bicycles.

67. A. NO CHANGE
B. at
C. with
D. in

68. F. NO CHANGE
G. who
H. which
J. for who

69. A. NO CHANGE
B. would
C. could of
D. might of

[5] Bike shares also <u>enable</u> workers to take public
⁷⁰

transit downtown on rainy days, then ride home later

when the weather improves.

[4]

[1] Moreover, many bike-share systems offer

subscriptions that make the first 30–45 minutes of use

very <u>inexpensive; these subscriptions also encourage</u>
⁷¹

riders to use them for short-distance trips. [2] In

contrast, those seeking a bicycle for casual riding over

several hours or days will often find that a traditional

bicycle rental is <u>cheaper then</u> a shared bike.
⁷²

[5]

Finally, bike shares are using new technologies to

<u>enhance their appeal</u>. Potential riders can use cellular
⁷³

phones to search for nearby bike stations and even

view how many bikes are available at each one. Since a

bike can be returned to a station with a free dock,

this information is <u>only</u> important for current riders as
⁷⁴

well.

70. Which choice would NOT be an acceptable
    alternative to the underlined word?

    F. permit
    G. allow
    H. create
    J. help

71. Which of the following would NOT be an
    an acceptable alternative to the underlined
    portion?

    A. inexpensive; and they encourage
    B. inexpensive. These subscriptions also
       encourage
    C. inexpensive and encourage
    D. inexpensive, encouraging

72. F. NO CHANGE
    G. cheaper as
    H. more cheaply than
    J. cheaper than

73. Which of the following best expresses the idea
    that new technologies make bike shares easier
    to use?

    A. NO CHANGE
    B. reduce their cost
    C. facilitate riders' access
    D. expand their market

74. The best place for the underlined word is

    F. where it is now
    G. before the word *be*
    H. before the word *dock*
    J. before the word *current*

Question 75 asks about the passage as a whole

75. Upon reviewing the essay and finding that some information has been left out, the writer composes the following sentence.

> Their fears are justified: as many as 2 million bikes are stolen each year.

The sentence should be placed after

A. Sentence 2 in Paragraph 2
B. Sentence 1 in Paragraph 3
C. Sentence 2 in Paragraph 3
D. Sentence 2 in Paragraph 4

235

Test 2 (answers p. 264)

Passage I

New York City Public Library

The origins of the New York Public Library date

back to the time when New York was emerging as one

of the world's <u>more larger</u> cities. By the second half of
1

the nineteenth century, New York had surpassed Paris

in population and was quickly catching up to London.

Among <u>it's</u> inhabitants was former governor Samuel J.
2

Tilden (1814-1886), <u>whom</u> left the majority of his
3

fortune to "establish and maintain a free library and

reading room in the city of New York." The site <u>chose</u>
4

for new Public Library was the Croton Reservoir, a

popular strolling place that occupied two blocks of

Midtown Manhattan. [5]

As director, Billings had a lofty vision of the new

building. <u>His design, first sketched on a scrap of paper,</u>
6

<u>became the blueprint</u> for the majestic structure.
6

1. **A.** NO CHANGE
   B. most largest
   C. more largely
   D. largest

2. **F.** NO CHANGE
   G. they're
   H. its
   J. there

3. **A.** NO CHANGE
   B. who
   C. which
   D. he

4. **F.** NO CHANGE
   G. to choose
   H. having been chosen
   J. chosen

5. Given that all of the choices are true, which
   one most effectively links this paragraph to
   the paragraph that follows?

   A. The library would feature collections
      of books from around the world.
   B. There were already many libraries in
      New York at the time, but nearly all
      charged an admission fee.
   C. Dr. John Shaw Billings, one of the
      most famous librarians of his day, was
      appointed to lead the library.
   D. The library was expected to be
      completed within three years.

6. **F.** NO CHANGE
   G. His design, first sketched on a scrap of
      paper, became the blueprint,
   H. His design, first sketched on a scrap of
      paper became the blueprint,
   J. His design – first sketched on a scrap
      of paper, became the blueprint

It called for an enormous reading room set atop seven floors of stacks, as well as the country's most rapid book delivery system.

Although some of the city's most prominent architectural firms competed to build the library, the well known firm of Carrère and Hastings was ultimately selected to design and construct it. The result was the largest marble structure ever built in the United States. Before construction could start however, 500 workers had to spend two years demolishing the reservoir. The cornerstone was finally laid in May 1902.

Work progressed slowly, but steady on the monumental structure. During the summer of 1905, huge columns were put into place, and work on the roof began. By the end of 1906, work on the interior rooms had begun. Four years later, 75 miles of shelves were installed to house the immense collections. 12

More than one million books were set in place for the official dedication on May 23, 1911.

7. **A.** NO CHANGE
   B. extremely famous
   C. relatively obscure
   D. OMIT the underlined portion

8. **F.** NO CHANGE
   G. start, however,
   H. start; however,
   J. start, however

9. Which of the following choices best conveys the idea that the workers took the reservoir apart one piece at a time?

   A. NO CHANGE
   B. dismantling
   C. obliterating
   D. annihilating

10. **F.** NO CHANGE
    G. slowly, but steadily
    H. slow but steadily
    J. slowly but steadily

11. **A.** NO CHANGE
    B. have begun
    C. has began
    D. begun

12. If the writer were to delete the words "monumental," "huge," and "immense" from the previous paragraph, the essay would primarily lose

    F. a sense of the library's magnitude
    G. a contrast between the reservoir and the library building
    H. an irrelevant description
    J. details supporting a claim

237

The ceremony <u>being</u> presided over by President
    13
William Howard Taft and was attended by Governor

John Alden Dix and Mayor William J. Gaynor. The

following <u>morning, the library officially opened</u>
        14
<u>its doors at precisely 9:08 a.m.,</u> the first patron filed a
        14
slip to request a book, receiving it only six minutes

later! [15]

13. A. NO CHANGE
    B. having been
    C. would have been
    D. was

14. F. NO CHANGE
    G. morning; the library officially opened
       its doors, at precisely 9:08 a.m.,
    H. morning, the library officially opened
       its doors. At precisely 9:08 a.m.,
    J. morning, the library officially opened
       its doors at precisely 9:08 a.m.

Question 15 asks about the passage as a whole.

15. Suppose the writer had wanted to compose an
    essay describing the opening of the New York
    City Public Library. Would this essay fulfill that
    goal?

    A. Yes, because the writer provides a list of
       officials who attended the ceremony.
    B. Yes, because the essay states that the
       library officially opened its doors at 9:08
       a.m.
    C. No, because although the opening of the
       library is mentioned, it is not the essay's
       primary focus.
    D. No, because the writer does not describe
       the public's reaction to the new library.

238

Creek Garden

Winter is the season when members of the Creek

tribe <u>spent time cultivating</u> the soil. Rejecting chemical
1

fertilizers and insecticides, they used hand-held tools to

work the land and drew bountiful harvests from

modest gardens. The methods used by the Creek could

revolutionize agriculture. [2]

[A] My Creek grandparents <u>lain</u> out their garden just
3

the way their ancestors did. [B] They planted corn

in straight rows <u>and other crops were arranged by</u>
4

<u>them in rectangular beds</u>. [C] To provide nutrients for
4

the soil, my grandmother threw leftover food,

including <u>bones and eggshells,</u> into the garden.
5

[D] Inspired by my grandparents, I decided to start my

own Creek garden a few years ago.

.

16. Which choice most effectively suggests
    that Creek cultivation techniques appeared
    to have a miraculous effect on the soil?

    F. NO CHANGE
    G. worked their magic on
    H. began to work
    J. took an interest in

17. At this point in the essay, the writer is
    considering deleting the previous sentence.
    Should this change be made?

    A. Yes, because the essay primarily
        focuses on traditional gardening
        practices.
    B. Yes, because the writer does not
        provide support for the statement.
    C. No, because Creek gardening methods
        do not use chemical fertilizers.
    D. No, because it explains why the writer
        took an interest in Creek methods.

18. F. NO CHANGE
    G. lie
    H. laid
    J. laying

19. A. NO CHANGE
    B. and other crops have been arranged by
        them in rectangular beds also
    C. and arranged other crops in
        rectangular beds
    D. and arranging other crops in
        rectangular beds

20. F. NO CHANGE
    G. bones, and, eggshells
    H. bones, and eggshells
    J. bones and eggshells

[E] I chose a spot by the empty chicken coop near my
21

house that had been previously used as a storage shed.
21

[F] The coop's floor was made of mineral-rich red clay,

a natural fertilizer. [G] To soften the clay, I occasionally

sprinkled it with ash, dusting it lightly. [H] I also
22

gathered clam shells, and decayed leaves, which I

I crushed and spread throughout the garden. [23]

Having thoroughly prepared my soil, I carefully

chose my plants. I filled trays with squash, spinach
24

carrot, and lettuce seeds. I quickly discovered that
24

the garden rarely required weeding. While
25

the vegetables were planted relatively dense,
26

they shaded the surrounding soil surfaces and

prevented weeds from growing.

21. A. NO CHANGE
    B. I chose a spot by the empty chicken coop, which was near my house and had been previously used as a storage shed.
    C. Near my house was an empty chicken coop, which had previously been used as a storage shed, and my choice was a spot by this.
    D. An empty chicken coop, which had previously been used as a storage shed near my house, was where a spot was chosen by me.

22. F. NO CHANGE
    G. ash while lightly dusting it
    H. ash, dusting it in a light manner
    J. ash

23. If the writer were to divide the preceding paragraph in two, the logical place to make that division would be at Point:

    A. C
    B. E
    C. F
    D. G

24. F. NO CHANGE
    G. with: squash, spinach, carrot, and
    H. with squash; spinach, carrot, and,
    J. with squash spinach, carrot and,

25. A. NO CHANGE
    B. Just as
    C. Whereas
    D. Because

26. F. NO CHANGE
    G. relative densely
    H. relatively densely
    J. relative dense

240

Moreover, the lack of chemical fertilizers drew toads,

turtles, and birds. They gobbled up insects that
                    27

might of eaten the plants.
  28

The results were phenomenal. After a month, my

squash vines were growing more than a foot per day.

In fact, they were growing so rapidly that they soon
                          29

covered an area twice the size of the original garden.

The vegetables not only grew quickly and were also
                                        30

delicious. I still use them in at least one meal every day.

27. Which of the following is the LEAST
    acceptable alternative to the underlined
    portion of the sentence?

    A. birds, which
    B. birds, they
    C. birds; they
    D. birds that

28. F. NO CHANGE
    G. might of ate
    H. might have ate
    J. might have eaten

29. Which of the followed would NOT
    be an acceptable alternative?

    A. magnifying
    B. spreading
    C. multiplying
    D. expanding

30. F. NO CHANGE
    G. in addition
    H. so
    J. but

Passage III - 4

John Cage: Revolutionizing Music

In a Woodstock, New York concert hall in 1952,

pianist David Tudor walked on stage, sat down in front

of a piano with a stopwatch in his hand – and

proceeded doing absolutely nothing. For four minutes
           31
and thirty-three seconds, the only sounds in the

auditorium were those of the audience members

31. A. NO CHANGE
    B. in doing
    C. with doing
    D. to do

shuffling their feet, clearing their throats, and they
32

would occasionally cough as they waited for the music
32

to start. In those four-and-a-half minutes

of silence, composer John Cage eluded
33
centuries of tradition by suggesting that musical

performance was not about creating sound but rather

for listening.
34

Cage had been working toward that moment for

years. While studying with classical composer, Arnold
35

Schoenberg at the University of California, Los Angeles
35

in the 1930s, Cage realized he wanted to invent a new
36
type of music, one that was completely different from

that of his time. Schoenberg discouraged his

pupil, however, insisting that Cage would eventually

overcome all of his obstacles.
37

32. F.   NO CHANGE
    G.   they occasionally coughed
    H.   occasionally coughing
    J.   occasionally coughed

33. Which choices best expresses the idea that
    Cage's work represented a sharp break
    from musical tradition?

    A.   NO CHANGE
    B.   drifted away from
    C.   ruptured with
    D.   condescended to

34. F.   NO CHANGE
    G.   in
    H.   about
    J.   to

35. A.   NO CHANGE
    B.   composer Arnold Schoenberg
    C.   composer, Arnold Schoenberg,
    D.   composer Arnold Schoenberg,

36. F.   NO CHANGE
    G.   1930s; Cage realized,
    H.   1930s, Cage realized,
    J.   1930s, and Cage realized

37. A.   NO CHANGE
    B.   begin to perform again
    C.   find himself at an impasse
    D.   have a breakthrough

Cage's teachers prediction was wrong, though.
38

In fact, Cage quickly discovered that other people were

just as interested than he was in creating art forms not
39
governed by the rigid rules of the past. He was

inspired by the idea that music did not have to

express internal ideas or emotions but could reflect the
40

sounds of everyday life.

41   As his experiments grew, however, Cage

started to reimagine the very idea of an instrument. In

"Imaginary Landscape No 4" (1951), therefore, he
42

played twelve radios at the same time.

In "Cartridge Music" (1960), one of his first

attempts to create electronic music, he inserted small

household objects into a record player cartridge and

manipulated them in a variety of ways. The sound

created by the objects jostling one another was picked
43
up by the cartridge and fed to an amplifier.

38. F. NO CHANGE
G. Cages teachers'
H. Cage's teacher's
J. Cages teacher's

39. A. NO CHANGE
B. that
C. and
D. as

40. F. NO CHANGE
G. ideas, or emotions, but
H. ideas or emotions, but
J. ideas or emotions; but they

41. Given that all of the following are true, which one provides the best transition between the previous paragraph and the paragraph that follows?

A. At first, Cage simply altered existing instruments.
B. One of Cage's early collaborators was painter Robert Rauschenberg.
C. In 1933, Cage travelled to New York to study with Adolph Weiss a former student of Schoenberg.
D. Cage also earned money by giving private lectures on modern art.

42. F. NO CHANGE
G. meanwhile
H. however
J. for example

43. A. NO CHANGE
B. mingling
C. repelling
D. slipping

Although Cage is considered one of the most

innovative composers of the twentieth century,

their legacy extends far beyond the world of music. His
44

belief that music could be everywhere and made from

anything, brought a sense of optimism to all of his
45

work. After him, no one could look at a painting or

a book without wondering how it might sound.

44. F. NO CHANGE
    G. our
    H. his
    J. your

45. A. NO CHANGE
    B. anything brought
    C. anything has brought
    D. anything will have brought

Passage IV

Rebecca Lee Crumpler

[1]

Rebecca Lee Crumpler was the first African

American woman to earn a medical degree at a time

when advanced education for women were rare. Born
46

in Delaware in the early 1830s, (her exact date of birth
47

is unknown), she was raised by an aunt. The two
47

women eventually settled in Pennsylvania.

46. F. NO CHANGE
    G. was
    H. have been
    J. having been

47. A. NO CHANGE
    B. 1830s (her exact date of birth is
       unknown), she
    C. 1830s, (her exact date of birth is
       unknown) she
    D. 1830s (her exact date of birth is
       unknown). She

Although <u>she</u> lacked formal medical training,
48

community members regularly consulted her for advice

<u>concerning and regarding their health</u>. Watching her
49

aunt, Crumpler later <u>wrote inspired</u> her to work in a
50
field that would allow her to "relieve the sufferings of

others."

[2]

<u>Crumpler moved to Charlestown, Massachusetts in</u>
51

<u>1852</u>, where she became a nurse. [52]
51

The doctors with whom she worked were so

impressed by her skills that they recommended her for

admission to New England Female Medical College.

<u>Thus</u>, her acceptance to medical school was highly
53

unusual. In the middle of the nineteenth century,

few medical schools existed in the United States,

and most of them did not admit African Americans or

women.

48. **F.** NO CHANGE
   G. we
   H. someone
   J. Crumpler's aunt

49. **A.** NO CHANGE
   B. concerning and in regard to their health
   C. with concern for and regarding their health
   D. about their health

50. **F.** NO CHANGE
   G. wrote, and inspired
   H. wrote, inspired
   J. wrote; inspired

51. **A.** NO CHANGE
   B. In 1852, Crumpler moved to Charlestown, Massachusetts,
   C. Crumpler moved to Charlestown, Massachusetts in 1852 and
   D. Crumpler's move to Charlestown, Massachusetts

52. At this point in the essay, the writer is considering inserting the following sentence

> Because there were no nursing schools at the time, she was forced to learn on the job.

Should the sentence be added?

   F. Yes, because it emphasizes the idea that Crumpler faced many obstacles.
   G. Yes, because it explains why Crumpler had difficulty performing her duties.
   H. No, because Crumpler later earned a medical degree.
   J. No, because the doctors were impressed by Crumpler's skill.

53. **A.** NO CHANGE
   B. Likewise
   C. Moreover
   D. Even so

[3]

When the Civil War ended in 1865, Crumpler

moved to Richmond, Virginia to help newly freed

slaves who, without her services, could not have

obtained medical care. In 1883, having returned to

Boston, she published *A Book of Medical Discourses.*

The book not only dispensed practical, medical, advice
                                                    54
for women but it earned Crumpler a place in history.

55

[4]

Crumpler began medical school in 1860, but as a

result of the Civil War, which expelled her classes,
                                      56
she did not graduate until 1864. Upon her graduation,

she became the first African American woman to earn a

medical degree as well as the only African American

woman to ever graduate from the New England

Female Medical College.

54. **F.** NO CHANGE
   G. practical medical advice
   H. practical medical advice,
   J. practical, medical advice,

55. Given that all of the following statements
   are true, which one provides the most
   relevant information at this point in the
   essay?

   A. It was the first medical book published
      by an African American woman in the
      United States.
   B. The book consisted of two volumes
      and described common childhood
      ailments.
   C. It was published by Cushman, Keating
      and Co., which was located in Boston.
   D. Notes from Crumpler's medical
      practice served as her inspiration.

56. **F.** NO CHANGE
   G. excluded
   H. interrupted
   J. revoked

Unfortunately, neither photos <u>or</u> other images of
57

Dr. Crumpler survive. For decades, she slipped into

obscurity, but today <u>much of</u> her groundbreaking
58

achievements are recognized. In 1989, two

physicians founded the Rebecca Lee <u>Society. The</u>
59
<u>organization supports</u> and promotes female African
59
American physicians. Each year, it grants a scholarship

in the name of Rebecca Lee Crumpler.

57. A. NO CHANGE
  B. nor
  C. and
  D. than

58. F. NO CHANGE
  G. too much
  H. more than
  J. many of

59. Which of the following would NOT be
  an acceptable alternative to the underlined
  portion of the sentence?

  A. Society, an organization that supports
  B. Society; the organization supports
  C. Society. The organization, which
    supports
  D. Society – the organization supports

Question 60 asks about the passage as a
whole.

60. For the sake of logic and coherence of the
  essay, Paragraph 4 should be placed

  F. where it is now
  G. after Paragraph 1
  H. after Paragraph 2
  J. after Paragraph 5

Passage V

Visit to the Recycling Plant

It's one thing to discuss, and encourage

recycling. It's quite another to see what really happens

happens when our papers and plastics are taken

"away." Last spring, the staff at the magazine where I

work received an invitation to tour the Keystone State

Materials Recycling Center (MRC), it serves

62

more than ten counties in northern Pennsylvania and

southern New Jersey. 63

Before the tour of began, me and them

64

donned hardhats, glasses, and gloves to protect

ourselves from flying debris. Nearly 1,000 trucks drop

65

over 3,000 tons of materials onto the processing

floor each day. Therefore, the Center has one of

66

the highest capacities of any MRC in the United States.

61. A. NO CHANGE

  B. discuss and encourage,

  C. discuss and encourage

  D. discuss, and, encourage

62. F. NO CHANGE

  G. (MRC). Which serves

  H. (MRC), which serves

  J. (MRC) and serves

63. Given that all of the choices are true, which one conveys the most specific information about the positive effect that Keystone has on the environment?

  A. Each year, Keystone workers save 372,000 cubic yards of landfill space.

  B. The facility opened in the 1970s but has expanded in recent years.

  C. I have an interest in environmental issues, so I was eager to go.

  D. Keystone MRC is located in Bristol, Pennsylvania, close to New Jersey.

64. F. NO CHANGE

  G. me and they

  H. me and my colleagues

  J. I and my colleagues

65. Which of the following would NOT be an acceptable alternative to the underlined word?

  A. deposit

  B. unload

  C. expend

  D. release

66. F. NO CHANGE

  G. Nevertheless, the Center

  H. Meanwhile, the Center

  J. The Center

As I was surprised to discover, Keystone State MRC

is a popular spot for tour groups of many different

ages. Elementary and middle school children are

frequent visitors, but unless they are senior citizens
                              67

from the local senior center. According to Amir Patel,

the community outreach coordinator with who we
                                        68

toured the facility, visitors often leave the center with a

new appreciation for the recycling process.

Utilizing a combination of manual and

mechanical technologies, up to 40 tons of material are
                         69

processed at the Center every hour – approximately
      69
half a million tons per year. Newspapers, telephone

books, and containers made of plastic and glass are all

processed with speed and efficiency under its roof. The

only materials, the Center cannot recycle are those
        70
that have been placed incorrectly in recycling bins,

which are dark blue and about eighteen inches high.
                71

Fortunately, this material can be sent to a nearby plant

that converts waste into energy.

67. A.	NO CHANGE
B.	visitors, and they
C.	visitors, but so
D.	visitors, but they might be

68. F.	NO CHANGE
G.	with whom
H.	with which
J.	that

69. A.	NO CHANGE
B.	the Center processes up to 40 tons of material every hour
C.	the Center processing up to 40 tons of material every hour
D.	40 tons of material, and maybe more, are processed at the Center every hour

70. F.	NO CHANGE
G.	materials, the Center,
H.	materials the Center
J.	materials, that the Center

71. A.	NO CHANGE
B.	these being dark blue in color and about eighteen inches high
C.	which are of a dark blue color and about eighteen inches high also
D.	DELETE the underlined phrase

One way that Keystone State MRC has improved its collection volume is to offer single-stream collection, this system allows paper, and plastic items [72] to be placed in one bin. By making the sorting process more easier, this tactic also increases communities' [73] enthusiasm about recycling. As Patel made clear, people have a choice: they can decide whether to put their recyclables in the garbage or in the recycling. [74]

72. F. NO CHANGE
    G. collection. This system allows: paper and plastic
    H. collection, a system that allows paper and plastic
    J. collection, a system that allows: paper and plastic,

73. A. NO CHANGE
    B. more easily
    C. most easily
    D. easier

74. The writer wants to provide a phrase here that will tie the conclusion to the essay's main theme. Which choice most effectively accomplishes that goal?

    F. Everything from tennis balls to car parts has been tossed into a recycling bin and sent to Keystone.
    G. If people are informed about how recycling works, however, they're more likely to participate in the process.
    H. Patel insists that items just need some cleaning to reveal their true value.
    J. It is important to check which items can and cannot be recycled in your area.

Question 75 asks about the passage as whole

---

75. Suppose the writer had wanted to compose an essay persuading people to recycle. Would this essay fulfill that goal?

    A. Yes, because it describes in detail the amount of energy that Keystone saves.
    B. Yes, because single stream collection encourages people to recycle.
    C. No, because the essay primarily describes the writer's experience at the recycling center.
    D. No, because Amir Patel states that people can choose between throwing items away and recycling them.

Answer Key

Preliminary Exercise (p. 11)

1. Pronoun
2. Verb
3. Preposition
4. Verb
5. Conjunction
6. Verb
7. Adverb
8. Adjective (not noun)
9. Adjective
10. Verb
11. Preposition
12. Adjective
13. Verb
14. Noun
15. Pronoun
16. Preposition
17. Adverb
18. Verb
19. Verb
20. Conjunction
21. Adjective
22. Preposition
23. Noun
24. Verb
25. Preposition

Drill 1: Apostrophes (p. 18)

1. its
2. beings, whose
3. their, correct (attempts)
4. correct (their), echoes that identify its
5. their, correct (its)
6. whose, correct (scientists')
7. its traffic jams, city's
8. whose, correct (its)
9. its
10. year's, there

Drill 2: Apostrophes (p. 20)

1.1 B
1.2 H

2.1 D
2.2 H
2.3 B

3.1 A
3.2 G

4.1 C
4.2 H

5.1 D
5.2 F
6.1 B
6.2 F
6.3 C

Is it a Sentence? (p. 22)

1. Sentence

2. Sentence

3. Fragment

4. Fragment

5. Sentence

6. Sentence

7. Sentence

8. Sentence

9. Sentence

10. Fragment

11. Fragment

12. Sentence

13. Sentence

14. Fragment

15. Fragment

16. Sentence

17. Sentence

18. Sentence

Punctuating Sentences and Fragments (p. 34)

1.1 B
1.2 J

2.1 B
2.2 J
2.3 D

3.1 C
3.2 H
3.3 A

4.1 B
4.2 H
4.3 D

5.1 B
5.2 G
5.3 D
5.4 G

Joining and Separating Sentences: Periods, Semicolons, and Comma +FANBOYS (p. 43)

1.1 D
1.2 J

2.1 D
2.2 F

3.1 C
3.2 F

4.1 B
4.2 H

251

5.1 A
5.2 J
5.3 C

6.1 B
6.2 F
7.1 C
7.2 J
7.3 A

8.1 C
8.2 J

9.1 A
9.2 J

10.1 B
10.2 G
10.3 C

Identifying Non-Essential Clauses (p. 52)

1.1 B

2.1 H
2.2 A

3.1 A
3.2 F
3.3 D

4.1 B
4.2 G
4.3 C

5.1 C
5.2 J
5.3 B

Commas with Essential and Non-Essential Clauses (p. 62)

1.1 D
1.2 J

2.1 A
2.2 H

3.1 C
3.2 F
3.3 D
3.4 J

4.1 C
4.2 J
4.3 A

5.1 B
5.2 F
5.3 D
5.4 G
5.5 A

6.1 A
6.2 G

Combined Drill: Periods, Semicolons & Commas (p. 71)

1.1 C
1.2 F
1.3 D
1.4 J
1.5 B

2.1 B
2.2 H
2.3 A
2.4 G
2.5 C

3.1 C
3.2 J
3.3 C
3.4 G
3.5 D

4.1 B
4.2 H
4.3 D
4.4 F
4.5 C
4.6 F
4.7 C

5.1 C
5.2 J

5.3 C
5.4 G
5.5 D
5.6 G
5.7 A
5.8 H

Colons and Dashes (p. 78)

1.1 A
1.2 J
1.3 C

2.1 A
2.2 G
2.3 B

3.1 C
3.2 G
3.3 D

4.1 B
4.2 H
4.3 D
4.4 F

5.1 C
5.2 J
5.3 B
5.4 H

Cumulative Review 1-7 (p. 81)

1.1 B
1.2 J
1.3 C

2.1 B
2.2 F
2.3 B
2.4 H

3.1 B
3.2 G
3.3 A
3.4 J

4.1 C

4.2 F
4.3 B
4.4 H

5.1 C
5.2 J
5.3 C
5.4 J
5.5 D

6.1 D
6.2 H
6.3 D
6.4 G

7.1 A
7.2 J
7.3 D
7.4 G
7.5 C
7.6 F
7.7 D
7.8 H

8.1 B
8.2 J
8.3 B
8.4 J
8.5 A
8.6 G

9.1 D
9.2 J
9.3 C
9.4 F
9.5 B
9.6 G
9.7 B

10.1 C
10.2 J
10.3 C
10.4 J
10.5 B
10.6 F
10.7 B
10.8 J
10.9 C
10.10 G

10.11 A
10.12 H
10.13 B
10.14 J
10.15 D

Verbs: Agreement and Tense (p. 105)

1.1 C
1.2 J
1.3 A
1.4 H

2.1 D
2.2 H
2.3 D
2.4 G

3.1 C
3.2 J
3.3 A
3.4 G
3.5 B
4.1 D
4.2 J
4.3 C
4.4 H
4.5 D

5.1 B
5.2 F
5.3 B
5.4 H
5.5 D

Pronouns: Agreement and Case (p. 117)

1.1 A
1.2 J

2.1 D
2.2 H
2.3 C

3.1 B
3.2 J
3.3 B

3.4 G

4.1 C
4.2 J
4.3 A
4.4 G
4.5 D
4.6 H

5.1 C
5.2 F
5.3 D
5.4 J
5.5 D
5.6 H

Adjective/Adverb Drill (p. 127)

1.1 D

2.1 H

3.1 D
3.2 G

Adjectives, Adverbs, Comparisons, Word Pairs (p. 131)

1.1 B
1.2 H
1.3 A
1.4 J
1.5 B

2.1 C
2.2 F
2.3 D
2.4 G
2.5 A
2.6 H

3.1 B
3.2 H
3.3 D
3.4 J

4.1 C
4.2 F
4.3 B

253

4.4 J
4.5 C

5.1 C
5.2 J
5.3 B
5.4 G
5.5 D
5.6 F

Modification (p. 139)

1.1 B
1.2 F
1.3 C
1.4 J

2.1 C
2.2 B
2.3 C
2.4 F

3.1 D
3.2 G
3.3 D

4.1 B
4.2 J

5.1 C
5.2 D

Parallel Structure (p. 144)

1.1 D
1.2 J

2.1 B
2.2 J
2.3 C

3.1 A
3.2 H

4.1 B
4.2 H

5.1 D
5.2 J

5.3 D
5.4 F

6.1 D
6.2 G
6.3 D
6.4 F
6.5 B

7.1 D
7.2 G
7.3 A
7.4 H
7.5 C

Relative Pronouns (p. 152)

1.1 B
1.2 J
1.3 A

2.1 C
2.2 J
2.3 A
2.4 G
2.5 C

3.1 A
3.2 J
3.3 B
3.4 F
3.5 C
3.6 J
3.7 B
3.8 H

Cumulative Review: Ch. 1-14 (p. 155)

1.1 B
1.2 J
1.3 A

2.1 A
2.2 H
2.3 D
2.4 F

3.1 C

3.2 J
3.3 D
3.4 H

4.1 C
4.2 J
4.3 C
4.4 G

5.1 C
5.2 F
5.3 D
5.4 J
5.5 C
5.6 G
5.7 B
5.8 F
5.9 C

6.1 B
6.2 G
6.3 C
6.4 G
6.5 A
6.6 H
6.7 C
6.8 H
6.9 D
6.10 J

7.1 A
7.2 J
7.3 C
7.4 H
7.5 B
7.6 H
7.7 D
7.8 F
7.9 C

8.1 C
8.2 G
8.3 D
8.4 J
8.5 B
8.6 G
8.7 C
8.8 H
8.9 B

8.10 A

9.1 C
9.2 G
9.3 C
9.4 H
9.5 B
9.6 J
9.7 D
9.8 H
9.9 B
9.10 F
9.11 D
9.12 H

10.1 D
10.2 H
10.3 A
10.4 J
10.5 B
10.6 F
10.7 B
10.8 J
10.9 D
10.10 G
10.11 C
10.12 H
10.13 B
10.14 F
10.15 D

Shorter is Better (p. 170)

1.1 D
1.2 J
1.3 A
1.4 J

2.1 D
2.2 H
2.3 D

3.1 D
3.2 J
3.3 A
3.4 J

Diction and Register (p. 178)

1.1 D
1.2 J
1.3 C
1.4 J

2.1 C
2.2 H
2.3 A
2.4 G

3.1 B
3.2 F
3.3 D
3.4 C
3.5 G

Transitions 1 (p. 186)

1: Contrast, B
2. Cause-and-Effect, B
3. Continue, C
4. Contrast, A
5. Contrast, D
6. Contrast, A
7. Cause-and-Effect, A
8. Contrast, C
9. Cause-and-Effect, D

Transitions 2 (p. 191)

1.1 B

2.1 D

3.1 A

4.1 D

5.1 C

6.1 B

7.1 D
7.2 H
7.3 C

8.1 A

8.2 H

9.1 A
9.2 G

10.1 D
10.2 F

11.1 C
11.2 G
11.3 C
11.4 J

12.1 A
12.2 H
12.3 C

Inserting, Deleting & Replacing Information (p. 209)

1.1 C
1.2 A
1.3 D

2.1 D
2.2 H
2.3 B

3.1 A
3.2 H
3.3 D
3.4 F
3.5 D
3.6 J
3.7 B
3.8 F

Sentence Order (p. 215)

1.1 D

2.1 H

3.1 A

255

Passage I: Cirque du Soleil

1. D: Parallel structure

The first two items in the list consist of single nouns (accordionist, stilt-walker), so the third item must consist of one noun as well. Only (D) fulfills that requirement.

2. G: Apostrophes, comma

Break this question into two parts: you wouldn't say "The Canadian circus famous for it is requirements," so *it's* is incorrect. That eliminates (F) and (J). (H) incorrectly places a comma after a preposition, so you can eliminate it as well. That leaves (G).

3. A: Adjective vs. adverb

Surprising is an adjective, and the adverb *hardly* must be used to modify it. That eliminates (B) and (D). In (C), the adverb *surprisingly* is incorrect because an adjective must be used to modify the noun *choice*. Only (A) correctly uses an adverb to modify an adjective.

4. H: Diction

The key phrase is "enthusiastic response," so you're looking for a word that has a clearly positive connotation, something similar to "motivated." *Allowed, directed,* and *led* all are relatively neutral and do not mean "motivated." Only *inspired* fits the necessary definition and is clearly positive.

5. A: Transition

Start by looking at the sentences before and after the one to be inserted – the correct answer will logically relate to both of them. The sentence before tells us that Laliberté was inspired by P.T. Barnun, the founder of the Barnum & Bailey Circus. The sentence after tells us that he began *producing* arts events in school. So logically, the correct answer will be related to the idea that

Laliberté wanted to be like P.T. Barnum. Only (A) contains that idea; the other answers are off-topic.

6. H: Transition

Start by considering the previous sentence as well as the sentence in which the transition begins. The previous sentence indicates that Laliberté was producing performing arts events at school, and the information after the transition indicates that he became a street performer, so the two sentences contain similar ideas. Both *in contrast* and *otherwise* are used to contradict, so (F) and (G) can be eliminated. Careful with (J): the second sentence is not automatically the result of the first, and there is nothing otherwise to indicate that Laliberté became a street performer because he produced performing arts events in school. (H) is correct because it creates a logical sequence, indicating that Laliberté became a street performer after leaving school.

7. D: Comma

The original version incorrectly places a comma between the items in a compound object. If that's too confusing, think of it this way: *comma + and =* period. If you replace *comma + and* with a period in the sentence, you end up with a fragment for the second sentence ("Accordion on the streets of Quebec.") (A) can thus be eliminated. (B) incorrectly places a comma before a preposition (*on*), and (C) incorrectly places a comma after *and*. No punctuation is necessary, so (D) is correct.

8. G: Comma splice, fragment, tense

The original version incorrectly places a comma between two sentences (comma splice). (H) incorrectly places a semicolon between a complete sentence and a fragment. (J) creates an unnecessary tense switch: the passage is written in the past tense, but *will* indicates future. (G) correctly uses the relative pronoun *where* to refer to Quebec and places a comma between an independent and a dependent clause.

9. C: Non-essential clause

However is used non-essentially here because the sentence still makes grammatical sense when that word is crossed out. Commas must be used before and after, and (C) is the only option that provides that construction.

10. J: Diction, idiom

Seized, grabbed, and *jumped at the opportunity* are all idiomatically acceptable ways of saying "take advantage of the opportunity." Only *held* is idiomatically incorrect.

11. D: Non-essential clause/comma around a name

Entrepreneur is used as an adjective that modifies *Gilles Ste.-Croix*, and commas should not be placed between adjectives and the nouns they modify. That eliminates (A). In (B), the two commas around the name would indicate that it is not essential to the meaning of the sentence, but the sentence no longer makes sense when it is removed. (C) incorrectly places a comma between the items in a compound object. No punctuation around the name is necessary, so (D) is correct.

12. H: Non-essential clause

Since the sentence still make sense if the clause "which Laliberté came up with while on vacation in Hawaii" is removed, the clause is non-essential. (G) is incorrect because the end of the non-essential clause is marked by a comma rather than a dash, and (J) is incorrect because it creates a fragment. Only (H) correctly places a comma at the start of the non-essential clause.

Shortcut: *which* must always follow a comma.

13. D: Redundancy

The words *at first* appear later on in the sentence, so the inclusion of a synonym here creates a redundancy.

14. G: Subject verb agreement

The subject of the plural verb *employ* is the singular noun *circus*, so the singular verb *employs* (don't forget that singular verbs have an *–s*) is required. Don't be fooled by the plural noun *continents*, which is part of the non-essential clause between the subject and the verb.

15. B: Comma, semicolon, colon, dash

In the original version, the colon signals an explanation (it makes clear the way in which Cirque du Soleil is unique) and separates two independent clauses. When a colon is used to set off an explanation, it is interchangeable with a dash, so (A) is fine. In (C) and (D), the semicolon and period are interchangeable, so neither answer can be wrong. (B) incorrectly uses a comma to separate two sentences (comma splice) and is therefore incorrect. Since the question asks you to find the unacceptable answer, (B) is correct.

Passage II: Modular Buildings

16. J: Comma

No comma should be used before, or before and after, an emphatic pronoun (*himself, herself, themselves,* etc.). Only (J) correctly omits any punctuation.

17. B: Comma splice

The original version uses a comma to separate two complete sentences. (C) creates a run-on because there is no comma before the FANBOYS conjunction *and*, and (D) creates a fused sentence. (B) correctly uses a semicolon to separate the two sentences.

18. H: Colon, comma

Although a colon can be used to set off a list, it must follow a complete sentence that makes logical sense on its own, and "Modular buildings may be used for temporary or permanent facilities such as" does not fulfill that requirement. (F) can thus be eliminated. (G) incorrectly alternates commas and semicolons between the items in the list, and when plugged into the sentence, (J) fails to place a comma between two items in the list (*classrooms, apartment buildings*). Only (H) correctly omits the colon before the list and provides consistent punctuation between the list items.

19. B: Pronoun agreement

The underlined pronoun refers to the plural noun *modular buildings* and must therefore be plural. Both (A), (C), and (D) all contain singular pronouns (*one, it*) and can be eliminated. Only (B) uses the plural pronoun *they*.

20. J: Redundancy (shorter is better)

Typical and *conventional* are synonyms, so only one of the words is necessary.

21. B: Verb tense

The gerund *being* in the original version creates a fragment, eliminating (A), and the gerund *having* creates the same problem in (D). Furthermore, the date 2010 indicates that the sentence is describing an action in the past, so a verb in the past is required. That eliminates (C), leaving (B), which correctly uses the past tense verb *were*.

22. G: Comma

No comma should be used before or after a preposition (*on*), so (F) and (H) can be eliminated. In (J), the period creates two fragments. Only (G) correctly omits any punctuation.

23. C: Subject verb agreement

The subject is the singular noun *construction*, which requires a singular verb. *Take* and *have* are both plural, eliminating (A) and (B). In (D), the gerund *taking* creates a fragment. Only (C) does not create a subject verb disagreement. (Note, however, that *can* is irregular in that its singular and plural forms are identical.)

24. H: Sentence order

What does Sentence 5 talk about? It describes what happens after the walls are in place. So logically, it must belong right after a sentence about the construction of the walls. Where is that discussed? In Sentence 2. So Sentence 5 belongs right after it, and the answer must be (H).

25. A: Verb tense (gerund vs. infinitive)

The infinitive (*to supervise*) rather than the gerund (*in/for supervising*) is necessary after the verb *required*, eliminating (B) and (C). (D) creates a fused sentence and can be eliminated as well.

26. J: Redundancy

The phrase *throughout the entire process* appears at the beginning of the sentence, making its repetition unnecessary. Be careful with the page turn, though; when a sentence runs onto a new page, it's very easy to miss important information if you don't look back.

27. C: Adjective vs. adverb

An adverb is necessary to modify the adjective *complete*, eliminating (A) and (B). (D) is incorrect because *complete* must be an adjective – you cannot say "When the modules are *completely*." (C) correctly uses the adverb *finally* to modify the adjective *complete*.

28. H: Dangling modifier

Who is using a crane? Workers. So *workers*, the subject, must come after the comma. Since it does not, however, the modifier is dangling, and (F) is incorrect. (G) creates a comma splice, and (J) creates a fragment when plugged back into the sentence. (H) eliminates the dangling modification and correctly places the word *foundation* before *where*.

29. C: Diction/register

The overall tone of the passage is moderately serious, and both (A) and (B) are too casual. Both those answers and (D) are inconsistent with the idea that the modules are constructed methodically and carefully. Only *placed* fits with that context.

30. J: Passage goal

Start by thinking about the main focus of the passage: modular buildings, and how they're constructed. We know that modular buildings are the focus because they're the sole topic of both the first and last paragraph, and because the word *modules* appears repeatedly throughout the passage. The passage does state that modular buildings can sometimes be used when traditional buildings can't, but that idea is restricted to a single sentence. In addition, the passage never specifically discuss how traditional buildings are built. That makes (J) the only possible answer.

Passage III: The Golden Spike

31. B: Verb tense

The phrase *by early 1869* is a tip-off that the past perfect (*had + past participle*) is required, making (B) the only possibility.

32. J: Non-essential clause

The sentence still makes grammatical sense when the clause *which stretched for 1,907 miles* is crossed out, so a comma is required both before and after it. That eliminates (F) and (H). In (G), the FANBOYS conjunction *and* should never be used after a semicolon. That leaves (J), which correctly places a comma at the end of the non-essential clause and does not include any unnecessary punctuation.

33. B: Colon, fragment

In the original version, the second clause is a fragment. Since a period and a semicolon are grammatically identical, both (A) and (C) can be eliminated. (D) can be eliminated because it creates

an extremely awkward construction and does not make sense. (B) correctly uses a colon to set off the list/explanation of the two railroad companies. Remember that a colon does not have to come before a full sentence, only after one.

34. F: Comma/FANBOYS, non-essential clause

The original version correctly uses *comma + and* to separate two complete sentences and later uses two commas to indicate that the name *Ulysses S. Grant* is non-essential – if it is crossed out, the sentence still makes sense. (G) is incorrect because it does not include a comma after *Grant*; (H) is incorrect because it creates a fragment; and (J) is incorrect because it places a semicolon between two fragments.

35. C: Diction

The sentence indicates that the underlined word is the result of "some debate." Logically, the companies must have agreed because "telegraph cables were sent out" to announce the railroad's completion. *Expanded* (made larger) and *wondered about* do not make sense, and *confirmed that* is grammatically unacceptable when plugged back into the sentence.

36. A: Correct emphasis

The key phrase in the question is *as soon as* – that tells you you're looking for a word that means "right away." That is the definition of *immediately*, so (A) is correct. *Eventually* and *ultimately* both imply that it took a while for the news to be sent, and *reluctantly* means "unwillingly," which is also the opposite of the correct idea.

37. C: Transition

The following sentence states that Hewes was "disappointed," so you're looking for a sentence that introduces that idea. (C) fits because *not happy* and *disappointed* convey similar ideas. In addition, that answer presents a contrast with the previous sentence, which states that newspapers "*proudly* displayed the news." None of the other answers has a clear connection to either sentence.

38. J: Comma: no "that" = no comma

The underlined portion can be written two ways: "*Hewes…was disappointed to discover no one had prepared an item…*" and "*Hewes…was disappointed to discover that no one had prepared an item…*" When the word *that* is optional and does not appear, no comma should be used in its place. (G) is incorrect because the colon is not preceded by a stand-alone sentence, and (H) is incorrect because *that* should not be followed by a comma. (J) correctly omits any unnecessary punctuation.

39. B: sentence division, comma splice

The original version places a comma between two complete sentences and creates an illogical division between those sentences. The correct version creates a new sentence at a more logical point and correctly places a comma between a dependent clause (*Using $400 of his own money*) and an independent clause (*he had a golden spike cast*). (C) creates a comma splice between *practical* and *using*, and although the semicolon in (D) correctly divides the sentences in the proper place, it creates a fragment by placing *and* after the comma.

40. F: Deleting information

What information does the sentence in question provide? It gives exact numbers (5 5/8, 14.03, 17.6) that describe the spike's length, weight, and purity – i.e. its physical characteristics. If it were deleted, that information would be lost. So the answer is (F).

41. C: Apostrophe, pronoun

Its' does not exist, so (A) can be eliminated immediately. You also wouldn't say *It is top was engraved…*, so (B) can be eliminated as well. In (D), *there* refers to a place and makes no sense in context. (C) is correct because *its* is the possessive form of *it*.

42. J: Transition/logical relationship

Consider the two halves of the sentence without the transition. 1) The ceremony was originally scheduled for May 8th. 2) Poor weather forced it to be rescheduled. Those statements are expressing contrasting ideas, so you need a contradictor: *but*. Both *so* and *since* are used to express cause and effect, eliminating (F) and (G), and *if* makes no sense in context.

43. B: Register

The overall tone of the passage is moderately serious, but the language is straightforward and not overly sophisticated. The use of high level vocabulary such as *arduous* and *verbose* is therefore inconsistent with the passage as a whole. At the other extreme, *mind numbing* and *totally boring* are both excessively casual. Only *dull and lengthy* fits the prevailing register.

44. G: Comma between adjectives

When two adjectives are separated by *but* or *yet*, no comma should be used to separate them, eliminating (F). (H) and (J) incorrectly mix adjectives and adverbs – both words modify the noun *swing*, so two adjectives are needed. (G) correctly uses two adjectives and omits unnecessary punctuation.

45. A: Inserting information

Since the question is asking you about how to end the essay, you need to consider the entire conclusion before deciding whether the sentence should be inserted. What is the paragraph about? It consists of a detailed description of the golden spike ceremony and indicates that Stanford was unable to drive the spike in himself. What is the sentence about? How a railroad worker drove in the spike and completed the railroad. The sentence should therefore be added because it explains what happened after Stanford missed the spike and provides a logical conclusion to the passage, which focuses on the events leading up to the railroad's completion.

Passage IV: Celebrating Tet

46. J: Deleting information

Although this question appears at the end of the first sentence, you must read the rest of the paragraph to establish context. What is the rest of the paragraph about? The fact that the writer's family came from Vietnam and that they still celebrate New Year's the way they did when they were living in Vietnam. If you read further, you can see that the writer is clearly focusing on Vietnamese New Year's. The phrase should therefore remain in the essay because it makes clear from the start that the writer is talking about Vietnamese New Year's, and the information is not explicitly stated elsewhere.

47. C: Dash

The beginning of the non-essential clause is set off with a dash, so the end of the clause must be set off with a dash as well.

48. G: Comma splice, sentence vs. fragment

The original version places a comma between two complete sentences. In (H), the gerund *lasting* turns the second clause into a fragment, and a semicolon can only be used between two complete sentences. (J) is grammatically correct, but the transition is unnecessary and creates an illogical relationship between the clauses. (G) correctly uses *comma + and* to join two complete sentences.

49. A: Correct emphasis

The key phrase in the question is *connection between throwing things out…and bad luck*, so you're looking for an answer that suggests that people who throw things away on Tet will have bad luck. Having one's fortune thrown away is consistent with the idea of "bad luck," so (A) is correct. The other answers have nothing to do with that focus.

50. G: Verb tense, comma splice

The original version contains an unnecessary tense switch: the surrounding sentences are in the

present, making the past perfect (*had put*) incorrect. (H) is incorrect because it creates a comma splice, and (J) is incorrect because the verbs are not parallel (*make…putting*). (G) is correct because the singular verb *puts* agrees with the singular noun *sound*, and *that* is correctly used without a comma before or after.

51. C: Deleting information

Make sure you pay careful attention to the question being asked: it's not about the sentence as a whole, only the specific words *new* and *freshly printed*. The writer mentions in the previous sentence that old things are put away. *New* and *freshly printed* therefore serve to reinforce that idea. In (A), it's true that the writer enjoyed the ritual, but the entire description wouldn't be lost if those words were deleted. (B) is simply incorrect; those words serve to continue the idea in the preceding sentence, so yes, they have a clear purpose. (D) might sound plausible, but the words in question simply emphasize the importance of new things on Tet – there's no actual comparison between Tet and any other day.

52. H: Correct emphasis

Blaring means "playing very loudly." None of the other words has that definition.

53. B: Replacing information

The fact that the majority of the passage is written in the present tense indicates that the writer still eagerly participates in Tet rituals. In fact, the entire passage is about how much the writer enjoys Tet. (B) is the answer most consistent with that idea. (A) indicates the opposite, and (C) and (D) are both off topic.

54. G: Adding information

The sentence to be added contains a lot of adjectives (*bright, shiny, red, tall*), indicating that it's providing a very specific description. Since it can be reasonably assumed that most readers won't know what a Tet shrine looks like, the sentence should logically be added. (F) is the opposite of what the passage says (*Like most Vietnamese families*…), (H) is incorrect because the writer only mentions that many different kinds of foods are cooked, and (J) is incorrect because the sentence is clearly linked to the previous sentence and adds to the overall description of the Tet celebration.

55. C: Pronoun consistency

The sentence starts out using the pronoun *you*; that pronoun should remain consistent throughout the sentence.

56. H: Idiom/preposition

The idiomatic expression is *blamed for*. Any other preposition is incorrect.

57. D: Transition

Consider the information before and after the transition. Before, the passage indicates that visiting people on Tet is not a good idea because visitors can be blamed for those people's misfortune. After, the passage indicates that the writer's family stayed home. Logically, the writer's family's choice to stay home is a **result** of the fact that they don't want to be blamed for bringing bad luck. *Consequently* is the only choice that conveys that cause/effect relationship.

58. G: Apostrophe

It can be reasonably assumed that the writer only had one father; since (F) and (H) are plural, they can be eliminated immediately. Second, the noun *father* is possessive – the stories belonged to the father. The possessive of a singular noun is formed by adding *apostrophe* + –*s* to that noun, so (G) is correct. (J) does not exist.

59. A: Adding information, main idea

What's the passage about? How much the writer loves Tet because it provides a link to his/her culture. Although the writer does mention other people, the focus is squarely on him/her. The correct answer must therefore have something to do with the writer. That eliminates (C) and (D). (B) is about the writer but has nothing to do with Tet,

leaving (A), which effectively includes the passage's main idea.

60. H: Passage organization

Paragraph 5 discusses what happens on the *first day* of Tet, so logically it belongs before a discussion of what happens on later days. Paragraph 1 discusses the preparations for Tet, and Paragraph 3 opens with the phrase *Only on the second and third days*, so logically Paragraph 5 belongs between them, i.e. before Paragraph 3.

Passage V: Bicycle Shares

61. C: Relative pronoun

Where should only be used to refer to places (physical locations), and a system is not a place. (B) creates an ungrammatical construction, and in (D), *when* should only be used for times/time periods. Because it is correct to say that something occurs in a system, *in which* is grammatically acceptable.

62. H: Fragment

In the original version, a period is incorrectly used to separate an independent and a dependent clause. (J) can be eliminated for the same reason. (You can also eliminate both answers immediately based on the fact that they are grammatically identical – there can't be more than one correct answer, so two identical answers must both be wrong.) (G) creates a run-on sentence; and (H) is correct because it separates an independent from a dependent clause with a comma.

63. D: Shorter is better

All of the answers express the same information, but (D) is the shortest and simplest.

64. G: Transition/logical relationship

Consider the two halves of the sentence without the transition. 1) The first bike share didn't last very long. 2) It served as an inspiration to cities around the world. Those are contrasting ideas, so a contradictor is required. In (F), *since* is used to indicate a cause/effect relationship; in (H), *despite* creates an ungrammatical construction when it is plugged into the sentence; and in (J), *when* is used to refer to the time an event occurred. (G) creates the correct logical relationship by placing the contradictor *although* between the two parts of the sentences.

65. D: Redundancy

Short-lived means "not lasting very long," so it is unnecessary to repeat that information.

66. J: Correct emphasis

The key phrase is remarkable growth, so the correct answer must emphasize the extent to which bike shares have grown. Only (J) accomplishes that goal effectively, by providing specific (large) figures to support the idea that bike shares have become very popular.

67. D: Diction/idiom

The idiomatic phrase is *participate in*. Any other preposition is incorrect.

68. G: Who vs. whom

Who, not *whom*, should be used before a verb (want), eliminating (F). Although *which* can correctly be used before a verb, it cannot be used to refer to people (city residents). In (H), *which* should be used for things, not people; and in (J), *for who* creates an ungrammatical construction when plugged into the sentence.

69. B: Diction: of vs. have

Would of, *could of*, and *might of* do not exist; the correct word is *have*. (B) is the only option that does not create this error.

70. H: Diction

Permit, *allow*, and *help* can all function as synonyms for enable and make grammatical sense when plugged into the sentence. In (H), create is not a synonym for enable and creates an ungrammatical construction.

71. A: comma, semicolon, dividing sentences

(A) incorrectly places a semicolon before the FANBOYS conjunction and. (B) correctly uses a period to separate two sentences; (C) correctly omits the comma before and because the subject is not repeated in the second clause; and (D) correctly uses a comma to separate an independent and a dependent clause.

72. J: Comparison, adjective vs. adverb

Than, not *then*, should be used in a comparison, eliminating (F). In (G), *than* rather than *as* should be used with the comparative form of the adjective *cheaper*; in (H), an adjective (*cheaper*) rather than an adverb (*cheaply*) must modify the noun *rental*. (J) forms the comparison correctly by pairing the adjective *cheaper* with the word *than*.

73. C: Correct emphasis

The key phrase is *easier to use*, so the correct answer must be related to the idea of making bike shares easier for riders to use. *Facilitate* means "make easier," so (C) is correct. None of the other answers expresses that idea.

74. G: Modification

Although the original placement of the word might sound ok, it actually creates a logic problem: the sentence states that the information is *important for current riders as well*. If it's important for them "as well," it can't be important "only" for them. The sentence makes far more sense if *only* is placed before *be*. This placement explains why "this information" (knowing how many bikes are available at each station) is important to current riders: if a bike can only be returned to a station with a free dock, riders need to know which stations have free docks – otherwise, they can't return their bikes.

75. C: Inserting information

The easiest way to approach this question is to determine where in the passage the idea of stolen bicycles is mentioned. That occurs in Paragraph 3, sentence 2, so the sentence in question should be inserted next to that sentence. Logically, it should be placed afterward because it expands on the idea of "concern" and provides a reason why riders are correct to worry about having their bikes stolen.

Test 2 (p. 236)

Passage I: New York City Public Library

1. D: Comparative, superlative

Either *adjective* + *–er/est* or *more/most* + *adjective* should be used, not both. That eliminates both (A) and (B). (C) is incorrect because an adverb (*largely*) cannot modify a noun (*cities*). (D) correctly forms the superlative *largest* and uses it to modify *cities*.

2. H: Pronoun

It is incorrect to say *Among it is inhabitants*, so (F) can be eliminated. Instead, the possessive *its* should be used. (G) contains errors in both pronoun agreement (*New York* = singular, *they* = plural) and in formation (*they're* = they are). In (J), *there* does not agree with *New York*, nor is it possessive.

3. B: Who vs. whom

Who, not *whom*, should be used before a verb. In (C), *which* can only be used to refer to a thing, not a person; and in (D), the placement of *he* after the comma creates a comma splice.

4. J: Verb form

The past participle *chosen* rather than the simple past *chose* must be used to modify *site*. In (G), the infinitive *to choose* is grammatically unacceptable, and in (H), the gerund *having* creates a fragment.

5. C: Transition

The following paragraph begins by mentioning Billings but does not explain who he is. In order for that information to make sense, he must be introduced in the previous sentence. Thus, (C) is the only possibility.

6. F: Non-essential clause

When the clause *first sketched on a scrap of paper* is removed, the sentence still makes sense. The original version correctly uses two commas to set off the non-essential clause. In (G), the comma after *blueprint* incorrectly places a comma before the preposition *for*; (H) contains the same problem and incorrectly places the non-essential clause; and (J) mixes a dash and a comma.

7. C: Replacing information

The word *although* indicates that the two parts of the sentence will express contrasting ideas. The first half of the sentence indicates that "some of the city's most prominent firms" wanted to build the library, so the second half must logically express the idea that Carrère and Hastings was **not** a prominent firm. *Relatively obscure* expresses that idea, so (C) is correct. Even though (A) and (B) might sound ok when plugged into the sentence, both *well known* and *extremely famous* are synonyms for *prominent*, creating an illogical relationship. Likewise in (D), if the adjective is removed, the contrast is also lost.

8. G: Non-essential word, comma

Because the sentence would still makes sense if *however* were removed, the word is being used non-essentially and must be surrounded by commas. Only (G) contains that construction.

9. B: Correct emphasis, connotation

The key phrase is *one piece at a time*, so the correct answer must have the connotation of taking apart something slowly and deliberately. Of the choices, only *dismantling* carries that connotation; the others imply a single act of complete destruction.

10. J: Comma, adjective vs. adverb

The verb *progressed* is being modified, so two adverbs are required. That eliminates (F) and (H). In (H), *comma + but* = period, but there are not two sentences. (J) is correct because it omits the comma.

11. A: Verb tense

The phrase *by the time* is a tip off that the past perfect (*had + past participle*) is required, making (A) the only option. The other answers contain additional errors as well: (B) because the plural verb *have* and the singular subject *work* disagree; (C) because the past participle *begun* must be used after any form of *to have*; and (D) because the past participle *begun* cannot stand on its own but must follow a form of *to be* or *to have*.

12. F: Deleting information

The adjectives in question are used to emphasize how *large* something is. Large = magnitude, so (F) is correct.

13. D: Fragment/gerund, tense

In the original version, the gerund *being* creates a fragment. In (B), *having* creates the same problem as (A); (C) creates an unnecessary tense switch and uses the past conditional where the simple past is required; and (D) correctly conjugates the verb and puts it in the correct tense.

14. H: Dividing sentences, comma splice

Although the sentences could be divided as they are in the original version, the comma after *a.m.* creates a comma splice; (G) incorrectly places a semicolon between a sentence and a fragment; and in (J), the comma after *morning* creates a comma splice. (H) correctly uses a period to separate two complete sentences.

15. C: Writer's goal

Think about the scope of the question vs. the passage. The question is specific: it asks whether the passage focuses on one event: the opening of the library. While the passage *mentions* this event, that mention is pretty much confined to the last paragraph. The majority of the passage talks about the background and construction of the library, making (C) the correct response.

Passage II: Creek Garden

16. G: Correct emphasis

The key phrase is *miraculous effect*, so the correct answer must be related to that idea. *Magic* is the only word in any of the answers that has a similar meaning, so (G) is correct.

17. B: Inserting information

The writer does not provide any specific examples of ways that Creek gardening methods could "revolutionize agriculture" but instead moves the discussion to his/her own experience planting a Creek-style garden.

18. H: Verb tense, diction

The surrounding sentences are in the simple past, so this sentence should be in the simple past as well. *Lie* is present tense, so (G) can be eliminated, and in (J), the gerund *laying* creates a fragment. Even if you're confused about *lie* vs. *lay*, you can still figure it out grammatically. Only past participles end in *–n*, and a past participle has to come after a form of *to be* or *to have* – it can't stand by itself. So (F) has to be incorrect. That leaves (H), which correctly uses the simple past of *lay*.

19. C: Parallel structure, shorter is better

The construction of the sentence before and after the conjunction *and* must match. The non-underlined portion of the sentence starts with a simple past verb (*planted*) so the underlined portion must start with one as well (*arranged*). Furthermore, the original version is a run-on because there are two complete sentences but no comma before *and*. (C) corrects both problems.

20. F: Non-essential clause

This is the very rare exception in which it is necessary to place a comma before a preposition. The comma before *including* signals the start of a non-essential clause, without which the sentence would still make sense (*My grandmother threw leftover food…into the garden*). As a result, a comma should be placed after *eggshells* to mark the end of the non-essential clause.

21. B: Misplaced modifier

The original version implies that the writer's house was originally used as a chicken coop. (C) and (D) both correct this error but contain wordy, awkward, and passive constructions. (B) corrects the original error and is the shortest and clearest answer.

22. J: Shorter is better

Sprinkle and *dust lightly* are synonyms, so it is unnecessary to use both.

23. B: Paragraph division

In the original version, the paragraph has two different focuses. It describes how the writer's grandparents followed the traditional Creek layout, and it describes how the writer's garden was modeled after that of his/her grandparents. Splitting the paragraph at (E) creates a logical division between the description of the grandparents' garden and the description of the writer's garden.

24. F: List

The original version correctly places a comma after each item in the list. In (G), the colon is incorrect because it is not preceded by a stand-alone sentence; in (H), a comma is incorrectly placed after *and*; and in (J), the comma is incorrectly omitted between *squash* and *spinach*.

25. D: Transition/logical relationship

Consider the two parts of the sentence without the transition. 1) The vegetables were planted densely. 2) The vegetables shaded the surrounding areas. Logically, the second part is the **result** of the first, so you need a transition that indicates cause and effect. Only *because* creates that relationship. *Just as* is used to indicate a similarity between two things, and *while* and *whereas* are both contradictors.

26. H: Adjective vs. adverb

How were the vegetables planted? Dense*ly*. So an adverb is required. That eliminates (F) and (J). Only an adverb can modify another adverb, so *relatively* must be used, making (H) the answer.

27. B: Comma splice, joining sentences

In (B), the comma before *they* create a comma splice. (A) correctly uses a comma to separate a complete sentence and a fragment; (C) correctly places a semicolon between two complete sentences; and (D) correctly uses *that* without any punctuation to join the two sentences.

28. J: Diction, have vs. of

Might have = right, *might of* = wrong, eliminating (F) and (G). (H) is incorrect because the past participle *eaten* rather than the simple past *ate* must be used after a form of the verb *to have*.

29. A: Diction

Although *magnifying* means "making larger," it does not fit grammatically into the sentence. An object can *be magnified* (e.g. the bacteria were magnified by the microscope) or it can *magnify something else* (e.g. the microscope magnified the bacteria), but it cannot simply *magnify*.

30. J: Word pair

Not only must be paired with *but*, making (J) the only option.

Passage III: John Cage: Revolutionizing Music

31. D: Gerund vs. infinitive

Proceeded should be followed by the infinitive (*to do*) rather than the gerund (*doing*). Any other construction is idiomatically incorrect.

32. H: Parallel structure

The other items in the list all end in *–ing*, so the underlined item must end in *–ing* as well. Only (H) contains that construction.

33. C: Correct emphasis

The key phrase is *sharp break*, so the correct answer must contain that idea. That is the definition of *rupture*, so (C) is correct. *Eluded* mean "evaded," *drifted* implies a slow movement, and *condescended to* means "talked down to."

34. H: Parallel structure

The prepositions on either side of the conjunction *but* must match. Since *about* is used on the non-underlined side, it must be used on the other side as well (musical performance is not <u>about</u> creating sound, but it is <u>about</u> listening).

35. B: Comma with name

Because the sentence does not make sense if *Arnold Schoenberg* is removed, the name is not used non-essentially and should not be set off by commas. (B) and (C) correctly omit any punctuation around the name, but when plugged in, (C) incorrectly places a comma before the preposition *at*.

36. F: Comma with independent and dependent clauses

The original version correctly places a comma between a dependent clause, set off by a subordinating conjunction (*While studying with classical composer Arnold Schoenberg at the University of California, Los Angeles in the 1930s*) and an independent clause (*Cage realized he wanted to invent a new type of music, one that was completely different from that*

of his time). Although both clauses are quite long, it is important to understand that long does not equal run-on. (G) incorrectly places a semicolon between an independent and a dependent clause; (H) creates a non-essential clause that results in an ungrammatical construction when it is removed from the sentence; and in (J), *comma + and =* period, and a period cannot separate a dependent from an independent clause.

37. C: Replacing information

Think about what the sentence is saying: logically, Schoenberg *discouraged* his pupil because he didn't think Cage would be successful, so the right answer must convey that idea. (A) and (D) are therefore exactly the opposite of what you want, and (B) is off-topic. In (C), finding oneself at an impasse means getting stuck, which would be a logical reason for Schoenberg to have discouraged Cage.

38. H: Apostrophe

Since it can be overwhelming to try to deal with both words as once, start with one word. How many teachers are discussed? One. So any answer with *–s* or *–s + apostrophe* at the end of *teacher* is wrong. That eliminates (F) and (G). Now look at the other word: is *Cage* singular or plural? Singular. So that eliminates (J) and leaves (H), which correctly makes both nouns singular and possessive by adding *apostrophe + –s*.

39. D: Word pair

As must be paired with *as*, making (D) the only possible answer.

40. F: Comma + FANBOYS

Comma + but = period, but when a period is plugged into the sentence, it turns the second clause into a fragment (*could reflect the sounds of everyday life*). (G) and (H) can thus be eliminated. (J) is incorrect because a semicolon should never come before a FANBOYS conjunction. No punctuation is needed, making (F) correct.

41. A: Transition

Be careful with the wording of this question. Although it appears to ask about both the previous paragraph and the paragraph that the transition begins, the information you need is only in the latter, particularly in the sentence following the transition. In that sentence, the word *however* indicates that it must provide information that contrasts with the information provided in the first sentence. Since the second sentence states that Cage *started to reimagine the very idea of an instrument*, the first sentence must contain the idea that Cage worked with traditional instruments earlier on. And that's pretty much what (A) says.

42. J: Transition

This question is potentially difficult because even though the transition occurs in the middle of the sentence, it is used to indicate the relationship between the sentence in question and the *previous* sentence. How do you know that? There's no obvious relationship between the information before and after the transition within the sentence, and there's also no option to remove the transition. So it has to connect to a different sentence. What information does the previous sentence provide? Essentially, that Cage invented new instruments. What information does the sentence in question provide? That Cage created a piece that involved twelve radios. Because Cage was using those radios as "instruments," that sentence logically provides an **example** of what the writer means by *reimagining the very idea of an instrument*. So *for example* indicates the correct relationship, making (J) correct.

43. A: Diction

Logically, the objects would make a sound when they hit against one another. That is the definition of *jostling*, so (A) is correct. Neither (B) nor (D) fit grammatically – things mingle *with* one another, and slip *past* one another. Although *repelling* fits grammatically, it does not clearly fit logically the same way *jostling* does. The fact that you might think *jostling* sounds weird is irrelevant. Meaning counts, not sound.

44. H: Pronoun agreement

The underlined pronoun refers to John Cage, who is a singular male. *His* is therefore correct.

45. B: Comma, verb tense

The original version incorrectly places a comma between the complete subject (*His belief that music could be everywhere and made from anything*) and the verb (*brought*). Both (C) and (D) contain unnecessary tense switches: the surrounding verbs are in the simple past, so the verb in question should be in the simple past as well. (B) keeps the tense consistent and eliminates the unnecessary comma between subject and verb.

Passage IV: Rebecca Lee Crumpler

46. G: Subject verb agreement

The original version contains a singular subject (*education*) paired with a plural verb (*were*); the plural noun *women* is part of the prepositional phrase between the subject and the verb. The verb must be singular and in the simple past in order to keep the tense consistent, making (G) the only option.

47. B: Comma with parentheses

No comma should be used before an open parenthesis, eliminating (A) and (C). (D) uses a period to incorrectly separate a dependent and an independent clause, leaving (B), which correctly places a comma only after the close parenthesis to separate the dependent clause from the independent clause.

48. J: Pronoun, ambiguous antecedent

Since passage alludes to "two women" in the previous sentence, it is unclear which of the women *she* refers to. (J) is the only answer that specifies which woman the writer is referring to.

49. D: Shorter is better

All of the answer express the same information, but (D) does so in the shortest and clearest manner.

50. H: Non-essential clause

Although the wording of the original version may be confusing, this is actually a relatively straightforward non-essential clause question. When the second comma is added after *wrote* and the clause removed, the sentence still makes perfect sense (*Watching her aunt inspired her to work in a field that would "relieve the sufferings of others"*). The correct way to fix the sentence is to add the second comma, making (H) correct. (G) and (J) are grammatically identical and can eliminated on that basis alone since no question can have more than one correct answer.

51. B: Misplaced modifier

The original version uses *where* to modify a time (1852), when *where* should only be used to refer to a place (Charlestown). In (B), *where* correctly modifies *Charlestown*. Both (C) and (D) create ungrammatical constructions when plugged back into the sentence.

52. F: Inserting information

Think about the sentence in context of the paragraph and passage as whole. The paragraph indicates that Crumpler was admitted to medical school at a time when most people of her race and sex were denied access to medical education. Furthermore, the passage later states that she was the only African American woman to graduate from New England Female Medical College. The passage therefore establishes that Crumpler faced – and overcame – significant obstacles, and the presence of a sentence indicating that Crumpler not only became an excellent nurse but acquired her skills on the job emphasizes that idea.

53. D: Transition

Consider the sentence in question and the previous sentence without the transition. 1) Crumpler's colleagues recommended her for admission to medical school because they were impressed by her skills. 2) Crumpler's admission was unusual. Those are two contradictory ideas: normally, if a candidate came highly recommended, it would be normal for her to be accepted. So *thus* is the opposite of what you want. *Likewise* and *moreover* indicate similarity, so neither makes sense. That only leaves (D), which you can choose by default even if you're not sure what *even so* means. The expression means *despite this*, which correctly indicates a contrasting relationship.

54. G: Comma with list

No comma should be placed between an adjective (*medical*) and the noun it modifies (*advice*), so (F) is incorrect. When plugged into the sentence, (H) and (J) incorrectly place a comma before the preposition *for*, leaving (G), which uses the adjective *practical* to modify the *adjective/noun* combination *medical advice*.

55. A: Inserting information

In order to figure out which choice is most relevant, you need to look at the context, so back up and read the previous sentence. It states that Crumpler's book earned her a place in history, so logically, the sentence to be inserted must explain why the book was so important. Only (A) provides a clear reason, one that fits with the passage's overall emphasis on Crumpler's role as a pioneer.

56. H: Diction

The sentence indicates that Crumpler began medical school in 1860 but did not finish until 1864 because the Civil War _____ her class. Logically, the word in question must mean something like "stopped." *Interrupted* comes closest to that definition, and none of the other words, although similar, have the correct connotation. *Expelled* means "kicked out," *excluded* means "not allowed to participate in," and *revoked* means "took back."

57. B: Word pair

Neither must be paired with *nor*. Any other word is incorrect.

58. J: Many vs. much

"Achievements" can be counted, so *many* rather than *much* should be used. *Too much* and *more than* do not make sense in context.

59. C: Joining sentences

(A) correctly places a comma between an independent and a dependent clause; (B) correctly places a semicolon between two independent clauses; and (D) correctly uses a dash to join a pair of independent clauses in which the second clause expands on the first. (C) is grammatically incorrect because it turns the second "sentence" into a fragment.

60. H: Paragraph order

Paragraph 4 describes Crumpler's experience in medical school in the early 1860s. Logically, this information must come after the description of her experience as a nurse in the 1850s (Paragraph 2) and her return to Boston in 1865 (Paragraph 3).

Passage V: Visit to the Recycling Plant

61. C: Comma

Comma + and = period, and plugging a period into the sentence creates two fragments. (B) incorrectly places a comma between a verb (*encourage*) and its direct object (*recycling*), and (D) is incorrect because *and* should not be used non-essentially and because no punctuation is necessary when only two items are listed in a parallel construction.

62. H: Comma splice

The original version creates a comma splice (as indicated by *comma + it*); (G) turns the second "sentence" into a fragment; and (J) creates a nonsensical construction when plugged back into the sentence.

63. A: Inserting information

The key words are *specific* and *positive effect*. As a shortcut, the precise figure "372,000" indicates that (A) is indeed very specific, and upon closer inspection, the information that recycling facilities save that much landfill space is consistent with having a "positive effect" on the environment. None of the other choices convey the correct emphasis.

64. J: Pronoun case

The underlined pronouns must be subject pronouns because they come before a verb (*donned*). (F), (G), and (H) can all be eliminated because *me* is an object pronoun. (J) correctly uses the subject pronoun *I* and specifies who "they" are.

65. C: Diction

Deposit, *unload*, and *release* can all refer to the action of placing large amounts of material onto a surface. *Expend* means "use up" and is typically used to refer to intangible things such as energy or effort.

66. J: Transition

Consider what the sentence in question and the previous sentence are saying with the transition. 1) Huge amounts of material are dropped onto the recycling floor. 2) The Center has one of the highest capacities in the US. Those two ideas are similar (eliminating (G)), but the second isn't necessarily the result of the first (eliminating (F)). The sentence has nothing to do with time, so *meanwhile* doesn't make sense. In fact, no transition is required, so (J) is correct.

67. C: Conjunction/logical relationship

(A), (B), and (D) all contain a serious logic error that turns the sentence into nonsense: they imply that the elementary and middle school students are, or can be, senior citizens. Only (C) creates a logical relationship and indicates that the students and senior citizens are two distinct groups, both of which visit the Center.

68. G: Who vs. whom

When a person is referred to, *whom* rather than *who* should be used after a preposition (*with*).

69. B: Dangling modifier

What utilizes a combination of manual and mechanical technologies? The Center. So *the Center* must immediately follow the comma. That eliminates (A) and (D). In (C), the gerund *processing* creates a fragment, leaving (B).

70. H: Comma

The underlined phrase can be written two ways: *The only materials that the Center can recycle*, and *the only materials the Center can recycle*. When *that* is optional and is not included, no comma should be used in its place. That eliminates (F) and (G). In (J), no comma should be used before *that*.

71. D: Deleting information

The physical description of the recycling bins is irrelevant to the paragraph, which focuses on the processing of recyclables at the Center.

72. H: Colon, comma splice

The original version contains a comma splice (as indicate by *comma + this*); (G) and (J) fail to place a stand-alone sentence before the colon; and (H) correctly uses a comma to separate an independent and a dependent clause.

73. D: Double positive, adjective vs. adverb

The underlined portion modifies the noun *process*, so an adjective is required. That eliminates (B) and (C). The original version incorrectly uses *more* in addition to the comparative form of the adjective. (D) correctly provides the comparative alone.

74. G: Inserting information

What is the passage about? The importance of recycling and the recycling "education" that the writer acquired by visiting the Keystone Center. So the correct answer must have something to do with the idea that learning about recycling is important. Only (G) fits that criterion.

75. C: Passage goal

Think carefully before you jump to answer. The writer is clearly a big fan of recycling, but the passage is specific, focusing only on the writer's experience at the recycling plant and his/her description of how the plant works. At no point does the writer address readers directly, or engage in a direct attempt to persuade them to recycle. And it's reading too far between the lines to infer that presenting a positive view of an activity is the same thing as trying to persuade people to engage in that activity. In order for the goal to fit the passage, the persuasion would have to be explicit. So the passage does not fulfill that goal.

Score Chart*

Raw Score	Scale Score	Raw Score	Scale Score
75	36	23-24	11
74-75	35	21-22	10
73-74	34	19-20	9
72	33	17-18	8
71	32	15-16	7
70	31	13-14	6
69	30	11-12	5
67-68	29	9-10	4
65-66	28	7-8	3
62-64	27	5-6	2
59-61	26	3-4	1
56-58	25	0-2	0
54-55	24		
51-53	23		
50-51	22		
47-49	21		
45-46	20		
42-44	19		
39-41	18		
37-38	17		
35-36	16		
32-34	15	*Scores are approximate
29-31	14	and based on scales from
27-28	13	a variety of administered
25-26	12	exams.

Apostrophes: Plural vs. Possessive

Test	Question #	Page
Test 1	6	153
Test 1	31	156
Test 2	17	294
Test 2	32	297
Test 2	41	299
Test 3	10	439
Test 3	13	440
Test 3	36	443
Test 5	19	723
Test 5	23	723
Test 5	48	727

Sentences vs. Fragments

Test	Question #	Page
Test 1	2	152
Test 1	27	155
Test 1	30	156
Test 1	48	159
Test 1	6	162
Test 2	1	295
Test 2	25	296
Test 2	38	298
Test 2	59	301
Test 2	61	302
Test 2	63	302
Test 3	17	440
Test 3	52	445
Test 3	61	446
Test 4	4	576
Test 4	26	580
Test 4	40	581
Test 5	4	720
Test 5	52	727

Joining and Separating Sentences/Clauses

Test	Question #	Page
Test 1	1	152
Test 1	39	157
Test 1	57	160
Test 1	63	161
Test 2	1	292
Test 2	10	293
Test 2	20	295
Test 2	26	296
Test 2	31	97
Test 2	55	301
Test 2	65	302
Test 3	5	439
Test 3	31	442
Test 3	40	443
Test 3	72	448
Test 3	74	448
Test 4	3	576
Test 4	10	577
Test 4	11	577
Test 4	16	578
Test 4	36	581
Test 4	38	581
Test 4	50	583
Test 5	16	722
Test 5	29	724
Test 5	41	726
Test 5	53	727
Test 5	59	729
Test 5	65	729
Test 5	66	730

Non-Essential Clauses

Test	Question #	Page	Note
Test 1	7	153	
Test 2	52	300	
Test 2	72	303	
Test 3	22	441	
Test 4	20	579	
Test 4	69	586	Comma with name
Test 5	34	725	
Test 5	20	723	Comma vs. dash
Test 5	67	730	Comma vs. dash

Commas: Additional Uses and Misuses

Test	Question #	Page	Note
Test 1	16	154	No that = no comma
Test 1	18	154	Prep.
Test 1	32	156	
Test 1	53	159	Subj. & verb

Test			
Test 1	61	161	Prep., subj. & verb
Test 2	2	292	No that = no comma
Test 2	7	293	Betw. objects
Test 2	19	295	Prep.
Test 2	36	298	
Test 2	75	303	Subj. & verb
Test 3	3	438	No that = no comma
Test 3	21	441	
Test 3	27	442	
Test 3	54	445	
Test 3	63	446	Sub. & verb, prep.
Test 4	1	576	Preposition
Test 4	10	577	
Test 4	21	579	Emphatic pronoun
Test 4	22	579	Prep.
Test 4	48	583	Prep.
Test 4	27	580	Betw. adjectives
Test 4	59	585	
Test 4	60	585	
Test 4	61	585	Preposition
Test 5	1	720	Preposition
Test 5	10	721	Compound subj.
Test 5	28	724	
Test 5	50	727	

Colons

Test		
Test 1	69	162
Test 3	53	445
Test 4	34	581
Test 5	28	720

Dashes

Test		
Test 5	20	723
Test 5	67	730

Subject Verb Agreement

Test		
Test 1	22	155
Test 1	47	159
Test 1	67	162
Test 2	74	303
Test 3	2	438
Test 3	68	447
Test 4	23	579
Test 4	39	581
Test 5	24	724
Test 5	31	724

Verb Tense and Form

Test			
Test 1	13	153	
Test 1	14	154	
Test 1	17	154	
Test 1	41	157	Gerund vs. infinitive
Test 1	44	158	
Test 2	3	292	
Test 2	12	294	
Test 2	33	297	
Test 3	29	442	Gerund vs. infinitive
Test 3	42	444	
Test 3	58	446	
Test 3	62	446	
Test 3	70	447	
Test 4	7	577	
Test 4	25	579	
Test 4	57	584	
Test 5	8	721	
Test 5	9	721	
Test 5	12	721	
Test 5	46	727	
Test 5	64	729	Have vs. of

Pronouns/Referents

Test		
Test 1	33	156
Test 1	51	159
Test 1	56	160
Test 2	9	293
Test 2	54	301
Test 2	62	302
Test 3	1	438
Test 3	12	439
Test 3	50	445
Test 3	37	443
Test 4	8	577
Test 4	49	583
Test 4	65	585
Test 5	33	725
Test 5	51	727

Adjectives vs. Adverbs

Test		
Test 1	19	154
Test 1	59	160
Test 3	8	439
Test 3	18	440
Test 4	72	587
Test 5	38	725

Comparisons

Test 1	25	155	Much, many, few
Test 2	16	294	
Test 2	47	300	
Test 2	60	302	
Test 3	51	445	
Test 4	33	581	
Test 5	14	722	

Word Pairs

Test 2	23	295
Test 5	61	729

Parallel Structure

Test 1	29	156
Test 2	57	301
Test 2	71	303
Test 3	24	441
Test 3	28	442
Test 3	44	444
Test 4	63	585
Test 5	56	728
Test 5	58	728

Modification

Best Placement for Underlined Word/Phrase:

Test 1	42	158
Test 1	72	162
Test 4	6	577
Test 4	14	578
Test 4	70	586
Test 5	21	723

Dangling Modifiers:

Test 1	12	153
Test 1	28	155
Test 1	34	156
Test 2	73	303
Test 3	35	443
Test 4	19	579
Test 5	27	724

Misplaced Modifiers:

Test 1	36	156
Test 2	11	293
Test 2	42	299
Test 3	45	444
Test 3	46	444
Test 4	32	581
Test 4	35	581
Test 4	55	584
Test 4	67	586
Test 5	18	723

Relative Pronouns

Test 1	3	152	Who vs. whom
Test 3	26	441	
Test 5	32	724	
Test 5	69	730	

Shorter is Better

Test 1	9	153	Redundancy
Test 1	20	154	
Test 1	35	156	Redundancy
Test 1	37	157	Redundancy
Test 1	50	159	Irrelevant info.
Test 1	55	160	Redundancy
Test 1	58	160	
Test 1	65	161	
Test 1	66	162	
Test 2	4	292	
Test 2	34	297	Redundancy
Test 2	43	299	Redundancy
Test 2	66	302	
Test 3	9	439	
Test 3	14	440	
Test 3	16	440	Redundancy
Test 3	34	443	
Test 3	41	444	Redundancy
Test 3	49	445	
Test 3	67	447	Redundancy
Test 4	12	578	Redundancy
Test 4	47	583	Irrelevant info
Test 4	66	586	
Test 4	68	586	Irrelevant info
Test 5	3	720	Redundancy
Test 5	7	721	
Test 5	26	724	
Test 5	39	725	Redundancy

Test 5	40	726	Irrelevant info
Test 5	71	730	Redundancy

Diction/Idioms and Register

Test 2	22	295	
Test 2	29	296	Register
Test 2	40	298	
Test 2	44	299	
Test 2	46	300	
Test 2	49	300	
Test 2	67	302	
Test 3	11	439	
Test 3	19	440	
Test 3	64	447	
Test 4	2	576	
Test 4	31	581	
Test 4	53	584	
Test 4	62	585	
Test 4	73	587	
Test 5	22	723	
Test 5	42	726	
Test 5	43	726	
Test 5	47	727	
Test 5	72	731	
Test 5	74	731	

Transition/Logical Relationship

Test 1	4	152	
Test 1	11	153	
Test 1	24	155	Betw. paragraphs
Test 1	52	159	
Test 1	54	160	Betw. paragraphs
Test 1	62	161	
Test 1	70	162	
Test 2	6	293	
Test 2	8	293	
Test 2	39	298	
Test 2	58	301	
Test 2	65	302	
Test 2	69	303	
Test 2	70	303	
Test 3	4	438	
Test 3	20	441	
Test 3	33	443	
Test 3	38	443	
Test 3	48	444	
Test 3	57	446	
Test 4	9	577	

Test 4	17	579
Test 4	37	581
Test 4	54	584
Test 4	58	584
Test 4	64	585
Test 5	6	721
Test 5	13	722
Test 5	17	723
Test 5	57	728
Test 5	63	729
Test 5	73	731

Inserting, Deleting, and Replacing Information

Inserting:

Test 1	15	154	Conclusion
Test 1	23	155	
Test 1	38	157	
Test 1	43	158	
Test 1	64	161	
Test 1	71	162	
Test 1	73	163	
Test 2	5	292	
Test 2	13	294	Conclusion
Test 2	18	295	
Test 2	48	300	
Test 2	53	301	
Test 3	23	441	
Test 3	25	441	
Test 3	30	442	
Test 3	39	443	
Test 3	43	444	
Test 3	47	444	Conclusion
Test 3	55	445	
Test 3	60	446	Conclusion
Test 3	66	447	
Test 3	69	447	Conclusion
Test 4	13	578	
Test 4	24	579	
Test 4	30	580	
Test 4	41	582	
Test 4	43	582	Conclusion
Test 4	56	584	
Test 5	2	720	
Test 5	55	728	
Test 5	68	730	
Test 5	75	731	Conclusion

Deleting:

Test 1	26	155
Test 1	40	157
Test 1	46	158
Test 2	15	294
Test 2	24	296
Test 2	35	297
Test 2	37	298
Test 2	50	300
Test 3	7	439
Test 3	15	440
Test 3	59	446
Test 4	5	577
Test 4	15	578
Test 4	29	580
Test 4	42	582
Test 4	44	582
Test 5	30	724
Test 5	36	725

Replacing:

Test 1	5	152
Test 1	8	153
Test 1	10	153
Test 1	74	163
Test 2	28	296
Test 2	56	301
Test 2	68	303
Test 3	6	439
Test 3	32	442
Test 3	56	446
Test 3	73	448
Test 4	18	579
Test 4	46	583
Test 4	52	584
Test 4	74	587
Test 5	5	721
Test 5	25	724
Test 5	37	725
Test 5	44	726
Test 5	49	727
Test 5	54	727
Test 5	60	729
Test 5	62	729
Test 5	70	730

Sentence Order and Placement

Test 1	21	154
Test 1	49	159
Test 2	14	294
Test 2	27	296
Test 3	65	447
Test 4	28	580
Test 4	71	586
Test 4	75	587
Test 5	11	721
Test 5	35	725

Paragraph Organization

Test 1	45	158
Test 4	51	584

Writer's Goal

Test 1	60	160
Test 1	75	163
Test 2	30	297
Test 2	45	299
Test 3	75	448
Test 4	45	582
Test 5	15	722
Test 5	45	726

Appendix B: Questions by Test

Test 1 (p. 152)

1. Comma splice
2. Fragment/gerund
3. Who vs. whom
4. Transition (modification)
5. Replacing information
6. Apostrophe
7. Comma (non-essential clause)
8. Replacing information
9. Shorter is better (redundancy)
10. Correct emphasis
11. Transition
12. Dangling modifier
13. Verb tense
14. Verb tense
15. Inserting information (conclusion)
16. Comma (no that = no comma)
17. Verb tense
18. Comma (preposition)
19. Adjective vs. Adverb
20. Shorter is better
21. Sentence placement
22. Subject verb agreement
23. Inserting information
24. Transition (paragraphs)
25. Many, much, few
26. Deleting information
27. Sentence vs. fragment
28. Dangling modifier, shorter is better
29. Parallel structure
30. Sentence vs. fragment
31. Apostrophe
32. Comma
33. Pronoun agreement
34. Dangling modifier
35. Shorter is better (redundancy)
36. Misplaced modifier
37. Shorter is better (redundancy)
38. Inserting information
39. Comma, semicolon
40. Deleting information
41. Gerund vs. Infinitive
42. Modification (best placement for underlined word)
43. Inserting information
44. Verb tense
45. Paragraph organization
46. Deleting information
47. Subject verb agreement
48. Sentence vs. fragment
49. Sentence placement
50. Shorter is better (irrelevant information)
51. Pronoun agreement
52. Transition
53. Comma between subj. & verb
54. Transition (paragraphs)
55. Shorter is better (redundancy)
56. Pronoun agreement
57. Comma, semicolon, parallelism
58. Shorter is better
59. Adjective vs. adverb
60. Writer's goal
61. Comma
62. Transition
63. Semicolon
64. Inserting information
65. Shorter is better, usage
66. Shorter is better
67. Subject verb agreement, parallelism
68. Fragment/gerund
69. Colon
70. Transition
71. Inserting information
72. Modification (best placement for underlined word)
73. Inserting information
74. Replacing information
75. Writer's goal

Test 2 (p. 292)

1. Comma + FANBOYS, joining sentences
2. Comma (no that = no comma)
3. Verb tense
4. Shorter is better
5. Inserting information
6. Transition
7. Comma (compound object)
8. Transition
9. Pronoun
10. Comma, Semicolon, Joining Sentences
11. Misplaced modifier
12. Verb tense, parallelism
13. Inserting information (conclusion)
14. Sentence order/placement
15. Deleting information
16. Comparative and Superlative
17. Apostrophe
18. Inserting information
19. Comma (preposition)
20. Comma, semicolon
21. Fragment/gerund
22. Idiom/preposition
23. Word pair
24. Deleting information
25. Sentence vs. fragment
26. Comma, semicolon
27. Sentence order/placement
28. Replacing information
29. Register
30. Writer's goal

31. Comma between dep./indep. clause (sentence vs. fragment)
32. Apostrophe
33. Verb tense
34. Shorter is better (redundancy)
35. Deleting information
36. Comma
37. Deleting information
38. Sentence vs. fragment
39. Transition
40. Diction
41. Apostrophe
42. Misplaced modifier
43. Shorter is better (redundancy)
44. Diction/usage
45. Writer's goal
46. Idiom/preposition
47. Comparative and Superlative, who vs. whom
48. Inserting information
49. Diction
50. Deleting information
51. Modification, shorter is better
52. Comma
53. Inserting information
54. Pronoun
55. Comma splice
56. Replacing information
57. Parallelism
58. Transition
59. Sentence vs. fragment
60. Comparison
61. Sentence vs. fragment
62. Pronoun, preposition
63. Sentence vs. fragment
64. Comma splice
65. Transition
66. Diction
67. Shorter is better (redundancy)
68. Replacing information
69. Transition
70. Transition
71. Parallelism
72. Comma (non-essential clause

73. Dangling modifier
74. Subject verb agreement
75. Comma (between subject and verb)

Test 3 (p. 438)

1. Pronoun consistency, shorter is better
2. Subject verb agreement
3. Comma (no that = no comma)
4. Transition
5. Comma betw. subj. & verb, fused sentence
6. Replacing information
7. Deleting information
8. Adjective vs. Adverb
9. Shorter is better
10. Apostrophe
11. Diction/usage
12. Pronoun consistency
13. Apostrophe
14. Shorter is better
15. Deleting information
16. Shorter is better (redundancy)
17. Sentence vs. fragment
18. Adjective vs. adverb
19. Diction (have vs. of)
20. Transition
21. Comma, apostrophe
22. Non-essential clause
23. Inserting information
24. Parallelism
25. Inserting information
26. Relative pronoun
27. Comma
28. Parallelism
29. Idiom/gerund vs. infinitive
30. Inserting information
31. Comma splice
32. Replacing information
33. Transition
34. Shorter is better
35. Dangling modifier, passive voice, shorter is better
36. Apostrophe
37. Pronoun

38. Transition
39. Inserting information
40. Comma splice, sentence vs. fragment
41. Redundancy
42. Verb tense, parallelism
43. Inserting information
44. Parallelism
45. Misplaced modifier
46. Misplaced modifier
47. Inserting information (conclusion)
48. Transition
49. Shorter is better
50. Pronoun agreement
51. Comparative and Superlative
52. Sentence vs. fragment, transition
53. Apostrophe, colon, comma splice
54. Comma
55. Inserting information
56. Replacing information
57. Transition
58. Verb tense, comma
59. Deleting information
60. Inserting information (conclusion)
61. Sentence vs. fragment
62. Verb tense, parallelism
63. Comma betw. subj. & verb, preposition, colon
64. Idiom/preposition
65. Sentence order
66. Inserting information
67. Shorter is better (redundancy)
68. Subject verb agreement
69. Inserting information (conclusion)
70. Verb tense
71. Gerund
72. Comma, colon, fused sentence
73. Replacing information
74. Comma, semicolon
75. Writer's goal

Test 4 (p. 576)

1. Comma (preposition)
2. Diction
3. Comma splice
4. Sentence vs. fragment
5. Deleting information
6. Modification (best placement for underlined word)
7. Verb tense
8. Pronoun (antecedent)
9. Transition
10. Comma, pronoun
11. Comma
12. Shorter is better (redundancy)
13. Inserting information
14. Modification (best placement for underlined word)
15. Deleting information
16. Comma, semicolon
17. Transition/logical relationship
18. Replacing information
19. Dangling modifier
20. Non-essential clause
21. Comma (emphatic pronoun)
22. Comma (preposition)
23. Subject verb agreement
24. Inserting information
25. Verb tense, parallelism
26. Sentence vs. fragment
27. Comma (between adjectives)
28. Sentence order
29. Deleting information
30. Writer's goal
31. Idiom
32. Modification (misplaced modifier)
33. Comparison (then vs. than)
34. Colon
35. Modification (misplaced modifier)
36. Comma, semicolon
37. Transition
38. Joining/separating sentences
39. Subject verb agreement, shorter is better
40. Sentence vs. fragment
41. Inserting information
42. Deleting information
43. Inserting information (conclusion)
44. Deleting information
45. Writer's goal
46. Replacing
47. Shorter is better (irrelevant information)
48. Comma (preposition)
49. Pronoun (antecedent), register
50. Fused sentence, sentence logic
51. Dividing paragraphs
52. Correct emphasis, replacing information
53. Diction/usage
54. Transition
55. Misplaced modifier
56. Inserting information
57. Verb tense
58. Transition
59. Comma (non-essential clause, comma splice)
60. Comma (betw. compound object)
61. Comma (preposition)
62. Diction/usage
63. Parallelism
64. Transition/logical relationship
65. Pronoun
66. Shorter is better
67. Misplaced modifier
68. Shorter is better (irrelevant information)
69. Comma with name
70. Modification (best placement for underlined word)
71. Sentence order
72. Adjective vs. adverb
73. Diction/preposition
74. Replacing information
75. Sentence order

Test 5 (p. 720)

1. Comma, semicolon
2. Inserting information
3. Shorter is better (redundancy)
4. Sentence vs. fragment
5. Replacing information
6. Transition/logical relationship
7. Shorter is better
8. Verb tense, parallelism
9. Verb tense, parallelism
10. Comma (betw. compound subj.)
11. Sentence order
12. Verb tense, parallelism
13. Transition
14. Comparison (then vs. than)
15. Writer's goal
16. Comma + FANBOYS, period, modification
17. Transition
18. Modification (misplaced modifier)
19. Apostrophe, pronoun
20. Non-essential clause, comma vs. dash
21. Modification (best placement for underlined word)
22. Diction/usage
23. Apostrophe
24. Subject verb agreement
25. Replacing information
26. Shorter is better
27. Dangling modifier
28. Comma betw. subj. & verb, semicolon
29. Comma splice
30. Deleting information
31. Subject verb agreement
32. Relative pronoun
33. Pronoun agreement
34. Non-essential clause
35. Sentence order
36. Deleting information
37. Replacing information
38. Adjective vs. adverb

39. Shorter is better (redundancy)
40. Shorter is better (irrelevant information)
41. Comma splice, period
42. Diction: of vs. have
43. Diction/usage
44. Replacing information
45. Writer's goal
46. Verb tense
47. Diction: of vs. have
48. Apostrophe
49. Replacing information
50. Comma betw. subj. & verb
51. Pronoun (antecedent)
52. Sentence vs. fragment
53. Comma, semicolon, colon
54. Replacing information
55. Inserting information
56. Parallelism
57. Transition
58. Parallelism
59. Semicolon, fused sentence, fragment
60. Replacing information
61. Word pair
62. Replacing information
63. Transition
64. Verb tense
65. Comma splice
66. Comma splice, transition
67. Comma, colon, dash
68. Inserting information
69. Relative pronoun, sentence vs. fragment
70. Replacing information
71. Shorter is better (redundancy)
72. Diction/Idiom
73. Transition
74. Diction/Idiom
75. Inserting information (conclusion)

Appendix C: Who vs. Whom

Who = subject pronoun, used before a verb

Who refers to the **subject of a sentence**. It can be replaced by the subject pronouns *she/he* or *they*. For example:

Sentence 1:   Martha Graham was a choreographer.

Sentence 2:   **She** revolutionized dance in the twentieth century.

To combine the sentences smoothly, we can use a relative clause (underlined below):

Combined: Martha Graham was a choreographer **who** revolutionized dance in the twentieth century.

Why use *who* rather than *whom*? Because *who* refers to back to Martha Graham, and Martha Graham is the subject of the sentence. Furthermore, if we were to split the sentence back into two clauses, the second clause – the one that the clause beginning with *who* replaces – would start with the **subject pronoun** *she*.

One more example:

Sentence 1:   The first African American woman to travel into space was Mae Jemison.

Sentence 2:   **She** trained as a dancer before becoming an astronaut.

Combined: The first African American woman to travel into space was Mae Jemison, **who** trained as a dancer before becoming an astronaut.

Even though *Mae Jemison* does not appear at the beginning of the sentence, she is still the subject of the second clause. We know this because we could also replace her name with the subject pronoun *she* (*she trained as a dancer before becoming an astronaut*). *Who* should therefore be used.

Whom = object pronoun, used before a noun or pronoun

Whom is used when a person is the **object of a verb or preposition**. It can be replaced by the **object pronouns** *her/him* or *them*.

As a general rule, *whom* is only tested as the direct object of a <u>preposition</u> (as discussed in Chapter 14), **not** as the direct object of a <u>verb</u> (as below). If a question contains answer choices that use both *who* and *whom* in this context, there will virtually always be an additional, unrelated factor (e.g. comma splice, redundancy) that makes one or both of the answers choices incorrect. See #40, p. 726 of the "Real Guide" for an example.

Sentence 1:   Squanto was a member of the Patuxet tribe.

Sentence 2:   The Pilgrims encountered **him** shortly after arriving in the New World.

Combined: Squanto was a member of the Patuxet tribe **whom** the Pilgrims encountered shortly after arriving in the New World.

In the example above, *whom* is the **object** of the verb *encountered*. Because Squanto's name could be replaced by the **object pronoun** *him* (*they encountered him shortly after arriving in the New World*), *whom* is correct.

ABOUT THE AUTHOR

In addition to *The Complete Guide to ACT English*, Erica Meltzer is the author of *The Complete Guide to ACT Reading* (2014), *The Critical Reader* (2013) and *The Ultimate Guide to SAT Grammar* (2011). Her books are used by tutors and tutoring companies throughout the United States and around the world. She lives in New York City, and you can visit her online at www.thecriticalreader.com.

Made in the USA
Lexington, KY
05 August 2016